Contents

Transforming children's lives: the importance of early intervention

Proceedings of a conference on the importance of early intervention, held in London, 12 March 1998

Conference organiser: Ceridwen Roberts
Report editor: Ros Bayley

Occasional Paper 25

FAMILY POLICY STUDIES CENTRE

Published by Family Policy Studies Centre
9 Tavistock Place, London WC1H 9SN

Tel: 0171-388 5900
Fax: 0171-388 5600

ISBN 1-901455-20-3

March 1999

British Library Cataloguing-in-Publication Data.
A catalogue record for this book is available from the British Library.

The Family Policy Studies Centre is an independent body which analyses family trends and the impact of policy. It is a centre of research and information. The Centre's Governing Council represents a wide spectrum of political opinion, as well as professional, academic, faith, local authority and other interests. This Occasional Paper, like all those in the series, represents the views of the authors and not necessarily those of the Family Policy Studies Centre.

Cover photographs by Format Photographers
Design and print by Intertype

Acknowledgements

The Family Policy Studies Centre thanks the Department of Health for its support of the conference and this publication. It also thanks all the conference speakers and contributors whose presentations form the basis of this report.

Introduction

Ceridwen Roberts, Director, Family Policy Studies Centre

Recently we have seen enormous changes in the rhetoric surrounding public intervention into the private arena of family life. Historically, family policy in Britain has been implicit rather than explicit, predicated on the assumption that 'the less intervention the better'. Government's job, therefore, was mainly to set the broad parameters for all families, usually through fiscal and benefit policies and a broad legal framework covering the obligations of married and unmarried adults and their children.

More explicit policies of intervention, through support and regulation, were developed for the small minority of families who experienced severe crisis and/or disfunctionality. Increasingly though, there has been concern that the considerable public resources expended on helping these families has not been effective enough. Intervention and help has usually only become available at a very late stage in the development of a problem – indeed when it has already become a crisis. This not only often fails to help parents and children adequately but is also not cost effective.

Over the 1990s there has been a dramatic increase in political and popular interest in family breakdown and failure. This has been matched by a concern to break the cycle of disadvantage that can trap a significant minority of families and children. Attention is now firmly focused on how best to help families give children a 'good enough' start. There has been a growing realisation that public services for vulnerable families and children needed to be re-orientated in a variety of ways to be more receptive to supporting parents so as to pre-empt problems. The different services need to be both encouraged and helped to work better together, crossing departmental and sectoral boundaries to deliver multi-agency programmes and solutions. And they need to re-focus their methods of working with families so as to tackle problems earlier.

It was against this background of growing interest in earlier intervention that the Department of Health and the Family Policy Studies Centre decided to collaborate to mount a national conference on 'Families and Early Intervention'. We knew that, whilst central and local government increasingly recognised its importance in theory, it is often very much more difficult in practice to change working partnerships and methods of funding so as to encourage a more preventive approach and multi-agency working.

The conference, which was held in London in March 1998, had four main aims:-

- to review the case for earlier intervention and preventive work in Britain;
- to examine current developments in the UK and USA in the move towards more focused services;
- to consider how central government is working across departments to promote better services;

• to discuss examples of good practice in five key areas – health, social services, education, the criminal justice system and the community.

And these themes were reflected throughout the day's mixture of plenary and workshop sessions.

The conference, which was chaired by Jon Snow, was over-subscribed. It attracted a very wide range of people working in the field, from the large-scale statutory to small-scale voluntary organisation or community project, and individuals with an interest in family support. Conferences, however are ephemeral. Too often they touch only those attending and there is a tendency for the conclusions to get lost and the same ground to be revisited several years later. We decided to try and prevent this by publishing a record of the proceedings and so give a flavour of the main points of the key presentations, the workshop sessions and the conclusions reached by the participants.

Paul Boateng, Parliamentary Under-Secretary of State at the Department of Health opened the conference with a wide-ranging review of the Government's role in early intervention. He stressed that 'families want and need preventive services' but recognised that 'prevention isn't necessarily cheap nor is it quick. It is about getting it right, so it lasts and endures in terms of the impact it makes'. A message with which conference concurred.

Mr Boateng also emphasised the importance of measuring success in terms of the outcomes for children, particularly for looked after children. Too often they figure in the indices of failure and deprivation. Nor are they, or children more generally, properly listened to. In the new culture of articulating and meeting service objectives Mr Boateng promised that there would be 'more opportunities for the voice of children and young people, and their needs and concerns, to impact on what we do' for 'it is only when you build structures that are responsive to children and young people that early interventions will deliver'.

Finally, Mr Boateng turned to consider the wide range of traditional sources of support for parents. He argued that 'we need to free up and resource professionals such as GPs, health visitors and teachers who are in contact with children and their parents and therefore well-placed to recognise and respond to their needs'. Parents too, often get support from other parents, and organisations such as Home-Start played a crucial role in supporting parents in their local communities. This type of voluntary initiative needs to be built on, the Minister concluded.

Professor Sir Michael Rutter of the Institute of Child Psychiatry, University of London reviewed the evidence on the preventive role of early intervention, beginning his presentation with a reminder about the causes of anti-social behaviour and the factors which inhibit it. Importantly he stressed that children have choices and their behaviour is influenced by social and structural factors which shape the costs/benefits of their actions. Both must be tackled if anti-social outcomes are to be prevented.

Among the interventions he considered were the effects of good pre-school education, programmes of parenting enhancement, the early treatment of disruptive behaviour, school programmes to enhance social competencies or tackle bullying, situational prevention and programmes to tackle areas of social disorganisation. His examples, therefore, spanned the psychological to the structural but underlying all his talk was an emphasis on the multi-factoral approach to early interventation.

The next speaker, Professor Carolyn Webster-Stratton, focused on the serious issue of conduct disorder in children, a problem which is growing in the United States where between 10%-25% of young children are held to be affected. The problem is also seen to be growing in the UK. Her detailed account of a clinical programme of early intervention to tackle disruptive behaviour in children as young as six attracted the attention of the conference, as did her video vignettes.

Her recommendations were clear – that 'we give more attention to the educative health model for families which begins when children are very young' and 'we switch the emphasis in schools from primarily a cognitive or academic competence emphasis to give more attention to social competence and the emotional well-being of children'. This primary and secondary level care provides essential early intervention which all helps to reduce the incidence of more serious problems in children.

Webster-Stratton felt very strongly that society in general, as well as parents and children, would benefit from the wider effects of early intervention – 'children who have learned effective relationship skills will be more likely to have happier marriages, less depression and divorce'.

The final plenary speaker approached the topic of prevention and early intervention from a rather different perspective. Dagmar McGill, Director of International Division, Big Brothers Big Sisters of America, spoke about her experience in running community-based mentoring schemes in North America. These match an adult volunteer to a child with the expectation that a caring and supporting relationship will develop which will help the child. Mentors spend between three and five hours a week with their matched child and also receive on-going supervision and monitoring. Each match relationship sets its own goals reflecting the changing needs of the child.

McGill reported on some of the recent evaluation studies of the schemes. Mentoring relationships which were developmental were more successful than prescriptive ones – they persisted longer and were highly valued by the young people. Mentoring was also shown to have a marked effect on the behaviour outcomes for young people. A random controlled study showed that mentored young people were 46% less likely to do drugs, 27% less likely to initiate alcohol use and about a third less likely to hit someone than the non-mentored group. Their school attendance and performance were also better, as were their relationships with their parents and peers. McGill concluded that programmes like mentoring should have a place in the canon of early intervention strategies.

These presentations set the scene. The workshops enabled conference participants to look in more detail at initiatives for particular groups or in specific settings. Five strands of workshops enabled a number of practical projects and experiences to be reviewed.

An important theme was community support for families. Two speakers explained their experience of developing locally-based initiatives. Martin Craig, Director and Co-founder of the Waterville Projects in North Tyneside, powerfully conveyed the dynamics of working with community activists to help families and children get the support they need. The spin-offs in helping people to help themselves had been enormous and this area had now seen both a number of projects for teenagers, young children, young parents and so on as well as a growth in individual and community confidence. However, the perpetual demand of short-term funding was draining; and this type of initiative also generated the explicit hostility of local criminals who need the instability which supports criminal activity.

Schools can also be an important resource for local communities and Graham Evans, Principal of Minsthorpe Community College in South Elmsall, talked about how, over the last five years, his school had become 'the educational, training, leisure and recreational centre of our community'. About five and half thousand people a week pass through the college attending a whole range of activities including a Family Learning Centre and a school–family learning programme for youngsters. This type of initiative not only tackles the home–school divide and puts learning on everyone's agenda, it also gives people hope.

The issue of early intervention for children in need was the theme of a second workshop. Dr Michael Little of Dartington Social Research Unit, presented the findings of his recent Department of Health-funded review of the research on what works and what doesn't work in early intervention. He outlined three key findings. 'First, no effective intervention is located within a single agency: it all has to be cross-agency work. Secondly, intervention works by intervening effectively within chains of effects' ie. by breaking a chain that is going to lead to later difficulties. And thirdly, 'practical things to help people solve practical problems' work best.

The value of this approach was illustrated by Colin Holt's presentation. Based at the Lawrence Weston Family Centre in Bristol, Mr Holt described the work he has been doing with fathers over the last eight years. Through supportive, often therapeutically orientated work, chiefly undertaken by a male specialist the Centre had engaged with a wide range of fathering problems. They had been successful in helping fathers to remain with their families, or in closer contact with their children, helping to change abusive behaviour and in providing vulnerable fathers with constructive support.

The theme of multi-agency working was central to the third workshop. This focused on early years provision and aimed to illustrate best practice. Virginia Makins, who had written *'Not just a nursery: multi-agency early years centres in action'* talked about her findings . She stressed the positive benefits that emerged from her case studies: in particular that this non-stigmatised source of early family support seemed to help even difficult and belligerent parents, and led to fewer children in these areas reporting difficulties at school. Though the centres were expensive to set up and run the longer term benefits were enormous for children, parents and professionals.

Makins' recipe for success, namely open access for all families in the area, good leadership, proper staff development and training, parental involvement, and responsiveness to local conditions and needs was borne out by Bernadette Duffy's account of her centre's work. Head of the Dorothy Gardner Centre in Westminster, which had recently been announced as an Early Excellence Centre, she illustrated vividly all the factors necessary to make this type of initiative work.

Funded jointly by education and social services the Centre is open to all families in its catchment area and sees itself as a resource for the local community, to be used as the community wants. Duffy described the variety of services on offer and the reactions over time of some of the parents and children. She finished with three main points: 'there is no off-the-shelf model', centres are successful because they reflect their community's need, but a 'centre cannot be all things to all people' ... 'you need to have a clear view about what the centre is best equipped to do and how it links with other related services in the community'. Finally, she said, centres cannot be set up in isolation and they take time to evolve.

The fourth workshop took the theme of 'Refocusing Children's Services' and reported on the recent initiative of the Department of Health to encourage new ways of working with families. Diana Robbins, who had conducted an evaluation of the Initiative's forty projects, identified the main findings. Many of the projects were very small, innovative in their partnerships or client group and were often only set up for a short period of time. However, the evaluation of what worked revealed the remarkable amount of creative energy and synergy that could be released when groups were tasked and funded to work in different ways.

This Initiative had handed the baton to the voluntary sector who in some cases were more aware of users' wants. It also enabled projects to work with 'families in the round' and to try and develop better ways of getting user-led provision. Robbins showed that there are lots of exciting new ideas though, unfortunately, the old problem of getting proper and continuous funding still applies. Some of Robbins' findings were illustrated by the work of the Ormiston Children and Families Trust based in East Anglia.

Sue Blake and Melanie Dopson spoke about their projects with 11 to 14 year olds in Peterborough and families in the Fen town of March. A clear emphasis here was on listening to young people's views about what they wanted as well as being responsive and accessible to families. This has enabled them to develop projects which more accurately reflect what young people want and also to identify new partners to work with.

The fifth workshop focused on healthy living initiatives. Professor Hilton Davis described an early intervention programme in the highly deprived areas of Southwark and Lewisham in south London. The Parent Advisers Service is staffed by health visitors and community doctors and aims to help families referred because of the emotional or behavioural problems of a child under five, or parenting problems, or problems in the parents. The service is based on home visiting and the family is visited once a week initially to build up the relationship.

The project had been independently evaluated and since there was a matched comparison group of families with similar problems it had been possible to assess the effectiveness of the intervention. Professor Davis reported on several measures where the intervention group showed more improvement than the comparison group including, the attitudes of the mother, the behaviour of the child and the decreasing rate of contact with the GP. All the evidence pointed the same way, showing that this intervention had proved helpful in reducing early child–parent difficulties.

Another family health intervention was reported by Lonica Vanclay and Alice Cook of the Family Welfare Association. Their WellFamily Service, aimed at families living in areas of high disadvantage, was initially based in Hackney in north London. The service works by locating a family support co-ordinator in a GP practice. Families are both referred and self-refer and the worker's role is to listen, to offer help and support, to work with families to sort the issues they want to deal with and how to tackle them.

Vanclay reported that while the service had not yet been formally evaluated, preliminary feedback suggested that the service was valued by families and GPs alike. Its non-stigmatising accessibility meant it was non-threatening and it was enabling the social and practical problems underlying some GP visits to be sorted out at more appropriate levels, often leading to quicker, cheaper solutions. The future for more joint working like this seemed bright as this work fits well into joint commissioning possibilities and primary care groups.

The conference ended with an Any Questions Panel which reflected the wish to develop 'joined-up thinking'. Six senior officials from the main government departments with policy or expenditure responsibility for families and children came together to answer conference participants' questions. Chaired by Rita Stringfellow in her capacity as chair of the Local Government Association's Social Affairs and Health Committee the panel comprised officials from the Departments of Health – Elisabeth Johnson and Georgina Fletcher-Cooke, Education and Employment – Rob Smith, the Home Office – Mark Perfect, the Treasury – Norman Glass, and the Social Exclusion Unit – Jon Bright.

This session provided a useful reminder of the challenges to policy and practice multi-agency or cross-departmental working brings. We are all on a learning curve about how to do things differently, often breaking out of long-held assumptions and ways of conceptualisng the world and working. The panel members responded gamely to the cross-departmental questions they were posed and, if central government officials can begin to do this, as their political masters have, the world may begin to change.

Transforming children's lives: the importance of eary intervention

Chaired by Jon Snow, Channel Four News

and

Rita Stringfellow, Chair, Local Government Association Social Affairs and Health Committee and Leader, North Tyneside Council

1 The Government's role in early intervention

Paul Boateng, Parliamentary Under-Secretary of State for Health

This conference is an important event, concentrating and focusing on some of the challenges that face us as a society: challenges around the family, challenges around social inclusion, and challenges about what we must do to bear down on some of the most intractable problems that face us at the end of the 20th century. We do so in the knowledge that we can make gains, and add real value to the lives of each and every one of us, as well as the lives of the most vulnerable, by recognising the importance of early intervention and the differences and the changes that it can bring.

This Government is committed to ensuring that we support families, especially in their parenting role, so as to give children the best start in life. We are committed to supporting families when they seek help, and before they reach crisis point, and to making the best use of scarce public resources. It is because of that that we see the importance of early intervention. The evidence is that early intervention works. Michael Rutter, Carolyn Webster-Stratton and Dagmar McGill will be providing that evidence clearly and unequivocally today.

The Government's political agenda in this field for the next few years includes early intervention, healthy living, community support, multi-agency working and the focus on families. We will seek to draw on the expertise and the commitment that is represented at this conference, in order that we take forward that agenda, in partnership, in a continuing programme of work. We end the conference today with a panel of key officials from across government, representing the multi-departmental approach that this government is characterised by, and that Tony Blair is absolutely committed to – departments working across traditional boundaries in order to focus on the challenges that face us. A panel of key central government officials, chaired by Rita Stringfellow, represents local government, an important partner in this endeavour. Local government, for too long under-valued and under-resourced, is seen as a major player in implementing this agenda, in partnership with central government, the voluntary and the independent sectors.

I want to share with you at the outset some concerns around re-focusing. The key message from Diana Robbins' evaluation of the Refocusing Children's Services Initiative is that the strategy works. Families want and need preventive services such as those aimed at helping parents, including teenage parents, with their parenting skills. But that prevention isn't necessarily cheap, nor is it quick. Early intervention isn't about a cheap, quick fix. It's about getting it right, so it lasts and endures in terms of the impact it makes.

Securing long-term funding is very important, particularly to the voluntary sector, which is very often best placed to deliver the sort of support that we are talking about today. We need to ensure that statutory agencies jointly provide the resources to ensure that all our children thrive. It is about getting health and social care working together. It's about getting the whole of the statutory sector energised across its boundaries, in order to make best use of that which is available. Making best use of universal services such as education, and intervening with additional social support at critical times.

We have to do that in a context which recognises the importance of measuring success in terms of outcomes for all children. As a government, we will make sure that we recognise and reward those voluntary and statutory agencies engaged in best practice, and that we do that through appropriate grant mechanisms. We need to be able to evaluate, we need to be able to assess what works and, where it does, to make sure that the resources are there to back it up.

Only two days ago we had a meeting of Area Child Protection Committees looking at this issue. The message was very clear: there are real gains to be made in the field of child protection by early intervention. But we need to recognise that we have to be in a position to assess, that intervention has to be sufficiently sensitive to meet childrens' needs and that it takes place at points where it can significantly enhance a child's welfare. We need to respond in a way that enables those children to access the range of services that guard and protect against the possibility of abuse, without necessarily being part of the child protection process. And it's not easy. Agencies working in this area work under a great deal of pressure. But working together, systematically assessing and responding to need, measuring their success through child development-oriented common goals and outcome measures, surely helps in handling that situation.

We are right to expect a high standard of professional practice. We are right to criticise poor standards, but we must be prepared to take informed risks based on thorough assessments, in order to allow proper priority to family support services. We have to do that in a culture which isn't a culture of blame and fear, that all too often puts a pressure on front-line workers, that causes the triggering-off of quite inappropriate responses, and that leads to too early, too hasty interventions, that aren't designed to meet wider needs.

Children living away from their own families are especially vulnerable. The State has failed as a parent and, as a society, we have let down looked-after children. This Government is determined to confront this. We must now begin to win back for those children a childhood that does not lead them to feature, as they do now, in every index of failure: the prison statistics, the statistics of those who have gained absolutely nothing from the education system, and all the indices of deprivation and disadvantage.

'Looked-after' children are obvious candidates for early intervention and we intend to make sure that we deliver on this. One example is to reduce the numbers of teenage pregnancies among looked-after children, an initiative led by my colleague the Minister for Public Health, Tessa Jowell. This is central to our work in this area, because teenage pregnancies continue the cycle of deprivation and disadvantage through generation upon generation.

The Safeguard Review (Utting, 1997) raised a number of wider issues. The Government will be addressing these through a ministerial task force. It's not only systems that need to be in place to promote the safety and development of looked-after children. When local authorities act as corporate parents, they need to be sensitive to any emerging problems and to act quickly, when necessary, just as any ordinary parent would wish to do.

And they need also to listen to children. No one's pretending it's easy. It's not easy listening to one's own children. But we have to do it as parents. And if we have to do it as parents, local authorities must do it because they are the 'parents' of these children. And it is only when you build structures that are responsive to children and young people that early interventions will deliver. It's not just an issue of local government. We are working together across government, looking at ways in which we as a government respond to children and young people. We will be making sure, in terms of the way that government departments work, that there are more opportunities for the voice of children and young people, and their needs and concerns, to impact on what we do.

The inter-agency approach is crucial if we are to meet the needs of young people. We are working with colleagues in the Department for Education and Employment, for instance, to remedy poor educational outcomes for looked-after children.

I want to say one or two words about planning because intervening, and knowing when to intervene, more often than not depends on information in possession of another agency. How good are the structures for ensuring that the agencies which are best placed to act receive the information they need to act effectively? That's a question we need to ask ourselves. Structures for joint working have to be put in place, if we are to ensure effective children's service planning. For younger children and their families, the new Early Years Development Partnerships and their Early Years Development Plans, offer a comprehensive and integrated approach to good quality early years education and child care. And by this September (1998), we will have put in place the system by which a high quality, early education place will be available for all our four year olds whose parents want it.

And we're also setting up a network of some 25 pilot Early Excellence Centres, in order to promote innovation and integrated early years services and high quality training. These Centres will act as beacons of excellence and models for cross-sectoral partnerships and dissemination of good practice. They will provide us with good examples of early intervention.

I talked about the importance of outcomes and measuring outcomes. We have to be in a position to ensure that we are better able to measure and respond to service objectives and performance. We need to articulate those service objectives more clearly. We want objectives that yield benefits for children and families. If you look at better basic educational attainment, that should be an objective, not only for looked-after children, but for all children in need, including those excluded from school. And we need to seek measures of social inclusion, and basic literacy and numeracy, for all children. To ask ourselves, if we are responsible for a local authority social services department, do we know how often a social worker has made contact with the school of the child looked after? Are we measuring effectively that child's performance and success in school?

We need also to consider other objectives: the need to reduce repeated incidents of significant harm, suicides, pregnancies amongst 16 year olds. Performance and outcome measures are being considered for these objectives and we'll be looking for year-on-year improvement. We're putting our mind as a Department to these issues now, with a view to sharing our thinking more widely in the summer of 1998.

It's a discipline for us. It will be a discipline for you. But it will be a discipline that we believe will pay real dividends.

This approach is very much a part of what we are seeking to achieve in the NHS White Paper *The New NHS: modern and dependable,* in the Green Paper *Our Healthier Nation.* There the Government's priority is to do more to stop people falling ill and that means tackling the root causes of avoidable illness. It means also putting an emphasis again, allowing us again, within the Department and within the field of public debate, to focus our minds on the issue of inequalities. It beggars belief that there were years in the Department of Health when officials weren't allowed to talk about inequality; as if, by not talking about it, it would cease to exist. We know the very reverse happened and the inequalities have got greater. But we are determined now that we should have a concerted attack on health inequalities, as an integral part of our new health strategy. Ill health is both a cause and an effect of social exclusion. The very worst-off in our society face unemployment, lack of training opportunities and poor housing and they are therefore more likely to fall ill. And in turn, illness reduces the chances of being able to get a job or to go back to college.

In this 50th year of our NHS, we need to recall and to reflect on the truths that were evident to the founding mothers and fathers. Aneurin Bevan was both Minister of Health and Housing. He recognised then, the Government recognised then, just as this Government recognises now, that we have to tackle these issues in a holistic way.

A few words about Health Action Zones, which present an opportunity to pilot some of the solutions that we are seeking to develop in these areas. As the Secretary of State has said, there will be pilots which fail, both in terms of the NHS White Paper and in terms of tackling inequalities under the aegis of the Green Paper. But we must be daring. We must be prepared to take risks, if we are to drive this agenda forward.

One or two words about Education Action Zones. They are seen as a means of driving up standards and achievements within schools. Schools often face additional problems, around unemployment or housing and unacceptable crime levels. If you are a child living in a high crime area, that will impact on your performance in school. If you are worried about what happens to you in the playground, or on your journey to school, that will influence your success or otherwise in class.

This Government is under no illusion that criminal justice issues are part and parcel of the overall problem that we face as a society, and that we need to address them. When we talk about bearing down on juvenile crime, we must be clear that the main victims of juvenile crime are other juveniles. The notion that to be tough on juvenile crime is to be tough on young people and undermines the welfare of young people, is the reverse of the truth.

No one can be under any illusions about the inhibiting and corrosive effect on the life of a young person, of growing up in an environment where crime is rife. We have to make sure that our early interventions there are designed to turn young people away from a life of offending. That's why we see the corporate role of the local authority as being very important, but working alongside the police, the education service and the health service. Education Action Zones are part of that process: zone partnerships based around clusters of schools in areas of relative deprivation, working closely together to shared and challenging targets.

The issue of school exclusion is one that we need to address, not least because a child excluded from school is a child likely to be at even greater risk. It wasn't for nothing that the Prime Minister sought to launch the policy in relation to social exclusion and the Social Exclusion Unit at Stockwell Manor School. This is a school which had been at the forefront in a deprived urban area, dealing with problematic issues and damaged young people, but that had managed to get to grips with the problem of school exclusion. It had identified those problems early on and focused the efforts of the school, social services and GPs around the needs of young people themselves. We cannot allow children aged eight and nine to languish at home or on the streets or in the gaming arcades, with their parents not knowing which way to turn, with a sense that the school has wiped its hands of them, with the child's prospect of a decent education slipping away as every day passes.

Such children are all too vulnerable to drifting into the criminal sub-culture. Our network of inter-agency youth offending teams will need to be particularly alert to the risks that present themselves to those children, and the risks that those children themselves can come to present.

The Prime Minister has given particular priority to family policy and parenting. We are working, again across government departments, to scope the role for a family policy. It's one of the most exciting areas, one of the most exciting places to be, in government at this time. Jack Straw leads a process which enables ministers and officials to think freely, to come together to exchange ideas and to work on the development of policy, in a way that crosses departmental boundaries. And that's a great privilege. It's a great privilege to be in government. But to be in government and to be able to think, that's marvellous. It is a great liberating force but we want it obviously to be a force that is directed to moving with practitioners and specialists in the field, and to moving for change on the ground.

A number of themes are already beginning to develop. In supporting better parenting, particularly in the area of young children, we need to free up and resource professionals such as GPs, health visitors and teachers, who are in contact with children and their parents and therefore well-placed to recognise and respond to their needs. This is an area where there is absolutely everything to play for in early intervention.

Health visitors are another exciting area of development. They are going to be playing a key role in working with parents and children in the community. We also need to recognise the importance of community-based regeneration. The Social Exclusion Unit is tackling deprived communities and the worst estates. The vision is that these deprived neighbourhoods will be places where people want to stay: where they want to raise families and send their children to decent schools, where they can get support to return to employment. Communities which aren't wrecked by vandalism, crime, drugs or racism, and the disadvantage and the discrimination that follows.

We recognise today that there are times when parents need the help of other parents working in partnership with them. Issues arise within the family that its members cannot always resolve immediately. This applies to all families. It must never become something that 'we' are doing to 'them' or for 'them'. It's something that we as a society have to do for ourselves: recognising that it is in the nature of family life from time to time to arrive at a point where you need help, where you need to be able to reach out and to know that help will be there for you.

And therefore we recognise that a sympathetic but dispassionate outsider can offer a friendly ear or a word or suggestion, or give an indication as to where help might be found or how an issue might be tackled. That can be enormously helpful. It can make all the difference between success or failure. We appreciate the work and the expertise that has been built up in the organisation Home-Start. It has done enormously valuable work in the wider community, drawing not only on professional expertise, but also on the voluntary impulse, the civic impulse, that exists within our society still, despite the pressures that have been brought to bear in our society.

We have to build on the track record of success that Home-Start represents. We have to recognise the importance of that voluntary and civic impulse and I am glad to be able to announce today, on behalf of the Joint Ministerial Team for the Department of Health and the Department for Education and Employment, that we intend to recognise the contribution that Home-Start has made by additional funding of £1,070,000, of which £800,000 is to be found in 1998/99, which will help expand their operation over the next few years.

This is in addition, not a substitution, for local government funding for Home-Start – over 90 per cent of the support for Home-Start comes from local government. But we believe that it is right that we should, as a government, put the resources that are necessary in order to take forward this work. Equally, this is not in substitution for Department of Health Section 64 grant funding powers, it is in addition to Section 64. I want to see a focus there on new projects in support of parents in partnership with other parents, projects strengthening family policy, projects aimed at reducing social exclusion, and new support for the mentoring of young children.

These are exciting, challenging times, times of partnership. We know from our own lives that partnerships can be demanding and difficult but we know that we get out of them what we put into them and that it's worth persevering. It's worth building together a partnership that will endure.

Reference

Utting, Sir William (1997). *People like us: the report of the review of the safeguards for children living away from home.* Department of Health and Welsh Office.

Discussion

In the discussion that followed, the Minister was asked whether the Government was planning to issue guidance to local authorities on managing partnerships with the voluntary sector, to make their support 'more coherent and homogenous' across the country. In particular, guidance was needed on best value, and outcomes and performance measurement.

Another delegate asked what could be done to give a more positive attitude to the professionals on the front line, who were often demoralised by 'the culture of blame' that had developed over the last ten years.

Another commented that it was difficult for organisations to move forward, when they lacked stable funding. They, for instance, had just been given government money to develop one aspect of its work while simultaneously losing core funding.

Mr Boateng said that best value would *'provide the sort of framework that will allow for local democracy and the meeting of local needs'*. It would create pressure to raise standards and give people a sense of what they're entitled to from local government. The Government was also developing a compact with the voluntary sector, that would seek to raise standards and clarify what people can expect from the voluntary sector and what the voluntary sector can expect from central government.

The Department of Health was due to publish a White Paper in the summer on social care, that will create a new set of priorities, redefining social work and social care around some of the issues under discussion at the conference.

Core funding would be one of the issues the compact with the voluntary sector would deal with, Mr Boateng said. However he was determined to reverse a trend that had led to Section 64 becoming the core funder by default, as government withdrew from other areas of funding, *'Section 64 is about innovation, it's about the development of services ... enabling and empowering and finding new ways of working'*.

The proposal to involve health visitors more in parenting was welcomed by a health visitor in the audience but she asked how they could be expected to do it, given current funding levels, *'We barely can do our jobs at the moment, much less to get involved in parenting.'*

'By freeing you up from some of the tasks and the paper pushing and the form filling that you're currently required to do,' Mr Boateng replied.

Could a body of funding be established to help projects evaluate their work?

The Minister said the balance in research and development should change. *'We need the emphasis being on development ... to find out what works,'* he said.

2 Preventing anti-social behaviour in young people: the contribution of early intervention

Professor Sir Michael Rutter, Institute of Child Psychiatry, University of London

My job is to try and set the scene for how we might think about prevention and to say a little bit about the different sorts of approaches that have been employed. The first point to make is that in thinking about anti-social behaviour, as indeed one might think about any behaviour, we need to recognise we're not talking about something for which there is a single basic cause. It does not work like that. There are individual differences in the liability to engage in anti-social behaviour. These are influenced both by constitutional factors and by experiences. Risk and protective factors are important. We need to recognise the phenomenon of resilience in children exposed to extreme adversity, and that liability changes over time.

But whether a child does or doesn't engage in anti-social behaviour will also be influenced by social factors, like being part of a delinquent peer group, and structural influences, such as vandalism being more likely to take place in premises that were previously vandalised. Anti-social behaviour involves a degree of choice and an assessment of cost benefits.

If we think about the features inhibiting anti-social behaviour, we need to think of both values and attitudes. A commitment to societal values, long-term planning and goals, and personal features such as anxiety and responsivity to stress are inhibiting factors, as are empathy for others, internal controls and effective social problem-solving. In addition, there are external constraints such as surveillance and monitoring – by others, by parents, but also by the community – and the availability of non-delinquent rewards, like being part of a pro-social peer group.

The factors influencing behaviour are many and various. We need to be concerned not just with the parents and with the family, important though those are, but with the school and with the peer group. In terms of internal features, we must consider social problem-solving, stress coping, the role of academic achievement and the cognitive processing of experiences. The last reminds us that we are none of us, at any age, simply the passive recipients of what happens to us. The way we think about, and feel about, experiences will matter in determining how we respond.

We need to be concerned about immediate disinhibition effects. I mentioned, in terms of the situation, previous anti-social acts and vandalised premises, for example. The social group has a substantial influence through the values transmitted by an ethos of anti-social behaviour and alcohol. One sees this most obviously in terms of riots and similar situations, but in lesser degree it applies in many other situations.

In terms of opportunity features, there is the lack of surveillance. Evidence is building up now that with young people, particularly during the adolescent years, unsupervised time plays a role, as something that makes it easy to commit a delinquent act.

In terms of the perception of cost benefits, I am not referring to rewards only in terms of material gain, although of course that's an important part of it, but a recognition that respect, fear, admiration, power, control, feeling that it's justified and the excitement, all play a role. But, so too does the individual perception of the risk of apprehension. Note it is the *perception,* not the *reality,* of what the individual thinks is the likelihood of getting caught and their perception of the severity of sanctions.

Risk level and proportion of potential criminals targeted

Risk level	Increase in risk	No. in risk group	% criminal	No, criminal
Very high	16.7 X	10	50	5
Medium	2.3 X	60	7	4
Low	1 X	30	3	1

So, we have a range of influences making anti-social behaviour more or less likely, each of which provides an opportunity for some kind of effective intervention. Before turning to what those interventions might be, let me just say a word about high risk groups, because there is a real dilemma in focusing interventions on high risk groups. It seems obviously to make sense and indeed, there is much to be said for it. The point about this table, however, is to indicate that even when you have an ability to identify a very high risk group, you actually miss a high proportion of potential criminals. On the top line, we have a nearly 17-fold increase in the risk of a young person becoming criminal. This is much greater than one has for most kinds of risks that we can measure. At the bottom is the standard level of risk, as it were, and in the middle, a medium increase of risk. And what you see is that the proportion who are criminal, in relation to these risk factors, differs greatly, 50 per cent as against 3 per cent. But, if you take into account the number of people in a high risk group, you are still picking up only about half the potential criminals. In thinking about focusing strategies, we need to be aware that although that may be part of what we should do, we are going to miss a lot and we need to think about a combination of approaches, including population-wide interventions.

With that as a background, let me turn to a range of different sorts of intervention, focusing on just over half a dozen. Pre-school education is something which achieved most prominence through the High/Scope Perry Project, a multi-faceted, high-quality intervention, involving work with children and families. It fostered active learning, children's independence, trying to encourage self-esteem and self-efficacy, effective problem solving, sticking with tasks and an integration between home and school. It was a relatively small scale study but with good evidence that this did have substantial, long-term benefits in reducing anti-social behaviour, particularly of a persistent, repeated kind.

We then have a series of interventions looking at parenting enhancement, trying to encourage good parenting in high risk groups. There are a range of different things being done here. The Syracuse University Programme is one that has been evaluated and has been found to be effective. Again, it is multi-faceted, focusing on homecare skills, parenting skills and quality, an understanding of children's development and trying to help parents recognise the different needs of children and the ways these vary from child to child. And also focusing on parental self-esteem and self-efficacy, recognising that parents too are under stress, and helping the parents function better is part of what one needs to be doing.

The early treatment of disruptive behaviour is also very important. Again, multi-modal, multi-faceted, methods work well, with a focus on parenting, on the inter-personal skills of parents and not just on the parenting role, as well as working with the children directly and with teachers.

The expert on this is Carolyn Webster-Stratton and she will be telling us more about her own pioneering work. I will simply say as an introduction to that, that it involves a number of different elements for monitoring children's behaviour, a simple use of praise, systematic sanctions and constructive family negotiations and social problem-solving. And again, there is good evidence that this is an effective mode of intervention.

School-wide interventions are also important. These have been subjected on the whole to less evaluation but a number of studies show evidence of benefits. They take a number of different forms and the evidence to date really does not show which of these is the most useful or, indeed, whether some combination may be the best of all. There are a range of approaches that focus on enhancement of social competence or social problem-solving. The Botvins Life Skills Training is perhaps distinctive in dealing particularly with peer group pressures and helping children resist those that are negative. The Yale New Haven Programme, by contrast, focuses much more on coping with stress, although both of these deal with social problem-solving in one aspect or another.

There are a number of interventions that deal more explicitly with the reduction of aggressive behaviour. The first is looking at pro-social behaviour, or dealing with life challenges. Kellam's Good Behaviour Game,which is a group behaviour classroom intervention, would be an example of this kind. And then there are school-wide programmes, like Dan Olweus' Norwegian Programme. This focused on the reduction of bullying in school, but also led to reductions in anti-social behaviour by children.

All of the programmes are indeed multi-modal but some have had a particular focus. The Seattle Social Development Programme, David Hawkins' work, or the Fast Track Programme, would both be examples of this kind. They have some half a dozen different things that they do:

- trying to foster scholastic achievement, recognising that good scholastic achievement is an important factor in making anti-social behaviour less likely;

- social coping, a recognition that children have a whole variety of negative situations with which they may have to deal;
- peer relations, both in terms of quality of friendships but also dealing with the peer group;
- home–school links, trying to get these to work together in an effective way;
- a focus on classroom behaviour;
- and a focus on parenting.

The Fast Track Programme is one that has an interesting combination of a more intensive approach with high risk groups and also elements of the programme that are applied school wide. It is a bit early to know how far this is successful, but the initial results are encouraging.

The next area that I want to mention is situational prevention. A range of things can be done, that can be conveniently summarised as:

- *increasing the effort:* ie. making it more difficult to commit anti-social acts;
- *increasing the risks:* the techniques summarised by Ron Clark include: making the target more difficult, such as steering locks on cars; access control, like entry phones to buildings; deflecting offenders through street closures; and preventing means, as through gun control. There are measures such as entry and exit screening, merchandise tags on goods in shops, formal surveillance in terms of burglar alarms and the like, surveillance by employers and close circuit TV and natural surveillance in terms of good street lighting;
- *reducing the reward:* again there are a range of possibilities: target removal – stealing from telephone boxes was a favourite occupation, much reduced by use of phone cards where there is no money to collect; identifying property, such as property-marking cars; reducing or removing inducements, such as the cleaning-up of graffiti; and rule setting, such as banning consumption of alcohol in public places.

The evidence is that, if done in the right sort of way, each of these can be effective. But there are a whole lot of details that need attention if this is to work and, in particular, there needs to be a concern that one is not simply reducing opportunities in one place and shifting it elsewhere.

The last intervention that I want to mention deals with community-wide effects, a recognition that there are marked area differences in rates of anti-social behaviour. This has been known since the turn of the century but, until quite recently, it's been hard to know to what extent this is a cause and effect relationship. The work from Rob Sampson and his colleagues in the United States has taken a huge step forward, indicating the importance of a range of features, all of which are concerned with what one might broadly call social disorganisation or lack of social cohesion.

And there are things that can be done to aid this, of which the avoidance of negative housing policies is as important as any of the positive features. Let me just end, as I began, by reminding you that we are dealing here not with *'a'* thing or *'a'* cause, but with a heterogeneous *range* of behaviours, in which there are a range of factors that operate, and they operate over time. The chances for intervention begin in early childhood and they continue right into adult life. There is now a good deal of evidence, for example, that a cohesive, harmonious marriage in early adult life makes a big difference to whether or not anti-social behaviour that begins in childhood continues into adult life.

So, there is no one time for prevention. It needs to begin early but it needs to continue well into adult life.

3 Early intervention in family life: experiences from the United States

Dr Carolyn Webster-Stratton, Professor and Director of the Parenting Clinic, University of Washington in Seattle, USA

I'm going to talk a little bit about the what, where, why and hows of conduct disorders in young children.

What do we know about the problem of conduct disorder?

Aggression in children is escalating. In particular, it is escalating in younger and younger children. Recent studies have reported that anywhere from 10 to 25 per cent of young children, that is pre-school children and early, elementary school children, meet the criteria for oppositional defiant disorder or early onset conduct problems – such children are highly aggressive, disruptive, oppositional and sometimes hyperactive and impulsive. These rates are highest in low socio-economic groups.

I thought that I would start with a tape showing you a couple of the aggressive children from my clinic, so we can all be sure that we know what we're talking about. Can anyone identify the target child there?

In that short, 30 second segment, we saw the boy put his face in the other child's face, throw toys and hit him. We saw the other child rejecting him and threatening to tell on him: 'I'm going to tell your Dad, you're always in trouble.' These two children are six years old. They were given this castle to play with, which was quickly destroyed, even though they were instructed to 'make something together'. This tape demonstrates the lack of appropriate social skills evident in aggressive children. We don't see any co-operation, sharing, turn taking, or helping one another. We don't see any friendly communication or interaction which is reciprocal. We have found in our research that aggressive children are at least two to three years delayed in their play skills, which partially explains why they experience so much rejection by their peer group.

Why do we need to intervene?

With that kind of picture in mind, I wanted to say a little more about what we know about aggressive children and why we need to intervene early. Early onset conduct problems in children as young as aged three have been shown to be predictive of drug abuse, anti-social behaviour, delinquency, depression and violence, in adolescence and adulthood. Acts of murder, rape, robbery, drunk-driving, arson and abuse are carried out to a much greater extent by persons with a history of chronic aggression, stemming from childhood, than by other persons (eg. Kazdin, 1995).

Thus the problem of escalating aggression in young children is a concern for society as a whole, because of what it portends for the safety of ourselves and our children, regardless of our ethnicity, economic situation or the community in which we live. Conduct disorder is one of the most costly mental disorders to society. A large proportion of these children remain involved throughout their lives, either in mental health agencies or within the criminal justice system. In other words, we all pay in the long run – personally, financially or both – when these children are left uncared for and their behaviour problems untreated.

Research suggests that certain family characteristics put some children at higher risk of developing conduct problems: family poverty, single parenthood, teenage parenthood, parental psychotic illness, and parental history of drug abuse or criminality (eg. Farrington, 1992). Children whose parents are inconsistent in their discipline, or physically abusive or highly critical also are at greater risk, as are children whose parents are disengaged from their children's school experience and provide little cognitive stimulation in the home (eg. Patterson, Capaldi and Bank, 1991). And yes, as was pointed out already, there are some biological factors in these children which place them at higher risk, namely learning disabilities, language and reading delays, attention deficit disorder and hyperactivity. Children with two of these risk factors are four times more likely to have a mental health problem, compared to children exposed to one or no risk factors. Children with four risk factors are ten times more likely to have a mental health problem.

It is therefore strategic to try to identify these high risk children at a young age before they develop diagnosable problems and to offer families intervention and support early on so that we can prevent the development of conduct disorders and keep children from continuing on that trajectory to delinquency.

What have we learned from the research about what works with these children?

There are two broad types of intervention for families. One is family focused, aimed at teaching parents more effective parenting skills and the other is child focused, aimed at teaching the child more effective social skills, problem solving and anger management. I'm going to summarise some of the research. These conclusions are based on looking at randomised control group studies, and studies where there are parent and teacher reports as well as independent observations of child behaviour in the home. Comprehensive evaluations are important so we can have confidence that our programmes are effective.

Parent training

Parent training for parents of young children is probably the most effective and efficient way of helping young children with conduct problems. Parent training for young children has been shown in the research to be more effective than parent training for adolescents who are conduct disordered. I'm not saying that we shouldn't help parents of adolescents who have anti-social behaviour but, rather, to point out that research evaluating parent programmes suggests that it is far easier to turn around aggressive behaviour problems when children are young than when they are adolescents. Thus, by providing intervention when children are young, we get faster results, with a less expensive intervention. However, if we wait until adolescence, at that point the agressive children have gone on to develop permanent negative reputations, to be in a peer group which is as deviant as themselves and to have experienced serious school failure. Moreover, parents have experienced years of pain, helplessness and may have given up hope. If we start early, we don't have such an uphill battle. Take the anology of laying cement. In the beginning, when we first lay the cement with a design on it and we want to change the print, it's malleable. But if we leave the cement there for a long time and it hardens, we will need to crow-bar it out in order to make a change.

At least 25 years of research by a variety of researchers in the United States has consistently shown that two-thirds of young children (age 3–10 years) will be significantly helped with parent training intervention programmes. When we look at follow-up evaluation, three to twelve years later, we find that about two-thirds of the children whose parents received parent training are in the normal range, according to standardised measures, parent reports, teacher reports and observations. In other words, these early programmes do have lasting effects for the majority of families (see Webster-Stratton, 1996).

Our own research suggests that family characteristics, such as IQ, education, social class, whether they're single or married, whether the mothers have mild to moderate depression or whether there's a past history of abuse for the parents themselves, do not affect the parents' ability to benefit from parent training. On the other hand, our own research, as well as others', has suggested that families with spouse abuse, severe maternal depression, drug abuse, mental illness and severe poverty, will show less successful results when *only* parent training is offered. For these high risk families, parent training needs to be broadened to include other services, such as help for depression, marital issues and training in social skills and problem solving for the children. Broader-based services to these families leads to increased improvements in the children (see review, Webster-Stratton and Hooven, in press).

Additionally, we have found that while parent training leads to significant improvements at home, it does not guarantee improved behaviour and peer relationships at school, unless the teachers are trained in the intervention alongside parents.

What are the common characteristics of the most effective parenting interventions?

Effective parenting programmes need to be broadly based, particularly when we are dealing with high-risk families where there are other family issues, such as marital problems or mental illness. In this case we need to offer more than just a parent skills programme, rather a programme that deals with more of the parents' interpersonal issues.

Parenting programmes need to combine cognitive, behaviour, and affective components. Research suggests the most effective programmes are longer than 20 hours, are collaborative and focused on parents' strengths not their failings. They need to be group based, focusing on building social networks and collaboration amongst the parents themselves. Involving partners in programmes is key. A number of studies have shown that when there is a partner involved there are longer lasting results. Programmes that are culturally sensitive, where the parents are involved in setting their priorities and goals for what they want for their children, lead to fewer people dropping out, higher attendance and greater satisfaction. Programmes that are based on performance training methods, such as video tape, modelling, rehearsals, direct feedback and practice lead to greater behaviour change than programmes that are only discussion based.

Programmes that use multiple learning methods, such as practice, role play, discussion, books, audio and video tapes will be better able to address the different learning styles of parents. Programmes that involve, as I said before, teachers and parents in partnerships, and programmes that are sensitive to the barriers for low socio-economic families will be more likely to attract high risk families.

The most effective parent programmes are:

- broader based
- cognitive, behavioural, and affective in focus
- greater than 20 hours in length
- collaborative with parents
- focused on parents' strengths (not deficits)
- group-based – building social networks
- involving partners (fathers, grandparents)
- culturally sensitive
- based on performance training approaches
- using multiple learning methods
- involving teachers and parents in partnerships
- sensitive to barriers for low socio-economic families.

We have been involved for the last seven years in working with Head Start families, which is similar to your Sure Start, I believe. It is a programme offering an enriched preschool experience for families on welfare. We conducted a randomised study, where we offered a comprehensive parent and teacher-training programme to Head Start families. The results of the study are highly encouraging. Seventy-five per cent of the parents who signed up for Head Start attended the parenting groups. Eighty-five per cent of those who came to the groups attended more than two-thirds of the sessions. A year later, 85 per cent of the parents wanted to give back to the programme in some way, either by offering day care for other parents, so they could attend the parent group, by going to orientations and trying to tell other parents what the programme was about or becoming co-leaders, in some way assisting in the group leader.

Observations at home and parent reports indicated significant improvements in children's social competence and reductions in conduct disorder which were maintained one year later. Moreover, parents were observed to be significantly less critical and punitive with their children and to be more involved in their children's education (Webster-Stratton, in press)

My experience with this population has totally changed my vision. We must get programmes out of mental health centres and into schools and communities. We need to realise what the barriers are for low socio-economic families and what makes it difficult for them to attend parent groups. For example, we provided dinners for the parents, transportation and day care for the children in order to eliminate as many of the barriers as we could, so that it would be easier for them to be at the group. We carried out the programme in housing units, churches and schools, as close to the neighbourhoods of the parents as we could. When those services are provided in the community and when there's continuity and comprehensiveness in the programme so that parents can begin to trust the other parents and the leaders, then you have programmes that work.

Next I'll show you a tape taken from our parent training programme. This is an example from the programme for training parents in how to problem solve with their children. There are a variety of topics that we cover, from how to play with children to limit setting, discipline and problem solving. We use these videotape vignettes as the trigger for the group discussion. We show this vignette and then pause it part way and ask the parents, 'What would you say next?' or 'What would you do now?' Then they would try it out with a role play and then we'd show more of the vignette. The group leader asks, 'What did you notice about what this mother did?' 'Did you like it?' 'Would you do something different?' In order to build on the parents' strengths, we ask them to improve on some of the interactions in the vignettes, and what they noticed that they felt was helpful.

So the vignettes are used to stimulate the parents' discussion, to try to get the ideas from the parents, if possible, and to empower them.

Child-centred teacher training

Child training

Programmes that are targeted at teaching children social skills and problem solving directly, do improve peer relationships and social competence – skills which are characterised as protective factors or buffers against the development of conduct problems. In a recent randomised control study, we showed that by combining parent training with child training, we got improvements at home in children's relationships with their parents as well as improvements in their peer relationships. These children were able to play together and had less negative conflict management strategies with peers after the child training intervention. These effects were maintained one year later (Webster-Stratton, 1997).

Teacher training

We are involved in an exciting study now where we're randomly assigning families to interventions where there is teacher training, child training and parent training and various combinations of each. Our preliminary results suggest that the combination of parent training, child training and teacher training produces the most sustained reductions in conflict problems, both at home and at school, and in peer relationships.

I can tell you from personal experience, having spent 15 years involving only parents in the intervention programme, that it feels substantially different now that we have partnerships with teachers and teacher training. The teachers come in for workshops once a month, we go with the parents to the schools to develop individual plans for these children with their teachers. It feels like everybody's on the same page, holding hands.

Prior to this we used to hear parents complaining about teachers, and teachers complaining about non-involved and uninterested parents, and so on. We are no longer seeing that and it's very exciting. It will be another year before we finish this study, so I'm hoping the quantitative data bears out what we think is happening.

What are the characteristics of the most effective child training programmes?

Effective child training programmes must be developmentally based. For young children, fantasy, puppets and role plays engage them in the learning. Lots and lots of practice is essential. Groups should teach children collaboration and problem solving among themselves. If what is learned is going to be applied outside that setting to the school or the home, there has to be involvement of the parents and teachers. Memory cues help children organise their thoughts. Home assignments help promote further learning with their parents.

Next I will show you a videotape vignette of one of my child groups. We are talking here about a child who is about to be kicked out of school. We happened to be talking about consequences and all of a sudden he brings up the issue that he's going to be kicked out of school for bad language. In this part, we're dealing with the children's cognitions quite a bit but we also do a lot of role plays and practice of problem-solving situations. For example, we practice how to respond to teasing and how they would handle it. In this particular group, two of the children have been expelled from school. One is from a Catholic school and they're kicking him out for his foul language, the other child for aggressive hitting. The mother of one of the boys is dying of multiple sclerosis and his parents are getting divorced. Another of the boys was severely abused. The last boy's mother is intellectually delayed, and he was running rings around her. All of them are getting treatment because they're aggressive, but each has a very different family situation. We see them sharing their problems and we're encouraging them to talk about how they can help each other and have good friendships.

The most effective child training programmes:

- are developmentally based
- include affective, behavioural and cognitive components
- provide lots of practice activities in a variety of settings
- utilise role plays and videotape modelling
- utilise fantasy and games (child-friendly)
- are collaborative – using group problem-solving
- involve teachers and parents in reinforcing newly-aquired skills
- provide memory clues
- are offered in small groups
- utilise incentives and consequences
- give homework

How has the research been implemented into clinical practice or real life?

This is the part that I'm most discouraged about. Less than 10 per cent of young children with conduct problems get help and less than half of those children get empirically validated intervention. Practitioners are extraordinarily slow at adopting research-based interventions, perhaps because academicians haven't been interested in training and disseminating. Moreover, most of the mental health resources or interventions go to older children and adolescents. There is an appalling lack of comprehensive mental health services in our country for young children between the ages of three and seven. Young children with behaviour problems have been largely neglected by the mental health community. Pre-schoolers are offered help only if they have serious cognitive or developmental problems. Frequently they are ineligible for programmes or dismissed as having age-appropriate problems that are likely to be outgrown.

There is a myth that mental health problems don't exist for young children – that children under six do not have emotional and behavioural problems of such significance that they require intervention. Obviously there is evidence to refute this and this myth is destructive. In some states it is codified as policy, meaning there is no provision of mental health services for children under six and staff are not trained with developmental knowledge and skills to help young children and their families. In particular, interventions are not reaching socio-economically disadvantaged families, because they are based in mental health centres, are too expensive, too far away from their homes, too stigmatising, and they are not offered at flexible times to accommodate parental work schedules.

Recommendation – where do we go from here

I have two broad recommendations to make. One is that we switch the emphasis from a crisis-oriented / pathology-oriented *child's* mental health model to give more attention to the preventive / educative health model for *families*, which begins when children are very young. We need to increase the understanding that positive emotional and behavioural patterns can be identified, promoted or discouraged long before a child enters school.

My second recommendation is to switch the emphasis in schools from primarily a cognitive or academic competence emphasis to give more attention to social competence and the emotional well-being of children. It must be understood that a child's emotional state affects his or her ability to achieve the level of cognitive competence necessary to learn.

Stable and nurturing teachers, who do this emotional teaching, may be able to help buffer some of the high risk children from the impact of parental psycho-pathology and family stress, and provide support when parents are relatively unavailable to their children.

How do we do this?

Provide universal interventions

We need to provide universal parenting programmes to all parents. Every single parent should be immunised with a parenting programme. We should do as good a job marketing parenting as we do marketing Frosted Flakes. Health care systems should offer parent education programme options to parents in schools, health centres, libraries, doctors' offices, churches, housing units, home visits and on television.

Schools should offer all children an educational curriculum which addresses emotional literacy, such as education regarding social skills, understanding of feelings, anger management, problem-solving and friendship skills.

Schools need to work in partnerships with parents – developing plans that individualise children's social, as well as their academic needs, and bridging the gap between home and school where possible. Parents need to be seen as partners, not problems.

Provide selected intervention

After that we need to identify the high risk groups. Additional parenting support and education options should be targeted at socio-economically disadvantaged parents, as families living under the stress of poverty are more likely to have their parenting disrupted due to these stresses. High risk children, those with a parent who is mentally ill, or abusive, or at risk because of their own developmental difficulties such as attention deficit disorder or reading delays, need additional support in strengthening their social competence through small group training that includes social skills and problem-solving.

Provide indicated intervention

That's our primary and secondary care. And finally, the tertiary, what we call indicated prevention intervention, where we deal with the children who are exhibiting behaviour problems. These include those with high levels of aggression, non-compliance, peer rejection or diagnosed with oppositional defiant disorder or early onset conduct disorder. These children need remedial help in social skills, problem solving, anger management and emotional literacy, just as we would offer remedial help if a child was language delayed. Parents of children with these high risk behaviours need to be targeted for parent training.

Who will do this and how and where? training implications

Multiple professionals need to collaborate in this endeavour, as the problem is not the exclusive property of any single discipline. We can expand family support and services by training health care professionals, teachers and mental health care professionals to utilise empirically validated interventions. Health care professionals can help offer parenting advice before problems develop, and can screen and identify children at high risk who might benefit from extra support.

Teachers should be trained in effective classroom management skills, so they can effectively manage misbehaviour in the classroom. Then they should be trained to offer a social skills and problem solving curriculum for all children in their classrooms. Child care workers, pre-school and nursery school teachers and nannies need training in parenting skills, and how to promote social competence in young children. Psychologists, educational psychologists and social workers trained in running parent and child interventions for high risk families and children should be prepared to offer these programmes in community settings.

For any of this to work, there needs to be broad inter-agency collaboration at the systems level. At the primary prevention level, health care professionals such as nurses and paediatricians will provide parent education in health centres and homes through home visiting. At school, teachers will provide emotional education for every child. High risk families will be identified for additional support.

At the stage a young child has behavioural symptoms, the family may be offered intervention in the form of child training, social skills groups and parent training. These programmes may be offered by teachers, psychologists, psychiatrists or social workers. Families with children who have diagnosed conduct problems, or who have multiple issues like drug abuse, violence, emotional or speech problems, will need additional mental health services from those specially trained in family work.

These early intervention prevention strategies will not just help children who are at risk from conduct disorders but will have wider effects and other positive benefits for all children and their families. These effects will include more confident and involved parents, who use less harsh and abusive discipline with their children, and happier home lives, with children doing better academically and socially because their emotional needs are taken into account. Children who have learned effective relationship skills will be more likely to have happier marriages, less depression and divorce.

Teachers will feel more satisfied because they will have the support of parents and classrooms which are better managed with fewer behaviour problems. Ultimately, I believe we all reap the benefits of helping to create a less violent and more caring society.

References

Farrington, D. P. (1992). Explaining the beginning, progress and ending of anti-social behaviour problems: stability and factors accounting for change. *Journal of Child Psychology and Psychiatry, 31*, 891–909.

Kazdin, A. E. (1995). *Conduct disorders in childhood and adolescence.* Thousand Oaks, CA: Sage Publications.

Patterson, G. R., Capaldi, D., and Bank, L. (1991). An early starter model for predicting delinquency. In D. J. Pepler and K. H. Rubin (eds.), *The development and treatment of childhood aggression*, (pp. 139–168). Hillsdale, NJ: Erlbaum.

Webster-Stratton, C. (1996). Early intervention for families of pre-school children with conduct problems. In M. Guarlnick (ed.), *The effectiveness of early intervention: second generation research.* Paul H. Brookes Company.

Webster-Stratton, C. (1997). Treating children with early-onset conduct problems: a comparison of child and parent training interventions. *Journal of Consulting and Clinical Psychology, 65*(1), 93–109.

Webster-Stratton, C. (in press). Preventing conduct problems in Head Start children: strengthening parent competencies. *Journal of Consulting and Clinical Psychology.*

Webster-Stratton, C. and Hooven, C. (in press). Parent training for child conduct problems. In T. Ollendick (ed.), *Comprehensive Clinical Psychology*, Oxford, England: Elsevier Science.

Discussion

The speakers were asked about gender differences and their implications for early intervention work with families.

Professor Rutter said one of the best documented risk factors for anti-social behaviour was being male, but surprisingly little research had been done on why this was so. It is pervasive across time and across cultures, but has also changed over time and across cultures. So, for example, the ratio of boys to girls in delinquency and crime in this country has dropped from about 11 to 1 in 1950 to about 3 to 1 now. In this country the sex ratio is most marked in those of Asiatic background and least marked in those of Afro–Caribbean background. Finding out what factors might be relevant to this is a high priority, Professor Rutter said.

Professor Webster-Stratton said in her age range, the four to eight year olds, they saw four boys for every girl. Girls do not externalise as much as boys but they have just as much verbal deviance and slightly more non-compliance. These girls are therefore more divergent from their same sex peer group, than the boys. Girls then have a big rise in delinquency at adolescence, suggesting perhaps that non-compliant girls get overlooked because their behaviour is not as challenging as boys'.

Another delegate asked what evidence there was from research, or elsewhere, about what was effective in getting people to work together with parents and particularly across professional divides.

Professor Rutter said how it was done was crucial. It has to be 'a working together and not simply working alongside'. Bronfenbrenner had found a quarter of a century ago that, when parents and schools worked together, parents often became demoralised because they felt they lacked skills, 'It needs to be a real partnership, not simply one informing the other,' he said.

4 Mentoring as an early intervention strategy: the experience of Big Brothers Big Sisters of America

Dagmar E. McGill, Director, International Division, Big Brothers Big Sisters of America

Previous speakers have adequately grounded us in the various aspects of children and youth in crisis, and what is needed at various age levels in the developmental span. I've been asked to present a model that has proven to make a difference – the involvement of volunteers in a one to one relationship with children over an extended period of time. Allow me to put my remarks in some societal context, which may have meaning for you, as you continue to forge public policies and programmes to address your concerns.

For the past 40 years in the United States, public policies and funding at the federal level have tended to be focused on deficits of children and youth – juvenile delinquency, teen pregnancies, substance abuse. We have been in a 'fix them' mode for many decades and the tendency to do the fixing was focused on the teenager: the adolescent who was dropping out of school, the adolescent who was having a baby, the teenager who was abusing alcohol, the gangs of teenagers who were engaged in acts of violence. But there was a concerted effort among the national youth-serving organisations in the United States during the current decade to move the focus to a more developmental approach. The problem, however, has always been the difficulty of showing that positive work with a young person prevented subsequent negative behaviour. We couldn't prove that we were going to make a difference as the young person got older. The national youth organisations, the Girl Scouts, Boy Scouts, the YMCA and the YWCA, all got together and began to work with legislators to craft what was called the Youth Development Community Block Grant. This was an exciting piece of legislation, that was going to direct money at the community level for already established programmes, to reach and serve more children and youth at an early stage in their development. Unfortunately this legislation, which did have bi-partisan support, did not survive because there was an unwillingness to trade funded programmes, that had not been proved to work, with programmes that have demonstrated their effectiveness. Nonetheless, the language of positive youth development has been sustained and has gained national recognition.

In April 1997 we had an interesting session in Philadelphia, which is where the national office of Big Brothers Big Sisters of America is located. This meeting was called The Presidents' Summit on America's Future. It was the first time in our history that current and former presidents of the United States came together to talk about public policy. It was an exciting time, and out of that meeting came agreement on five resources that all American young people should have. Every child and adolescent in America should have the confidence, character, competence and connections needed to live a healthy fulfilling life and contribute positively to society. As a result of that summit, the alliance for youth – America's Promise – has identified five fundamental resources that, if consistently provided, will not only contribute to youth development but also significantly reduce problems facing America's youth. Here are the five resources:

- ongoing relationships with caring adults;
- safe places and structured activities;
- a healthy start for a healthy future;
- marketable skills through effective education;
- an opportunity to serve.

The goal of America's Promise is to connect two million additional young people from birth to age 20 to all five fundamental resources. These connections will occur primarily through the natural support systems in neighbourhoods and communities, families, youth organisations and so forth. Thus America's communities will work together to provide these resources for our children and adolescents. Following the summit, literally thousands of companies, organisations, civic and social groups, have come forward and have made a promise that by the year 2000 they will have made a significant contribution towards these resources for young people.

One of the active efforts in this early intervention work has been the work of the Search Institute in Minneapolis. In 1990 they introduced the concept of developmental assets for young people aged 12 to 18, demonstrating that these have powerful influences in adolescents' lives, and become the foundation for these young people to reach their full potential. The Search Institute was very much involved in the Presidents' Summit and helped craft the five resources. In the past few years, the Institute further developed these assets and they now include the full range of years from birth to 18. There are 40 developmental assets that have been identified through a great deal of research. Twenty of these assets are referred to as external, and comprise constant exposure to the interlocking systems of support, empowerment, boundaries and expectations – literally a web of safety and support that is important for stimulating and nurturing healthy development. However, the responsibility for children does not end with the provision of external assets. There needs to be a similar commitment to nurturing internalised commitments, values and competencies to guide young people in making their choices and to create a sense of centredness and purpose. Adults, who model these assets when children are young, lay the foundations for children to observe, learn and gradually internalise these assets. That is where the Big Brothers Big Sisters work comes in. The twenty internal assets are clustered around four building blocks: commitment to learning, positive values, social competencies and positive identity. Big Brothers Big Sisters of America is particularly interested in the internal assets model because it includes the involvement of caring adults in a child's life.

Big Brothers Big Sisters of America began in 1904 but during the 90 years of our national organisational development and localised service delivery, the word mentoring has not been part of the nomenclature. It was not until the late 1980s, when funders and researchers decided that mentoring might be a promising approach for children at risk, that the word mentoring found its way into the Big Brothers Big Sisters of America rhetoric for describing our service. There was a strong inclination on the part of local Big Brother Big Sister agencies – we have 505 of them across the United States, in every state in our union – not to be confused with more loosely fashioned mentoring programmes that were being developed around the country. They fought this notion of being referred to as a mentoring programme, because mentoring has various definitions, depending upon the emphasis that a particular community youth programme has as its goal. Mentoring is often used interchangeably with tutoring, and sometimes with a goal of apprenticeship. Mentoring tends to be an 'add-on' to programmes that have specific goals and objectives, with mentoring being seen as only one of many ingredients. Historically, mentoring has had a 'helping to learn' aspect to it, for example an older person guiding a younger person around some prescribed activity or aspect of life. Big Brothers Big Sisters' work, however, focuses on friendship. Friendship is the primary aspect of the relationship, which should lead to a feeling of trust over time, and which then may lead to some aspects of learning, regardless of the subject or behaviour. But the relationship, the trust, the mutually shared experiences of everyday life, is the essence of the Big Brothers Big Sisters service. While the word mentoring is now used, for the most part interchangeably with Big Brothers Big Sisters, the emphasis continues to be on the quality of the relationship between the volunteer and the child and not on a set of prescribed activities.

Big Brothers Big Sisters is a community mentoring programme which matches an adult volunteer, known as a Big Brother or a Big Sister, to a child, known as a Little Brother or Little Sister, with the expectation that a caring and supporting relationship will develop. Hence the match between the volunteer and child is the most important component of the intervention. Equally important is the support that the match receives in terms of on-going supervision and monitoring from a professional staff member. The professional staff member makes 'matches', monitors, supervises and closes the relationship between a volunteer and child, and communicates with the volunteer, the parent or guardian and the child throughout the match relationship. Although Big Brothers Big Sisters of America was not developed with academic theories of delinquency in mind, or any of the other deficits that I spoke of earlier, the programme's rationale most closely resembles social control theory. According to this theory, attachments to prosocial others, commitment to socially appropriate goals and involvement in conventional activities restrain young people from engaging in delinquent activities or other problem behaviours because they have socially bonded. More socially-bonded young people have more to lose by misbehaving. The operational rationale that has been guiding Big Brothers Big Sisters' service for nearly a century has been that the consistent presence of a non-familial caring adult can make a difference in the social and emotional development of a child or young person, particularly one growing up in a single parent family or in an adverse situation. Over the years the development of Big Brothers Big Sisters' service has been based upon the overriding belief that this consistent and frequent volunteer contact is a powerful influence. This belief has been based predominantly on anecdotal reports from parents, teachers, case managers and children themselves.

So the mission of Big Brothers Big Sisters of America is 'to make a positive difference in the lives of children and youth, primarily through a professionally supported, one to one relationship with a caring adult, and to assist them in achieving their highest potential as they grow to become confident, competent and caring individuals by providing committed volunteers, national leadership and standards of excellence'. In practice the volunteer intervention in the traditional one to one relationship with a child is three to five hours a week, on a weekly basis, over the course of a year or longer.

The generalised activity of the relationship is related to the goals that were set initially when the match was established. These goals are identified from the extensive case manager interview held with the parent or guardian and the child, and also with the volunteer. The foremost goal usually set is to develop the relationship – one that is mutually satisfying, where the parties come together freely on a regular basis. More specific goals might relate to school attendance, academic performance, relationships with other children and siblings, general hygiene, learning new skills or developing a hobby. The goal is established for a specific match and developed into an individualised case plan, which is updated by the case manager as progress is made and circumstances change over time. Generally speaking, the professional staff do not tell a volunteer what activities to engage in with the child during their time together, but they guide the volunteer and make suggestions of possible activities and approaches based upon the child's, and the volunteer's, interests and needs. Consistency in the relationship over time is a higher priority than the types of activities in which they participate. Once the match has been initially agreed upon in the presence of the child, volunteer and the child's parent, it is the responsibility of the professional staff member to maintain ongoing contact with all parties in the match relationship. To quote a volunteer, 'The last six months have been especially difficult for my Little Brother, too many foster homes, life has been very transient, he seems so susceptible to negative influences. My role is to be steady and to be there, I am his current lifeline, I apply no pressures, I show up, we go out, this is a long process because of my Little Brother's troubled background.'

At the local level, the agency may set outcome goals for specific children, or a specifically designed mentoring service. This might focus on a specific problem or situation, such as children having been abused, children of an alcoholic parent, children who are hearing impaired or disabled. However, even in these examples of a specialised one to one service, the emphasis is on developing the relationship prior to setting specific goals or objectives that relate to a potential risk factor. Although not necessarily explicit for every match, the non-directive objectives most frequently cited by agency staff include decreasing or delaying anti-social activities, improving academic performance, attitudes and behaviours, improving relationships with family and friends, strengthening self-concept and providing social and cultural enrichment.

The local Big Brothers Big Sisters agency develops its own criteria that define the type of child appropriate to be matched with a volunteer. Although most agencies have as their criteria that the child be from a single-parent family, many agencies serve children from dual-parent households when there is some type of stress in the family such as illness, poverty or other circumstances that make it difficult for parents to provide ongoing nurturing and support for the child. Our current figures are that 80 per cent are from single-parent families but 20 per cent now are from dual-parent families. Ongoing supervision and monitoring of the match help to ensure a more fulfilling and longer lasting relationship. Currently the average length of the match is two and a half years, with many lasting much longer. Case managers often deal with difficult situations that arise in the relationship, troubleshooting and solving problems that may have the potential to escalate into major problems and lead to the termination of the match. Even if a match should end prematurely because of problems in the relationship, the case manager helps the young person and the volunteer make that transition of closure and asks both parties if they care to be re-matched.

There are five major components or process points in the Big Brothers Big Sisters programme where decisions are made by the professional staff. The first point is during *enquiry:* this is an entry point for potential children and volunteers and is usually made through a telephone enquiry. After the enquiry, and when they've received information about the service, the next process point is *intake,* a process to determine the eligibility of the child and the suitability of the potential volunteer. The third process is that of *matching:* this is a process for determining the appropriate match of volunteer who will meet the needs of the child, and facilitating a positive beginning for all parties involved. The fourth is the match *supervision,* a process through which the case manager monitors and evaluates the progress of matches. The fifth point is *closure.* This officially closes the match relationship and either closes the files altogether for all parties or determines their desire to be re-matched.

In the late 1980s Public/Private Ventures, a youth development research firm located in Philadelphia, was intrigued by the potential of mentoring but concerned about the lack of solid information about its implementation, cost or effectiveness. So they developed a research agenda to explore what they called Created Adult–Child Relationships. Central to their research agenda was an examination of Big Brothers Big Sisters of America's service delivery at the local level, because it is the largest and most extensive mentoring programme, not only in our country but in the world. While they came to Big Brothers Big Sisters to carry out part of their research agenda, they did research on about three or four other kinds of mentoring programmes in the United States.

As a result of their four year initiative, four studies on Big Brothers Big Sisters work were published. Two of the studies are of particular interest to this discussion. Study number three was on building relationships with youngsters in programme settings. In this study, 82 matches, supervised by eight Big Brothers Big Sisters agencies across the country, were examined in detail over a nine-month period. This study found that matches could be separated into two broad categories, identified as developmental in approach or prescriptive. *Developmental relationships* are those in which the adult volunteer holds expectations that vary over time in relation to the needs of the youngster. The emphasis of the volunteer is first and foremost to establish a good relationship with the child. Other goals are not addressed until the relationship has been solidified. Developmental relationships also tend to be more egalitarian, with consideration given to youngsters' preferences about what they do together. The *prescribed relationships* are defined as those in which the adult volunteer views their goals for the match rather than the youngster's. Volunteers possess high expectations for behaviour change in the youngster, that is transformative goals, and they set these goals and ground rules for the relationship.

The research indicates that the Big Brothers Big Sisters of America's emphasis on the mentor's role as a friend is a focus that is likely to lead to a higher rate of developmental relationships than might be found in a mentoring programme with more transformative goals. The findings indicate that the successful volunteers took time to establish and maintain the youngster's trust. They were far more likely to listen, rather than risking judgement or lecturing the youngster. They respected the youth's desire to have fun, they encouraged their participation in making decisions about activities and they negotiated with the youngster until mutually satisfactory activities were agreed upon. These outcomes appear to be highly valued by the young people. Most developmental matches – 50 out of the 54 – persisted and continued to develop, while the majority of prescriptive matches – 22 out of 28 – faltered or closed. At the time of the second interview, one and a half years into the match, the majority of the youngsters in developmental relationships sought their adult friend's assistance or accepted their efforts to advise, guide or intervene.

Study number four was called Making a Difference, an impact study of Big Brothers Big Sisters. The impact study used a classical experimental design, in which young people were randomly assigned to either treatment or a control group. The youngsters were 10 to 16 year olds drawn from those applying to the eight study agencies. Young people who were selected to receive a match were matched as quickly as possible, and the control group were placed on a waiting list for the duration of the study. Control group studies are not very popular and we even lost one of our agencies, as their board of directors decided that they did not want youngsters to be a part of the control group. But, ultimately, 1,138 young people were enrolled in the study over a 17-month period. Information was collected from the youngster, parents and case managers at three points in time: the time of random assignment, the time of the match and at follow up. There were 959 youngsters in the analysis sample. The largest percentage, 60 per cent, were either ethnic minority youngsters, that is African–American, Hispanic–Latino or Native American. More than 60 per cent were boys. Many were poor, with 40 per cent living in homes receiving public assistance. These young people often experienced other problems as well: 40 per cent lived in families with a history of substance abuse, 28 per cent in families with a history of domestic violence and 27 per cent were themselves victims of emotional, physical or sexual abuse.

The research showed that Little Brothers and Little Sisters fared better than the youngsters in the control group, as a result of their participation in the Big Brothers Big Sisters programme. Findings indicate that matched youngsters were 46 per cent less likely than control youngsters to initiate drug use during the study period. A stronger effect was found for ethnic minority youngsters, who were about 70 per cent less likely to initiate drug use than ethnic minority control youngsters. Matched youngsters were 27 per cent less likely to initiate alcohol use than the control group, and female ethnic minority youngsters were half as likely to initiate alcohol use. Matched young people were almost one-third less likely than the control group to hit someone. Little Brothers' and Little Sisters' academic behaviour, attitudes and performance were better than those of the control group. Matched youngsters skipped half as many days off school than did the youngsters in the control group, felt more competent about doing school work, skipped fewer classes and showed modest gains in grade point averages. I understand from the researchers that that was significant because non-classroom activities usually don't produce much in the way of academic change. The gains in academic performance were strongest among ethnic minority females. The quality of the Little Brothers' Little Sisters' relationships with their parents or guardians, such as levels of trust in parents, was better at the end of the study period than it was for the control group. This effect was strongest for white males. The quality of the Little Brothers' and Little Sisters' relationship with their peers was better at the end of the study than it was for the control group: this effect was most strongly evidenced among ethnic minority males.

In conclusion, given the benefit that research shows that youngsters derived from caring and consistent relationships with adults, and the scarcity of such relationships in the lives of many young people, there is a significant need for interventions like mentoring. We believe that well implemented programmatic relationships, designed to address this need, play an important role in any broader strategy designed to serve the needs of young people, especially young people in high risk environments. Evidence of effectiveness like that contained in this research, especially around issues of drugs, violence and schooling, may influence the public's view of what can be accomplished. It also stimulates policy-makers to begin shaping a new and more effective social policy approach for young people – one that focuses less on specific problems after they occur and more on meeting young people's most basic developmental needs.

References

Beiswinger, George L. (1985). *One to one: the story of the Big Brothers/Big Sisters movement in America.* Philadephia: Big Brothers / Big Sisters of America.

Benson, Dr Peter L. (1990). *The troubled journey: a portraint of 6th–12th grade youth.* Minneapolis: Search Institute

Leffert, Nancy, Benson, Peter L. and Roehlkepartain, Jolene L. (1997). *Starting out right: developmental assets for children.* Minneapolis: Search Institute

McGill, Dagmar E., (1997). *Blueprints for violence prevention: Big Brothers Big Sisters of America.* Colorado: Centre for the Study and Prevention of Violence, Institute of Behavioural Science, University of Colorado at Bolder

Morrow, Kristina V, and Styles, Melanie B. (1995). *Building relationships with youth in programme settings: a study of Big Brothers/Big Sisters.* Philadelphia: Public / Private Ventures

Sipe, Cynthia L. (1996). *Mentoring: a synthesis of P/PV's research: 1988-1995.* Philadelphia: Public / Private Ventures.

Tierney, Joseph P., Grossman, Jean Baldwin, with Resch, Nancy L. (1995). *Making a difference: an impact study of Big Brothers/Big Sisters.* Philadelphia: Public / Private Ventures

Discussion

Two questions came up in the brief discussion that followed. A delegate asked whether research had showed whether the sex and the cultural background of the mentor, and other variables, were important.

Dagmar McGill said the Public/Private Venture research had considered these variables, and they didn't make a difference.

The second questioner asked whether Big Brothers Big Sisters had experienced problems with volunteers abusing children.

Ms McGill said there had been a few cases of paedophiles abusing male children, among the very large number of mentoring relationships established over the years, 'There is no way to give an individual a test, so we do a very stringent screening process, we check records and we do a lot of interviewing.'

Community support

Workshops chaired by Jon Bright, Social Exclusion Unit

5 Meeting the needs of children and young people in their community

Martin Craig, Project Leader, North Shields and Meadow Well Health Project,Co-Founder, The Waterville Projects for Children and Young People, North Tyneside

I lead a community health project in the Meadow Well estate in North Tyneside. Meadow Well is a run-down and deprived area, between Newcastle and the sea at Tynemouth, that is in the middle of an extensive regeneration programme.

The area consists of two electoral wards, and both of them have better housing outside of Meadow Well. If you put the whole lot together and called it Meadow Well and drew a ring round it, it would be one of the bottom five communities in the country in terms of deprivation, and its health statistics are similar. There are a lot of young people aged between 12 and 24 and quite a high average of single-parent households. The Probation Service say that 70 per cent of those given supervision orders are unemployed, illustrating the link between crime and unemployment.

There is a large amount of absenteeism. When the area was written about two years ago, school exclusions weren't such a big deal. They have become a very big deal and we are addressing that problem with local people.

What worries me most as a health worker is that, in the poorest regions, young males ages 15 to 44 have a lower life expectancy than their fathers. We've all become used to longer life expectancies with each generation, and we now have a generation in deprived areas (and the males particularly) whose life expectancy is not as good as that of their parents. This is a very worrying trend, one that we've not had since the Great Depression.

The Health Project uses community development methods, although we were not a community development project to begin with. A health visitor and I were 'parachuted' into Meadow Well in 1989, to 'sort out' problems relating to heart disease. Within one month I did the one piece of group work I've ever done in that community, and realised that I knew what I needed to know and that other things needed to happen instead of group work.

I was working with a group of residents, asking them the main causes of death in the UK, and they quickly listed heart disease, strokes, cancers and accidents. Prior to this session I'd been warned about this community by a local GP, who said that Meadow Well people were the 'ignorant, uneducated, criminal fringe of society'. Yet they knew the main causes of death without me telling them. So then I put on a blank transparency and wrote 'heart disease – causes?' and they listed the causes and their list was as good as a Professor of Primary Health Care could give me.

One difference was that the professor used words like sclerosis and the Meadow Well residents didn't; but they knew what the causes were. The other difference was that they joked about the causes. They laughed when they talked about smoking, they thought being overweight was quite a funny topic, they giggled at 'naughty but nice' cream cakes. They stopped laughing when they came to talk about stress. When they mentioned stress, the whole group immediately became introverted and depressed, and started volunteering experiences from their own lives to give me an idea of what they meant by stress. These were, without exception, horrific stories. They stopped my colleague and I in our tracks. We thought afterwards that we should resign. We felt, 'what they need here is mental health workers and neither of us are that. To be here, under false pretences, waving a leaflet called *Beating Heart Disease* is an insult to this community. They know the information that's in it, but they can't do a lot about it'. The residents told us that the reason they behave in the way they do; smoking a lot, eating the 'wrong' food and all the rest of it, is to do with stress.

Out of that session came a way of working that we've adopted ever since, which we call *Working Upstream*. We begin with what the statistics tell us – heart disease is the problem. They tell us what their problem really is – and heart disease is a long way down the road from there – and then we start following the trail. It began with heart disease, it led to mental health, and eventually we learned that the stresses were not about neurotic people unable to cope, or lack of fulfilment through being in the wrong job, or the wrong relationship, or whatever. Their stresses were bricks through windows, having your son brought home by the police, being burgled or raided or having your house set alight, or being intimidated out of your house by criminals. Actual stresses that would floor most of us, rather than just being someone who was not very well able to cope with normal life. Relaxation classes wouldn't have done much good. Assertiveness training wouldn't do much good, if the person you're helping to become assertive is threatened by a brick or a knife. A lot of the normal responses, which are valuable in some communities, weren't appropriate to this estate.

We also realised at that early stage (and this has changed dramatically since then) that the policing of this area was very poor indeed. It was extremely reactive. Policing was described by one lady from the estate as 'blue lights doing 90 miles an hour down Waterville Road'. She felt that the estate was a police no-go area, despite their protestations that there was no such thing in the UK. She felt that the police were reluctant to attend any kind of crime in Meadow Well. In one incident witnessed by me police took 45 minutes to travel two miles in response to a 999 call about a violent attack on a local woman.

Meadow Well is a complicated place. Three years ago a house was set alight by children, none of whom were over the age of 10, and they stayed in the burning house at an upstairs window. When the Fire Brigade came the children threw bricks at the fire engine while the house was blazing. At that time, we were planning youth work with the 16+ age group, and suddenly realised 'Help! There's a group coming up here that are scarier than the 16 pluses. Something needs to be done about that'

If you look at part of the Meadow Well today, there are various pieces of local sculpture, provided through the regeneration scheme, and the houses are being regenerated quite well: cavity wall and loft insulation, double glazing, better alarms, thicker doors, better locks. It's a mixture of community safety and better living conditions.

Regeneration does take a long time. You can't just wave a wand with something called City Challenge or the Single Regeneration Budget, or any of these schemes – which are all excellent – and suddenly solve it. One of the problems I have is with colleagues saying 'How long have you been there now? Shouldn't you be moving on? Isn't it sorted?' And this word 'sorted' sticks in my throat – the idea that you can 'sort' a community that took 60 years to reach the point where a riot happened in two or three years with a bit of government cash. It isn't going to happen as easily as that.

It's a complicated place, and there are complications within community work as well. Take a woman with whom I have worked closely and regarded as a friend for several years. She grew up in Meadow Well, has chaired a resident-led community group and has taken an active part as a paid worker in the area's regeneration. She is clearly successful in terms of her community work. But last year one of her sons died of a drug overdose. It is not yet clear at the time of talking to you whether or not he died under suspicious circumstances (for instance through somebody attacking him and using drugs as a way of killing him) or whether he just died because he overdosed on drugs. He certainly did not have a history of injecting; as far as we know the injection that killed him was the first he ever had. Despite this, his mother hasn't given up her work, although many people advised her to pack it in, saying, 'you've done enough, let somebody else take over, it's someone else's turn now' and she hasn't become evangelistic either. She has just carried on in the way she was before, as a community worker.

In Working Upstream, we began with heart disease and realised that giving leaflets out, showing videos or running the odd exercise class clearly was not enough. Working back from that realisation, we worked with local residents to set up a neighbourhood MIND group, a mental health group. The residents themselves decided to affiliate to national MIND, rather than become a local 'stress busters' group or something similar. MIND are quite strict. They don't make any kind of allowances for particular communities. They said, 'If you are a MIND group, you'll have to have committee procedures, chairs, treasurers, proper accountancy. Do you really want to do that, or would you rather just sit and have cups of tea?'. And the residents said, 'Don't insult us. We'll become a committee, we'll become a MIND group'. It's been going since 1990 and our health project supports it.

The next piece of work was community safety. We had to lobby like mad to get more effective policing: this included meeting people from the Home Office and saying to them, 'If you don't want repeats of the 1991 riots, things must be different here. It must be much more community oriented. The police must be unarmed; not in cars but walking around, and here when there isn't trouble.' I said, 'I'm a health worker; I'm not just around when people are dropping dead, I'm here all the time. Youth workers are here when the young people aren't in trouble. We would like some police here on the ground when things are normal'. So we got it. In the end, it happened. The police were based in our clinic, and they managed to get on with almost everyone in the community, except some of the teenagers. The police tried hard with the teenagers, but there was an 'us and them' brick wall between them.

During that time, due to successive poll tax capping, the local authority had to lose its youth service so we were in a position where there were no youth workers in an area that had had a riot 12 months earlier. A lot of young people were still very disaffected, with some experience under their belts of causing quite serious trouble.

This is where my voluntary work, and that of other people in the community (including the church) came in. We had contacts with the Sainsbury Family Charitable Trusts; and, after some meetings with them, we got enough money to employ two youth workers and put them back on the patch they had been working in. That initiative has grown from two staff in 1993 to now, where there is a Detached Project, a Children's Project (which I'll talk about briefly in a minute) and a Health Resource (linked to a small community gym in our clinic building). The Waterville Projects overall employ more than 20 people, with an annual turnover of about £330,000. This has meant a fund-raising nightmare for the directors, who are longing for a time when there is some kind of national strategy that would fund work like this.

The Children's Project came about because residents and workers organised a Family Fun Day in Meadow Well. There was a big marquee in a field, it was a nice sunny Saturday in the summer of 1993. It was meant to be fantastically good fun. Instead the marquee was very nearly dropped from its pole on to the heads of people underneath it by children under 10, who then tried to set light to it with gas lighters turned up high. They were torching the canvas, while their parents and others were inside. It was difficult to stop that happening, even though there were carefully planted police-horse displays and police-dog displays at the event. Despite this it nearly got out of control. The residents were saying to me, and to people like me, 'You fund-raised for work with 16 pluses – it's the little ones we're scared of'. The little ones were much more disaffected. Even teenagers who had been in quite a bit of bother were saying to me, 'All I did was nick cars. You should see my little brother, he's really scary.' We thought we were going to have something like a Bulger case at one time, and we had a contact with one of the social work team who had worked on the Bulger case. Their message was that it wasn't two uniquely evil children, it was children who felt that, for whatever reason, they could do almost as they liked. They were very scared that it wasn't just those two kids, that there may well be others like them.

We felt that the only thing to do was to throw something very positive at it. We got some money out of the local City Challenge, the Employment Service (interestingly) and the local TEC, to fund a Children's Project. We employed six local young people, who were just out of their teens themselves. They were well known on the estate already, they were not outsiders. We got them some training and set them up in male and female pairs as Play Development Workers.

As earlier speakers have already talked about we just provided positive play experiences as an act of faith that, if children were co-operating, learning to wait their turn, sharing things and generally learning to work with each other rather than against each other, something good ought to come out of it. We didn't have time to set up any evaluation or any studies, we just threw what money we could raise at providing workers on the ground from within the community. Since then, it has developed a great deal, and the young workers have developed enormously as individuals and as a team. We have always raised sufficient money to take them out of the poverty trap, so they can declare their income and play their full part in society. For example one of the lads has bought his own BMW – it's not new, but he bought it legally, he has a full licence, he is fully insured, and he's proud of his achievement.

We have a caseload-free Health Visitor on our project team who was keen to do three things: one on home safety, one in support of parents and some much needed work with older people. Safety Crackers is a loan equipment service for new parents which gives them stair-gates, fire-guards, smoke alarms and practical things like that for a one-off payment of £5.00. They can keep the equipment, which is worth about £70.00, for as long as they need it.

The Community Mothers Programme is a parenting initiative developed at Bristol University and pioneered in Ireland, London and other parts of the UK. It is basically about training local people with some experience and success in parenting to work with their peers. It doesn't bring in an expert, it trains local people as volunteers on an expenses-only basis to work with new families. The work is done in a non-directive way. If the problem is that a baby won't sleep, the Community Mother talks the parents through that, about what they can do, and if a parent says 'I could smack the baby' the Community Mother would ask what would happen then, give them a range of choices and then help them work out alternative ways of coping with the situation. Later the Community Mother would come back for another chat, talking about whether the plan has worked and, if it hasn't, helping the parents to modify the plan.

We have developed an older people's initiative (MOPI) but it has proved infinitely harder to fund-raise for work with older people than it is for children and adolescents. Hundreds of thousands of pounds have been raised for youth and play work, but the older people's initiative has made just £4,000 since its inception, and that's been a real struggle. Older people are a neglected group, certainly where we work. Because of this some older people tend to get antagonistic about youth work, saying 'Oh yeah, more money yet again thrown at criminals'. They use phrases like 'Goodies for baddies' . We have to argue with that, but it does cause problems when older people have difficulty raising enough money for a bus trip, and they see young people doing all sorts of exciting things like building hovercraft.

The Health Resource is centred around a community gym, which is built into the health clinic. You can use it if you're 16 or over. If you're on benefit it's entirely free. Rather than employ typical 'Look After Yourself' trainers we employed skilled people with experience in the worlds of fitness figure competition, boxing and (non-steroid assisted) body-building. The workers have received training in health promotion; they are excellent role models and the gym has developed a large membership. It is very popular, and like the NHS itself, we are fighting to keep it free at the point of delivery, because we know that the people who need it most would not be able to come if there were any charges.

Our biggest problem has continued to be related to crime. The estate suffered rioting in 1991 and this inevitably attracted national attention and generated new money. This brought new people with new ideas and there was a honeymoon period which I remember as the time when I could safely park my car outside the clinic! For about six months, we could just lock our cars, walk away and not worry about their safety ….

After that brief period we couldn't understand why, with all this good feeling, we started to get more intimidation and it was quite nasty stuff. All sorts of different things were happening, to the point where some residents threatened a rent strike against the council and lobbied health workers and other non-council staff to support them. We said 'We can't support you with a rent strike' (one of the dangers of community development is that, if you bite the hand that feeds you, you get closed down). We did say that we would go with residents to a meeting with housing staff and police to discuss the problems. What seemed to be happening was that criminals from outside the estate were encouraging, and sometimes paying, children and young people to cause trouble in selected areas. They were then coming along under the guise of security companies, to get contracts to allegedly clear the trouble up. It was a kind of protection racket. When we found out about that we talked to a criminologist who said that similar things had happened in places like Broadwater Farm, where there had been riots, trouble, new money, and where the criminals had tried to get their hands on some of that money. We organised a neighbourhood conference to discuss how we could avoid that, and we got death threats from the criminals for doing that. We got directly warned off, that we had to drop it now or our families were at risk. It was interesting that the threats came to families rather than to individual workers – I was never personally threatened over this issue, but was warned that things would happen to my wife and kids if I pursued it. We naturally talked to the police about these warnings and, on their advice, the conference on organised crime was cancelled.

Ever since then, all our community safety work has been almost clandestine. We've had to go off the estate, change venues, move around and there have been times when a car load of known criminals have followed those meetings from hotels to police stations and other venues. The criminals are keen on stopping us doing this kind of work. They also don't like our work with young people, who are good fodder for them. Criminals sponsor young people to do petty crime to keep the instability you need in an area in order to carry out more serious criminal activities. We had to talk to the police about that.

The danger of this cycle is that, because of their families, workers feel pressured to change their jobs. Sadly, some funders said for a while 'It's a black hole. They had a riot, we threw money at it, now there's more trouble , we can't throw any more money there, we are going somewhere else.' And then your money goes and then the workers can't stay any more because their jobs are gone. And the residents are left even more isolated and depressed than they were when the whole cycle started.

Our goal is to try and flatten out this circle, so that we don't go all the way round again and end up having another riot in five years time, followed by fresh appeals for money and all the rest of it. It's time to move on and that is the goal. The Meadow Well people don't want to live in a ghetto. They want to integrate with the outside community. We believe that the good work that is happening in Meadow Well can easily be expanded outside the estate. That will make the community proud that something it came up with is being exported, rather than depressed about trouble coming in. Through the Healthy Living Centre initiative, and in partnership with several agencies and community groups, we are hoping to address all the issues that impact on health in three sites within the boundaries of our local Riverside Primary Care Group. Getting into these communities, getting under the skin of their problems, with any research being action research – that, I hope, will be the framework of any bids we may make into the New Opportunities Fund (which will be launched later this year) and the future direction of our Health Project's work.

6 Reaching out to families: schools as a community resource

Graham Evans, Principal, Minsthorpe Community College, South Elmsall, West Yorkshire

Schools in the later part of this century have tended to concentrate on the national curriculum, but at Minsthorpe Community College we've also done a lot of other things. The core activity is the education of young people in the 11 to 19 age range. When I took over five years ago, the credibility of Minsthorpe was at rock bottom. It had no esteem in the local community whatsoever. To do a lot of the things that I and the governors and other people wanted to do, we had to get the core business right. In our particular situation, the keystone was the education programme of the large number – it was 800 then, it is 1,600 now – of students in the 11 to 19 age range. Whether you like it or not, GSCE results, A level results, are indicators of success. I like it, of course, because mine are going up. Schools should work in leagues rather than in tables, I believe, but everybody is into performance indicators. My teachers say, 'We shouldn't be judged on league tables', then scour the papers to move house and put their children into the school that gets the good results.

There is a whole range of things that we have now that we didn't have before. Five and a half thousand people a week use my site now. There is a music centre on a Saturday morning with 400 people, a sports complex, a training and conference centre, a family learning centre. A lot of my time in the last five years, and a lot of the time of the people who work with me, has been to turn dreams into reality. It's easy to say, 'we would like to be the educational, training, leisure and recreational centre of our community'. To turn that from a dream into reality takes a lot of hard work. If there was an Olympic gold medal for bidding, we would be in there because, like Martin Craig, I spend a lot of time bidding. If you want to give the people what the people want, you have to go out and get the money to do it. You can say, 'Oh, it's not my job.' You can say that all day. I go to head teachers' meetings and I sit there, and they say, 'I haven't got enough money for biros, or computers'. If you want it, you go and get it. There is money around. It's putting the work in to get it. We have raised about £3.5 million so far.

For example, we have obtained the biggest lottery grant that has ever come into

Yorkshire, £1.4 million. We have also developed a fantastic after-school family learning programme for my youngsters. Four hundred kids a night go to it. I am not going to say to one of my French teachers, 'Oh, by the way, five nights a week, after you have finished teaching six periods a day, run a family learning centre for 400 kids, will you?'. I'm going to get the money to hire a Family Centre Learning Co-ordinator, who can do a far better job than a French teacher, when she is tired at the end of a day.

Jon Snow wrote about the regenerative role of education in the *Times Education Supplement* in August 1997: 'This is where the great millennium opportunity is so far being missed ... using education to revive the community and the community to revive the country. The millennium could so easily be a moment when every child and every community is touched in some way by a new resource that will represent a tangible turning point in their lives.' We are now going to mount a major initiative to enhance the value of learning. It is called 'Creating a Learning Dome' over the SESKU area (South Elmsall, South Kirby and Upton). SESKU is a mining area, where learning traditionally was not valued in any shape or form. It has amazed me how people in the area have warmed to this concept.

We have now reached the stage where people are talking about a multi-million pound bid to set up neighbourhood learning centres based upon the primary schools. We are talking about young children being taught about life earning profiles – not using the words 'life earning profiles' but talking about the fact that learning pays. There has recently been a major research programme by Leeds Metropolitan University – the title of that project is Learning Pays. People 'like us' are now better paid than we have ever been. The gap between the qualified and unqualified has started to increase, for the first time since the Second World War. My counterparts from Europe laugh at the attitude towards learning in this country, and the academic/vocational split. If you are an undergraduate of a university or an apprentice painter on the Volkswagen production line, you are still a learner in Germany. Over here, we have this divide between vocationalism and academia. All of my full-time teaching staff for this year, including me, have been through a training programme on IT. One of the points that I keep stressing to the community is that we are all learning, even people with high academic qualifications.

Education is the key to economic and social regeneration in Europe. When Tony Blair came to Minsthorpe Community College, I talked about delivery to him. People want us to deliver. They are not always sure what they want us to deliver, but they know that they want us to deliver something. Whatever organisation you belong to has got to deliver, and by delivering I think we have got to give people hope. I regularly link the two words together now. I'm talking about *delivery giving people hope.*

Discussion

What needs to be done to make local services more accessible and better co-ordinated, what role should education have in commissioning or co-ordinating that service delivery?

Martin Craig said local government hadn't failed, because it was working in partnership with his project, and had helped by providing premises and seconding staff. 'The future for us is working in partnership. Without it we wouldn't survive,' he said. His project had found the Council was more au fait about what was needed than other organisations.

Graham Evans said professionals worked too much in boxes, and he would like to destroy the walls of those boxes. Regeneration was the aim and people needed to go for it in a big way. Although there were frustrations working with local authorities, they were the organisations that had to lead this regeneration drive and sell it to their communities.

A mental health fund raiser asked how developing young people's self esteem and emotional competence was addressed at Minsthorpe, and what links the college had with other agencies to promote children and young people's well being?

Mr Evans said not all his staff were teachers: there were also youth workers, nursery staff, crèche workers. On the question of self-esteem and competence, he gave the example of the After School Learning Programme. Young people had their own management committee, produced agendas for courses that they wanted to be run, brought in outside speakers. The College had a PSE programme and had drugs education within the curriculum, but even so there was a serious drug problem in the area.

Should parenting skills be part of the National Curriculum?

Mr Evans said parenting was part of the curriculum at Minsthorpe but it was difficult with youngsters who didn't live with their parents, or in the normal family model. The College worked with today's kids, who are going to be the next generation's parents, but also with the present generation of parents. There were parental programmes, parents and youngsters came together through the Family Learning Centre, and the College worked with Home-Start, particularly with young single mothers with low levels of parental skills.

Martin Craig said parenting work was needed, but the title should be broader, perhaps parenthood, rather than parentcraft. When working in the prison service, he had found that men who rejected parentcraft as a topic were ready to discuss whether they might want to be parents and the whole issue of whether as a male you had anything to do with the family, other than procreating and disappearing.

Creating opportunities for children and adults in deprived communities could be vulnerable, unless local authorities took it on, if it depended on the fundraising skills of people like Mr Evans.

Martin Craig said barriers seemed to be coming down with the Government keen to integrate work across disciplines. This was happening with Health Action Zones and the broader role being given to primary health care. And local authorities were back in the regeneration partnerships and the NHS, after years of exclusion. Another excellent trend was the current rehabilitation of group work and participative and non-curriculum dominated learning, which had been frowned on for a period. This ethos was helpful, for instance for drug education, Mr Craig said.

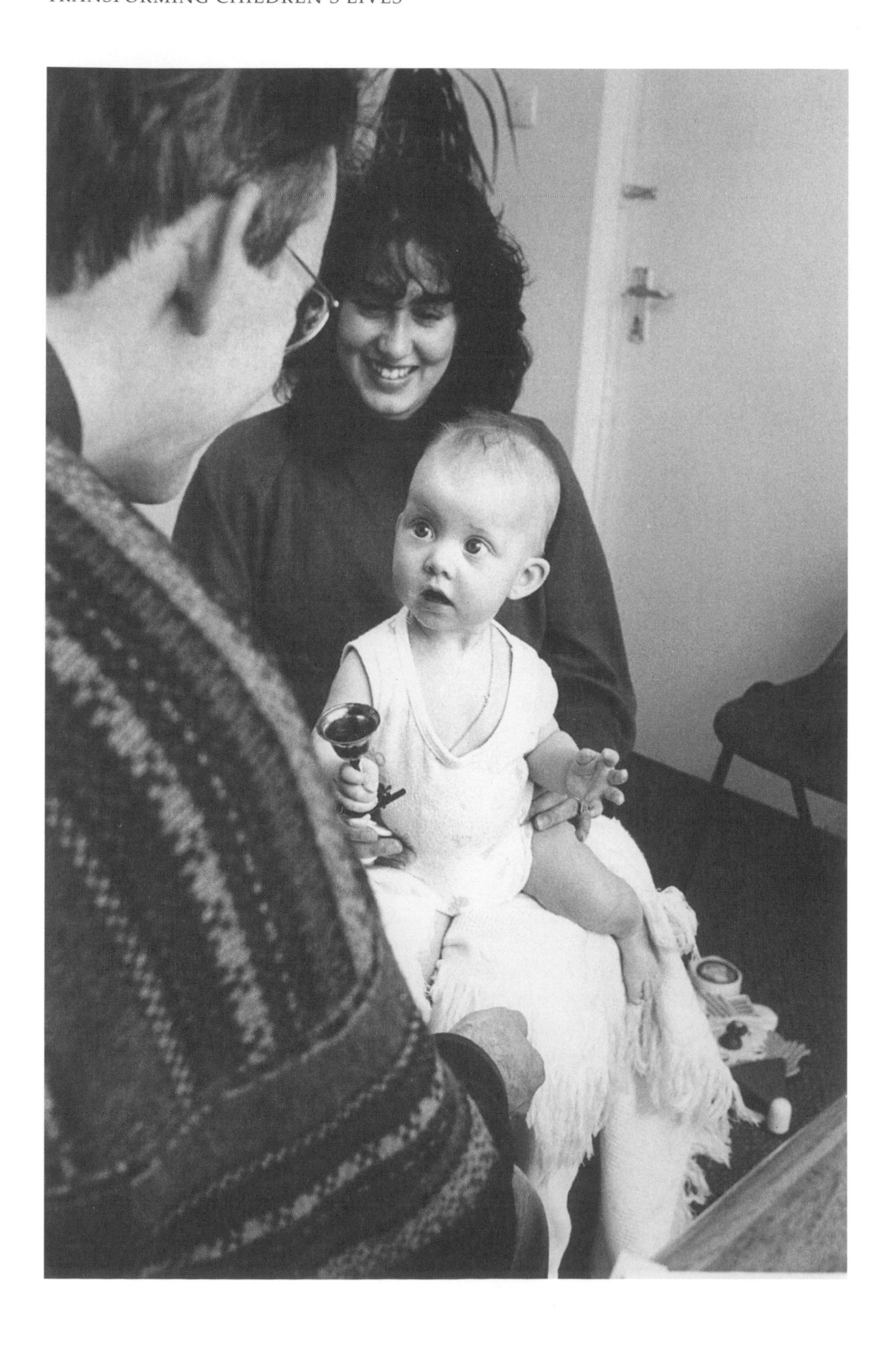

Early intervention for children in need

Workshops chaired by David Matthews,
Children's Services, Department of Health

7 The experience of early intervention: a review of practice in the USA and UK

Dr Michael Little, Dartington Social Research Unit

By removing the handle from a water pump, the Victorian doctor John Snow greatly reduced the incidence of cholera during an outbreak in a small area of central London. Snow intervened early. By preventing people drinking bad water he succeeded in preventing the transmission of a disease. Some aspects of the story may be apocryphal, but the central image of John Snow rolling up his sleeves before the Broad Street pump is very striking and it has encouraged many scientists, policy-makers, managers and clinicians to seek similarly forthright solutions to other health and social problems. Far better to take decisive preventive action than to wait for a disease to take hold.

Snow studied the incidence of cholera by location. His concern was less for the experience of the individual than for the connection between groups of people who died after experiencing similar symptoms: in this case, those caused by the cholera bacteria. His map marking each death in its approximate location and relating the deaths to the position of street water pumps, represented an important breakthrough in his understanding.

In the health world, some of the greatest advances have come from prevention strategies. By instructing physicians in a Vienna hospital to wash their hands before delivering a baby, Ignatz Simmelweiss saved many millions of lives – even by changing so small a detail of medical practice.

George Albee, an American expert on prevention, concludes from this and other evidence that 'no mass disorder affecting humankind has ever been eliminated or brought under control by treating the affected individual'. A logical conclusion to be drawn from this maxim is that early intervention holds the answer to many social problems.

One reading of the experiences of Snow and Simmelweiss would suggest that their discoveries were made in a Eureka-like flash. In fact, the advances followed careful research into the individual chains of effects involved in disease transmission and were made in the light of improving knowledge about the susceptibility of certain groups to particular types of disease. Their findings were treated with scepticism – and there are indeed a number of reasons to doubt the benefit of early intervention:

This diagram attempts to show how a range of interventions, some early, some later, coupled with an improvement in diagnosis, changes the pattern and reduces the prevalence of disease, but does not eradicate it

This stage is often referred to as primary prevention. which means intervening with an entire population to stop a problem emerging. Thus, a very early intervention to stop people drinking infected water would be to treat the water.

This stage is often referred to as secondary intervention, which means intervening to stop a problem becoming worse. Early intervention to increase resistance to the effects of drinking bad water might be to make available inoculation.

This stage is usually referred to as tertiary intervention, which means focusing on the particular circumstances of the individual. An intervention to treat cholera might involve rehydration.

This stage has variously been described as primary or secondary prevention depending on the context. Social prevention to stop those with cholera infecting others might involve an education programme.

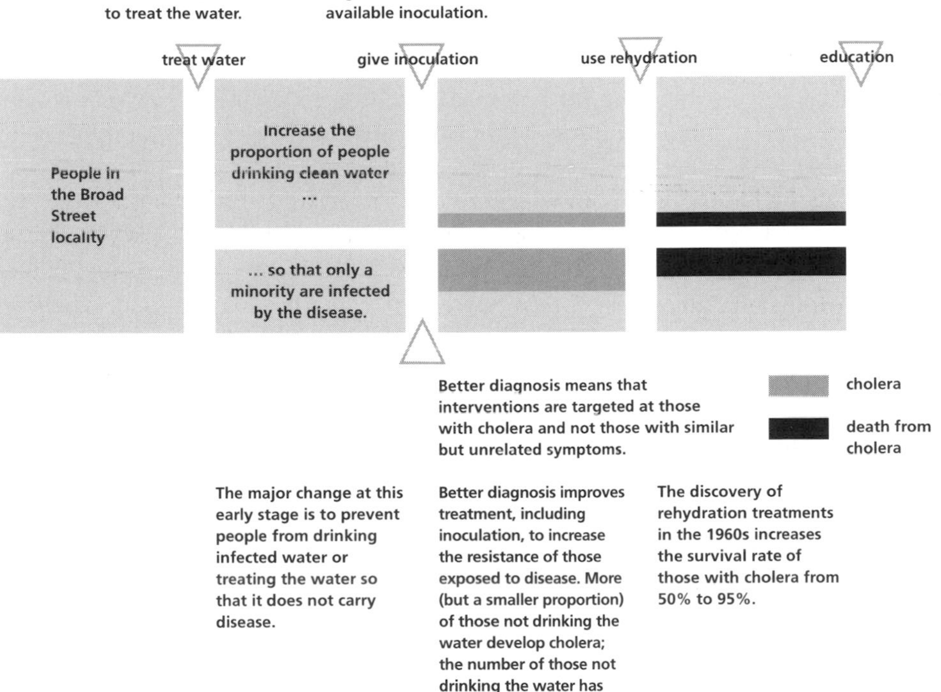

- There is seldom a single cause of death, illness or social disadvantage, so that even after the supply of diseased water had been cut or doctors began washing their hands, many more people died in the Broad Street locality and in the Vienna hospital.
- Typically, a significant proportion of people put at risk of disease, say by drinking water carrying cholera bacteria or by having a baby delivered by a doctor with dirty hands, do not become ill. Something protects them from the bad outcome.
- Although taking the handle from the water pump and improving standards of cleanliness in the hospital radically reduced the incidence of disease, some still developed cholera and childbed fever.
- Largely ineffective as they may have been, some treatments saved some of those who succumbed to disease. Some women infected by doctors during childbirth survived to raise their children. Half of those developing cholera would have lived to tell the tale.

The literature review by Little and Mount (forthcoming) considers different types of activity that have changed the incidence/prevalence of disease or social problems. It suggests that:

- primary prevention to intervene with an entire population;
- **plus** early intervention with those displaying the first symptoms;
- **plus** treatment for those who succumb to illness or social need;
- **plus** social prevention to minimise the damage that can be done to the wider community and better diagnosis to be clear about the precise nature of different problems;

in combination provide the most effective route to change.

In our book we summarise the sequelae of children's problems and prevention, early intervention treatment and social prevention that have been shown to operate in different aspects of children's lives, namely those stemming from:

- where they live
- their family relationships
- their social behaviour
- their health and that of their parents, as well as
- their education and employment opportunities.

Several specific strategies for effective change utilising the existing resources of housing, social services, education and health services are suggested.

It is a cornerstone of the argument that the confluence of several risk factors in a child's life is a necessary condition for later social psychological difficulty. For example, only a very small proportion of children exposed to poor parenting but whose school experiences are generally happy eventually become delinquent or suffer the other problems described. But children brought up badly, who suffer family discord and/or divorce and who fail to do well at school have a high likelihood of displaying serious antisocial behaviour in adolescence (or to other sorts of problem). This confluence is expressed in terms of chains of effects.

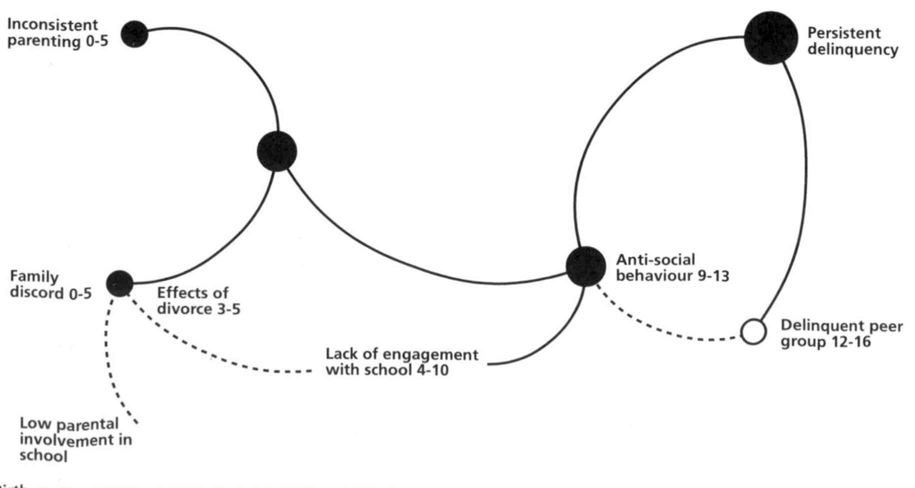

For example, assume that the above chains of effect can be identified as contributing to persistent delinquency in adolescence. The youth justice worker, picking up the end of the chain, is faced with a series of risk factors most of which are very resistant to intervention. Then make a second assumption – that a young person has a dormant protective factor in terms of his or her educational ability. A failure to engage with school will mean that this protection is never exploited, but it would be unrealistic for the youth justice worker to contemplate achieving very much in relation to the young person's schooling as late as his or her sixteenth year.

Organising services to bring out dormant protective factors so as to break or loosen chains of effect leading to social psychological problems in adolescence are at the heart of the approach. In this case, it might simply be the engagement of the parent in the child's education during the pre-school phase and its continuation thereafter. Such an approach is likely to improve the child's regard for and use of education and will bring out the protective factors of reasonable education ability. It may not reduce the risks generated by inconsistent parenting, family discord or the negative sequelae of divorce, but it is likely to widen the child's social network and so reduce the chances of drift into a delinquent peer group. Creating mechanisms to test new contributions of prevention and early intervention activity so that local and health authorities learn from each other as the evidence base increases would also improve the situation.

Reference

Little, M. and Mount, K. (forthcoming, 1999) *Prevention and Early Intervention with Children in Need.* Aldershot, Ashgate

Discussion

In the discussion that followed, a delegate asked whether British research had looked at European, as opposed to American, work on early intervention and whether any of this was going to be part of the model of intervention adopted here?

Another delegate said one of the problems with research was that it tends to be academically orientated and driven. Local authorities, unlike health authorities, have little if any capacity or funding to direct their own research or to be involved with academic partners.

Dr Little said one of the reasons for looking to the United States was the robust evaluation that takes place there. The attitude in the UK, that services were obviously good so what's the point in evaluating them, would have to change, although he acknowledged that some good evaluations were available here.

The connection between research and practice was a fundamental weakness, Dr Little said. Rather than researchers telling practitioners what to do, they needed to say: 'These kinds of methods are fairly simple to apply in your own context, why don't you build them in to your interventions as you get them started?' Dartington Social Research Unit now had four test sites where it offered advice and strategy about how to mount research but local authorities undertook the work themselves, he said.

David Matthews pointed out that the Department of Health's £2.5 million, five year research programme on families and supporting parents will provide some evidence in this area, although they won't follow children over long periods of time, or be subject to random control processes, as some of the American studies do.

The Department of Health funded some early intervention schemes for young people at risk of drug misuse a couple of years ago, and a delegate had been responsible for producing good practice recommendations from the evaluation. The key conclusions were the need for staff training, and integrated guidelines and procedures for the relevant people. 'In the research that we've done, there's a lot of skill out there but it doesn't get filtered down to the practitioners actually in the field, and that's where the problem is.'

A writer about parenting, suggested that government departments' rush to spend budgets at the end of the financial year, and consequent short-term funding of initiatives, worked against proper evaluation. 'I hope that the new government will pay more attention to the practicalities of making the money available to projects.' In America funders preferred funding evaluation to funding projects, she said.

Mr Matthews said that the workshop led by Diane Robbins would report on the evaluation of the Government's Refocusing Children's Services Initiative. An extensive evaluation of Home-Start three years ago had shown that schemes of that kind were very cost effective.

On Europe, Dr Little said the evidence differed. There was good evidence from northern Europe, though it was not as robust on the whole as that from the United States, while there was little from southern Europe. On the relationship with practice, he said researchers were often not good at writing, while the way work was presented, for instance by using journalists, was important. This answer did not satisfy one questioner, who said the key was getting the practitioners' angle, and translating it into practice, not making research readable.

One delegate suggested that race played a greater part than Dr Little's analysis suggested. Lone parents and inconsistent parenting did not explain why so many black children were excluded from school or were in youth custody. 'What about expectations, what about positive images, what about praising the black child, what about saying you can do it?', she asked. The focus tended to be on the child but sometimes a family's lack of infrastructure – home, benefits, nurseries – was the reason they couldn't look after the child properly.

Another delegate queried Dr Little's figures, claiming that divorce has no effect on children aged three to five, if you discount extreme disadvantage and children who have been in care.

On the race issue, Dr Little argued that the method of looking at the chain of effects could be used to determine what worked for different groups and so could help address the different outcomes for children in different ethnic minority groups. He took issue also with the questioner over infrastructure, arguing that in this country, particularly compared to the United States and southern Europe, there was an 'enormous' infrastructure of social services, family support, health visiting and specialist education.

Another questioner asked what impact free, nursery education with qualified teachers would have on children?

Dr Little suggested it was going to be important for certain high risk groups of children but would probably have relatively little benefit for other groups of children.

A participant from Kent asked about the overlap of services, with some children receiving help from social services, health and education.

Dr Little said in Kent £50 million was spent on children in need, but £38 million of that went on the 800 children looked after, and the rest on the 4,200 who were supported in their own homes. *'I don't know whether that's the most effective use of resources, but that is a question we have to start asking ourselves very seriously,'* he said.

Another participant said early intervention could become a self-fulfilling prophecy: by seeking to identify children who might develop problems later, those children might be labelled as potentially delinquent. A proactive plan to deal with that danger was necessary.

A head teacher said nursery education for all three year olds, as they had had for long time in his/her area, did make a difference. His/her school had contact with parents at an early stage, and worked closely with health visitors

Dr Little said social services should try to identify more clearly the different groups of children they were trying to help, and compare likely outcomes with or without the intervention. One way to get round the labelling problem was to include all six and seven-year-olds in outcome targets, and to make a bit more effort with the most deprived children to bring them up to the basic standard.

8 Working with fathers of children in need

Colin Holt , Project worker, Lawrence Weston Family Centre, Bristol

The Lawrence Weston Family Centre, in Bristol, has been involved with fathers for the last eight years. The Centre opened in 1982, as a response to a lack of provision for under-fives and a large number of young children on the Child Protection Register in our area in Bristol. The Centre is managed and run by Barnados but it is also joint funded by Bristol Social Services Department. We are therefore primarily a child protection agency, with 70 per cent of the children we work with on the Child Protection Register. The Family Centre's main aim is to promote the development and potential of young children and their families in the community and prevent the need for children to be looked after by their local authority.

Family centres are very diverse in what they do and could be put broadly into community work, neighbourhood work or therapeutic work. Ours is very clearly based in therapeutic work. Because of its child protection focus, we have employed very skilled, experienced social workers who carry out intensive assessments and interventions with families experiencing severe difficulties with their parent–child relationships. The approaches and methods of work reflect this particular therapeutic model in that the Centre responds to a wide range of parenting issues in a variety of ways, combining individual, couple, group, and family work, as well as play work and group work with children according to assessed and expressed needs.

The following are some excerpts from a video we have made for this conference, of men talking about how you engage men and what they are looking for in services, which is what most people want to know about working with fathers.

When a family is running into difficulties, there is usually enough support for the mothers and children: what is lacking according to some is enough support for the dads. Some fathers need help because they find they suddenly have to cope with the running of the household. They may need help to cope with difficult children. Some dads even need help because they are frightened of their own tempers, they are scared of what they might do in the heat of the moment. The Lawrence Weston estate near Bristol is the sort of place where those problems can boil over.

Many of the families who live here don't live here out of choice. They live here because they've come out of bed and breakfast, they've got nowhere else to go and many of the families say how lonely it is, just being here in the middle of nowhere.

Mike needed a hand with little Josephine because her mother is ill. Debbie and Brian needed help with their family because Brian had become extremely violent at home.

> *'He'd get upset if somebody said something slightly out of place – it got really bad – so I was glad he had someone to talk to about his violence and why he did it.'*
>
> *'The only problem I have found is that you've got to come and swallow your embarrassment and go into a group of women. You can't get away from the fact that you're a man amongst about 10 to 15 women. I really wish there were more fathers' groups around.'*

The group begins with a play session. Some fathers have previously found themselves too preoccupied or angry, tense or embarrassed to play with their children.

> *'I enjoy coming here with my little one, Terry. I've never seen the other two grow up, I was always at work. But now I'm between jobs, hopefully not for too long. I'm always doing things out in the garden so you tend to let them get on with it by themselves. Whereas here you tend to respond to the children, and you are given a specific time to play with children and they love it.'*
>
> *'Many more fathers are being involved and I think responsibility is the key word, they are taking responsibility for their children, they are taking them to school, they are picking them up, they are taking them to the dentist and all the things which in my family, my mother did. I think that it is really imperative for men to come together, as it is extremely important for women to come together, to talk about and exchange ideas. There isn't a right and a wrong way of doing it. If there was one text book, then it would all be easy. There isn't.'*

Halfway through the morning the men break off for a chat amongst themselves. To direct the conversation, they've developed a ball game, an ice-breaker. Today it's sort of a young parents quiz.

> *'All children to be potty trained by the time they are two. These are true or false?'*
>
> *'False.'*
>
> *'Why is that false?'*
>
> *'Because, Owen's two and he's not potty trained yet.'*

Admittedly these chaps don't look the sort to sit around having a young parents' quiz but that's probably the whole point.

What they actually say is that they can talk a different language. That they feel that, if they go to the pub or other social places, they get caught in a relationship with other men which is often competitive, which is often mickey taking, which is often about putting each other down, and here they come to talk about themselves, to talk about their feelings, to learn about their feelings. A lot of men find difficulty in identifying their feelings, to feel that they have feelings, let alone to express them.

> *'Well, men work, playing with kids for a few hours. They go to bed and they think they are close to kids. When you come here, you realise that you're not really that close to the*

> *kids. You come home for an hour then you go to bed. That's the same as baby-sitting. You want to try looking after them 24 hours a day, then you know what kids are and that's what you learn here.'*

Some of the difficulties that men experience are to do with their own background. Quite a lot of them will say that they experienced fathers who either rejected them, didn't live with them or who were absent or not directly involved. Which says something about that generation. I think that fathers have enormous potential for looking after children, I actually believe that the majority of fathers can look after children equally.

> *'But a fathers' group is a little bit of peace and quiet in lives that may have precious little of that. Some say it simply saved them from the edge of despair.'*

> *'I think that without Barnardos I wouldn't have anything, I wouldn't have the kids, I wouldn't have a relationship, I really believe that I'd be dead now or I'd be in jail.'*

Our mission statement is that the Centre works with fathers because we acknowledge the fundamental and significant role they play in family life. Over the last eight years, we've established an equal service delivery for fathers, mothers and children. In 1996-97, the Centre worked with 50 fathers and 60 mothers and 100 children. And our success in engaging and working with fathers is largely due to the Centre creating a male specialist post for this work over this eight year period. The Family Centre provides a wide range of services which address the many and various problems encountered by fathers which directly affect their parenting: providing support systems for primary carers and stepfathers, as well as structured therapeutic work for fathers who are physically, emotionally or sexually abusive to either their partners or to their children. If we have a key, it's partly that we work with all fathers. I want, now, to go briefly through the counselling, the group work and the feedback that I've got from fathers, which was largely on the video.

Our counselling is the central component and offers continuity, support and a flexible approach to the needs of the individual. The emphasis is on judging the behaviour and not the person. Developing a therapeutic alliance is crucial to enable the man to explore and change his behaviour. The feedback that we've got from the majority of fathers is that the one to one relationship with the male worker was the foundation for engaging and creating change. Fathers placing trust in the worker, and feeling listened to and understood, was the most important factor, closely followed by the worker's ability to be clear, honest and talk straight. Some fathers saw the worker's role as an advocate, spokesperson or support worker at formal meetings and case conferences.

The Centre has found group work is the most effective way of teaching fathering skills. The group is specifically designed to take experienced fathers who may be looking for support, as well as those who are first time fathers or where there is a child protection issue. By including a wide range of fathering skills, attitudes, abilities and ages of fathers, positive role models may be presented. The majority of fathers said the group had influenced and affected positive change in their parenting skills. Feedback, particularly from health visitors, showed that the group members had demonstrated child development knowledge outside the group.

The Centre provides a specific model of work with fathers who are emotionally or physically abusive to their partners and to their children. Fathers who have been abusive to their children reported that they felt they'd been labelled as dangerous, without anyone talking to them or assessing them, and that the decisions were often based on the mother's account only. Fathers said that they appreciated a fair and balanced assessment, and clear measurable goals to achieve change. Some of the fathers identified long-term work – which is between two and four years – as the most positive experience. Others viewed the work as helpful but too interfering and confrontational. Fathers viewed the work as enabling them to remain living with their families or to maintain close contact with their children.

Most mothers viewed the work with fathers as positive and beneficial to the family. Some mothers were concerned that fathers should not receive more or better services than the mothers. Some mothers were concerned about abusive men using the Centre and felt that they should attend separate centres. Enabling fathers to have a clearer relationship with their partner, fathers actively being more involved with their children and parents developing clear parenting roles were seen as the main benefits by the majority of the mothers.

In conclusion the Family Centre has been clearly successful in engaging and working with a wide range of fathering problems over an eight year period. We have been successful in enabling fathers to remain with their families or enabling fathers to maintain close contact with their children, where appropriate. We have also been successful in stopping some fathers abusing their children. The Centre has maintained contact with many of the fathers two to four years after the Centre's intervention and our information through this contact confirms success has been maintained. We haven't had any formal evaluation, which is what we desperately need. We are too busy doing the work and we need some help and support in that. But from our evaluations at the Centre, from the fathers, outside agencies and the professional workers, we have been successful in providing services, changing abusive behaviour, offering support and providing information and practical advice to fathers who would normally remain ignored or forgotten.

Discussion

What is available for the men when they finished at the Lawrence Weston Centre, for example, opportunities for adult education, job training, or child care to allow them to rebuild their lives?

Mr Holt said the Centre had other services, including adult education, in the building and a male adult literacy group was being set up. A lot of the Centre's work involved linking into other resources in the community.

One delegate commented on the lively positive presentation in the video, and said she had come across the same style in the United States. 'I think our forms of delivery need to be exceptionally positive because otherwise people will walk away,' she said. Mr Holt agreed that if you were confrontational or competitive with men, they wouldn't come back a second time.

A child health adviser asked how the Centre got men to come – was it the carrot, the stick or a combination of both – and whether staff were all from social services, or whether there was a multi-agency focus with health visitors involved?

Mr Holt said if you provide the right services for men, they will come along. But, 'If they see it's a service for mothers, and not for them, then they are not likely to come along.' Experience working with men showed similarities with working with women, for instance the crucial role of individual counselling and developing a relationship from the beginning. Health visitors ran separate groups on positive parenting for men and women, but so far integrating groups for mothers, children and fathers had proved problematic, he said.

How far does the project depend on Mr Holt's own presence, as initiatives often collapse when key people with will and drive leave?

Mr Holt said he thought the service was well established, as it had been running for so long, 'I'd like to think that the men wouldn't allow it to drop, if I left tomorrow.'

Mr Matthews said the challenge for central government was to find a structural mechanism for achieving delivery in areas where it was not possible to rely on the goodwill of individuals.

Three delegates commented that:

- **the general level of skills and training of all the staff was important, as well as the pivotal role of individuals. Getting the right balance between being positive and enabling people to confront their problems was also down to skills and training;**
- **there was a tremendous commitment to multi-agency working, and policy documents from central and local government were constantly promoting it. The problem as a practitioner was often to keep track of problem families, because they move, children change schools and fathers were in and out of prison. Did anyone have examples of good practice, where agencies share information about families without breaching client confidentiality, and keep track of difficult families?**
- **Research showed that the relationship, the skills, the training and the personal qualities of the person working with the families, or in other therapeutic situations, was more important than the type of therapy used. If Mr Holt disappeared, the work might not continue in the same way, but it was important to find people who could do it as well.**

Multi-agency working – early years centres

Workshops chaired by Michael Hipkins, Schools Directorate, Under-fives, Department for Education and Employment

Introduction

Michael Hipkins, Schools Directorate, Under-fives, Department for Education and Employment

I wanted to say a few words about the background to Early Excellence Centres, to put in context what will be said in a moment or two. After the present government was elected, in May 1997, there was a rapid process of moving from the previous government's policy to a system where early education was planned. At the end of October 1997, we issued a booklet on early years development plans with guidance on the plans for 1998/99. We've now received a large number of plans in the Department, which are under review.

What we've been asking early years development partnerships to do is to secure an early education place for every four year old. But plans should not stop there. They should look at early education places for three year olds as well. Targets here are to be set by the local authorities themselves, since there is no additional government funding for that yet. They should also look to the integration of early education and care and then, when it can be done, to look wider in terms of the age range of children that the plan covers, and the range of services as well. Some of the things that have been talked about in the plenary session, help for families and such like, are already set out in this guidance document for early years development partnerships to be thinking about. It's a big agenda, and a challenging one, but it is aimed at providing more and better services for young children.

However, there is on top of that the specific initiative of Early Excellence Centres with a pilot programme of 25 of them over the next three years. Seven have been announced already, starting in the present financial year, and we are in the process of going through proposals for starts in 1998/99.

These Early Excellence Centres have to be very good at their job, providing good quality early education and daycare, and various family support services as well. Over and above that, they must have a role in training early years workers and also in the dissemination of good practice in their area. Early Excellence Centres are not something that the government has suddenly plucked out of the air. Good centres already exist, with staff, premises and children that can be found everywhere. The programme is intended to identify this good practice and try to make it more widespread.

9 Multi-agency early years centres in action: the benefits and difficulties of working together

Virginia Makins, independent writer

The early years centres I visited weren't all offering the Full Monty of care, education, health and social services. They were chosen for variety. But they did all involve professionals from health, education and social services working together, and in almost all of them that multi-agency working was going very well. Here, I am going to concentrate on positive benefits, rather than barriers, to this kind of multi-agency working, but I think a few barriers will emerge as we go.

One barrier which people always mention in the context of starting new early years centres is cost. I can't tell you exactly how much a new centre would cost, because some are open all year, some only in term-time, some have services that care for under-threes on their own, and others don't. What I can tell you is that one of the centres with a very wide range of services, and open all year, spends £1,000 a year for each family that uses it.

However I can tell you a bit about what early years centres can save. I think Michael Rutter's estimate, that about two-thirds of the difficulties professionals try to tackle as children get older might be prevented by early intervention, makes a lot of sense. Removing two-thirds of the caseloads of special needs teachers and social workers would mean an awful lot more time for skilled professional work with the remaining third.

At present, special educational needs cost local education authorities more than £2.5 billion – 12 per cent of their education budgets. Child protection costs a great deal in resources, including social workers' time. The cost of one 'looked after' child is over £35,000 a year. Social workers up and down the country told me they were drowning in child protection work. If some of those children were removed from the register, more effective work could be done with the rest.

School exclusion – now costing more than £48 million each year – is closely linked with early educational failure, and with family difficulties. Many studies say that exclusion often leads straight to juvenile crime and delinquency.

Almost all the preventive measures that research studies have found to prevent crime and delinquency, including most of those mentioned by Michael Rutter, can be implemented very successfully in early years centres. They include parent education, high quality pre-school education, programmes for young children with impulsive and aggressive behaviour, early support for parents in difficulties, and advice on diet and health. Most important, early years centres offer all these things in a way that is accessible, acceptable and appreciated by parents.

What services can the centres offer? I have divided them very roughly into three parts – services for children, services for parents and the community, and services for professionals. But I'm sure you all realise that these are closely interlinked: improving a parent's self-esteem brings an improvement for the child; improving a child's behaviour helps relations with its parents; improve both self-confidence and behaviour and professionals have fewer cases and can spend more time on the genuinely difficult ones.

Services for children

Services for children include day care, nursery education, education for nought to three year olds, toy libraries, quality playgroups, after-school and holiday care, integration for children with special needs and strong policies on equal opportunities.

Not all the centres I visited thought it was appropriate to their local communities to offer day care, but where it was offered, it was very high quality. It had a strong education input, and there were social workers on hand to work with some parents and children.

The centres were very strong on nursery education. With their comparatively large staff teams, they were good places for curriculum development, unlike many nursery classes where a lone teacher is outnumbered by colleagues pressing to get on with Key Stage 1.

When it comes to education for under-threes, I can't stress too much how impressive it is to see what happens when parents come in with children from the time their babies are born. There is plenty of time for the staff to talk with parents, look at individual concerns, and perhaps put together a group of parents who are having problems with feeding, or tantrums or whatever. Parents see staff modelling successful ways of handling children, and the children have wonderful opportunities for play, and growth and physical development, particularly if they live in cramped housing. They get very carefully planned educational programmes. This work with the youngest children is a vital aspect of what these centres do. There are very few quality services for children in the critical stage from nought to three, and these centres provide them within buggy-pushing distance for all parents in the neighbourhood.

The benefits of a toy library are obvious. Many of the centres offered a base for playgroups, often independently run, but with skilled professional help and training on the site for playgroup leaders (generally parents), and the quality of the groups was good. Some also offered after-school and holiday care – again there is supervision and training for leaders, professional input, and good resources and they were put to good use.

Health clinics work much better in places where mothers are totally comfortable and know everyone, and they and their children have friends and coffee on tap. With the best will in the world, so many baby clinics are rather bleak and full of queues.

When children with special needs come to a place from birth onwards, where integration is a 'dyed in the wool' part of the fabric and parents have professional help early on, it is of obvious benefit for them. The need for strong equal opportunities policies is very important. A particular aspect is that when centres in multi-ethnic areas set out to recruit multi-ethnic staff, it makes a big difference to parents and children from minority groups.

Services for parents and the community

I talked a bit about informal help and advice from children's babyhood, and I would like to stress the *informal*. In early years centres members of staff become friends, other parents provide advice too, and a neighbourhood support system is built up.

The staff in the centres can identify children with special needs very early on – and anyone dealing with special needs says the sooner the better. Here, help is offered in places where the children with disabilities or behaviour problems won't be stigmatised or ostracised. And the everyday routines in the groups for toddlers in themselves help with potential behaviour problems – sitting with a group, having a story or biscuit and drink, chatting to each other, prepares children very well for being one of a large group in school.

Most centres also offered informal medical services and family support. Even if there aren't health visitors and social workers on the staff – the best solution – they often come in for sessions at a centre. If the centre's staff can't deal with something, there's a familiar social worker or health visitor who can take over. Even primary head teachers told me how nice it was to have a friendly social worker in a local early years centre, who knew the local families well and who they could consult informally, if they were bothered about a particular family, without bringing down the full weight of child protection procedures straight away.

The centres provide informal social and support networks for parents and other carers. You only have to visit one of these places to see the jokes, and friendships, and mutual support that have developed. I think Paul Boateng mentioned the importance of this earlier today.

They also provide formal and informal education and training. Here, the availability of high quality crèches was very important to parents. A lot told me they wouldn't have taken part in the adult education and training the centres offered unless they knew their children were being looked after by qualified people they knew well.

Some of these centres offered a huge range of courses, including leisure activities, basic family literacy and parent education, NVQs, GCSEs, computer training, and offered them to people who would never, ever, have taken part otherwise. Many were tied to young children, and couldn't get to local colleges, and often they didn't start with the self-confidence it takes to sign up for adult education classes. But once they had taken part in a baby massage or aromatherapy group, it often led on to literacy classes, or training, or access courses for further education. I met a number of women who had gone from what they said was severe depression and low self-esteem to confidently moving into further and higher education.

Some parents are just too troubled and isolated to walk into a centre in the first place. The centre's staff can go out to them. Parents also told me that if they were worried about a neighbour, or neighbour's child, it was nice to know they could encourage them to come in, or tell the centre about them and arrange a visit, rather than 'reporting' their worries formally.

The centres also offered space for childminders and other community groups involving children. I saw centres with groups for recent Somali immigrants, for Asian women, for Portage groups (for families with children with special needs). There were special times for childminders to bring in their charges and run their own group. The centres were a terrific local resource.

Services for professionals

Several social workers told me that the centres were great places for supervised access visits or for child protection work: parents and children were comfortable there. Staff in many of the centres played a big role in case conferences, and in observation and assessment. They saw the parents and children over time, and knew them well. Doctors and health visitors and speech therapists and occupational therapists also valued the centres very highly. Again, they said that their work was much more effective in a place where the parents came anyway, and were comfortable. Adult education workers said that they could reach parents in the centres who would never go to classes elsewhere.

Some of the bigger centres set out to offer training to other professionals working with young children and their families. In others, multi-professional training was more informal. One centre I visited had just taken on three autistic children, and had arranged for an expert to come in and run a workshop for staff. While I was there, two social workers, a health visitor and a local playgroup co-ordinator, who had heard about the workshop, dropped in angling for an invitation, and of course they were warmly invited. The centre was big enough to provide quality training for its own staff, and the others benefited.

When different professionals work in one place, it does a lot to reduce the barriers between them, even if some of them only come in once or twice a month. And the centre staff can easily refer parents on to other professionals. For example, a mother who lived near Cromwell Gardens in Gloucester told me her child started to have bad nightmares while the Fred West murders were in the news. She said she would never have bothered a doctor about it – but she talked to the centre head, who said: 'There's this really nice child psychiatrist down the road – shall I arrange for you to have a word with him?' So she did, and the mother said it was very reassuring and helpful.

These are the kinds of things people said to me about the centres I visited:

'It's not just a nursery, it's our life.'

This was a parent who gave me the title for my book. Her husband wanted to move from inner-Coventry, but she said she wouldn't move until the children were through nursery. 'He says: "But it's only a nursery." And I tell him: "It's not just a nursery, it's our life".'

'They have very listening ears.'

This was a mother who had been too depressed and shy to come in the main door of her centre at first, but had slipped in round the side to the family support room. But then she joined in more and more, and had ended up doing courses at the further education college.

'If I didn't have this place I'd be belting him at the end of the day.'

This mother had a little boy with some kind of nightmare brain damage, who was impossibly hyperactive. The early years centre accepted him, and made sure other parents did. They also assigned a member of staff to give him one-to-one attention, while the mother went to a yoga class.

'The only way to free social workers from the child protection juggernaut is to attach them to this kind of project.' Area social work manager.

This one speaks for itself: we all know, and the Audit Commission has confirmed, the terrible treadmill of child protection procedures. Working at a centre allows for real preventive work.

'Since the centre opened, many fewer children have been referred to us at the age of eight or nine.'

Several social work managers in different places said, like this one, that they were seeing fewer children than colleagues in comparable areas, and credited the work of an early years centre.

'It's all right here: they like playing with the other children.' Father – child protection case.

This was a very belligerent man who had stormed out of a social services 'stigmatised' family centre. In desperation, social workers had referred him to this centre, where young nursery nurses were doing supposedly 'light' family support. The day I was there, he had cooked some faggots for his young family worker – she was appalled, since she was a vegetarian and had to eat them. He was happy to come for family support when the centre offered his children integrated, good nursery provision, used and valued by everybody in the neighbourhood.

'We haven't seen the escalation in numbers of young children with special needs that colleagues in similar areas report.'

Several primary heads said, like this one, that the work of the local early years centre seemed to prevent special educational needs and behaviour problems.

'Parents now want to share responsibility for children's progress and behaviour – they don't just blame the school.'

This primary head teacher said that parents, who used to go all belligerent when things went wrong, now wanted to share in the education of their children, and solve problems together. She also made the interesting comment that although by no means all her parents had used the local centre – which had quite limited services and didn't suit everyone – she thought the ones that did had formed a critical mass, and affected the general culture of parenting in the neighbourhood.

'We're all in the same business, providing for young children and their families. There's no place for empire builders and ego trips.'

Everybody working with families and young children ought to hear this remark by a primary head of a grant-maintained school, who had built an amazing relationship with the local authority early years centre on the premises. He had opened a nursery class, with staff employed by the school, but had handed it over to the head of the centre to manage. I wish people in local authorities and in central government would listen to him too.

Factors for success

There are of course blocks to starting new multi-agency early years centres, or there would be many more of them. There is no time today to list them. But if we look at some of the reasons the centres I visited were successful, they also show some factors that overcome potential blocks.

A supportive management framework was crucial. It turns out that the actual management structures of the managing local authority, or voluntary body, don't make much difference. What matters is that the managers understand the enterprise, see its benefits, and want to make it work. One local authority can carefully integrate responsibility for services into a single early years committee, and people still turn out to be defending their particular professional patch. In another, with a traditional division between social services and education, integration works fine because both officers and councillors see the multiplier effects of putting services under one roof, and understand that the costs of an integrated centre can't be directly compared to a conventional 'stigmatised' family centre, nursery class, or day nursery.

It is absolutely critical that the centres offer open access to all families in a neighbourhood. There are two main reasons. First, open access avoids the stigma of referral. Second, centres that have moved from taking only social services referrals to open access have discovered a number of families with problems as severe, or more severe, than the families who had already been identified as needing support.

Leadership is crucial. There is plenty of talk about the difficulties of running these centres. You have staff from different professional backgrounds, with different training and attitudes, and very different terms and conditions of service. That doesn't matter so much when there is good leadership, and when leaders have a clear vision they communicate to staff, and make sure staff have time to explore and develop it. I met some brilliant leaders in nine of the ten centres I wrote about. The tenth did not have an overall head of centre, and it showed. People with management responsibility for an early years centre have to realise that its leadership is a difficult job, and give the head good and understanding support.

Staff development and training is key to the success of the enterprise. A lot of the work with some very stressed, difficult, depressed or even violent parents is done by nursery nurses, and it is astonishing what they achieve, given time for training and reflection and development. The best centres I visited all put a huge emphasis on training, and several had followed the model pioneered by Pen Green in Corby and shut for one afternoon a week for the staff to work on planning and development.

The need for clear equal opportunities policies goes without saying – but an equal opportunities policy must be strongly and continuously reinforced, if it is to be genuinely embedded in all the work of the staff and communicated to parents and children.

Parent involvement is also essential, although there are different levels of involvement. A few parents become involved in a centre's management. I met a number of school governors who said they would never have had the confidence to take on the role, if they hadn't got involved in an early years centre. But even more important, there needs to be a continuing emphasis on genuine partnership with parents, and genuine acceptance of parents' own knowledge about their children and their child-rearing practices, unless of course those practices are actually damaging to the children. Staff need to get alongside parents and build on their strengths – not an easy job.

Finally, there must be responsiveness to local conditions and needs. There is no blueprint for a multi-agency early years centre. In some areas it may be appropriate to focus more on family support and less on day care. In others, there is a big need for day care. In areas without any decent jobs for women, adult education and training, with good care for children while parents take part, may be more valuable than day care or five days a week nursery education.

This is another task for leaders: to respond to their communities, and provide opportunities that adults in that particular community will respond to, and benefit from – alongside providing high quality services for children. I shall end there: there is no ideal model early excellence centre, but there are different models that can successfully meet many of the needs of families and young children in different neighbourhoods.

10 Running a neighbourhood education and care service for children under five and their families

Bernadette Duffy, Head, the Dorothy Gardner Centre, Westminster

My brief is to give you a feel of one of these centres. Dorothy Gardner is one of the Government's Early Excellence Centres. It opened back in 1975, so it's not a new idea, and its aim has always been to provide high-quality integrated care and education for children under five, and to work in partnership with their parents and carers. The Centre had, however, an interesting history for its first 15 years, when it managed to have three heads in one building. Having three heads in one building is a great way to learn how not to run an integrated centre. So we were restructured in 1992 and now work as a fully integrated centre.

The Dorothy Gardner Centre is situated in an area of cultural and economic diversity in the north part of Westminster. We are open all year round, apart from a week at Christmas and a week at the end of August, from 8.00 am. At the moment, the last child goes about 5.30 pm., but that varies depending on the needs of the families that use the Centre. At present, the Centre is used by approximately 150 families a week, quite a large number. Our aim is to be accessible to the local community, and the families who use the Centre do reflect the religious, linguistic and racial mix of the community. It's in an area of tremendous diversity and it makes for a very rich environment for the staff, the children, the families, for everyone working there. That's certainly one of the strengths of the Centre, and one of the delights of working there.

The Centre is open to all the families within the catchment area. Professor Jack Tizard, who was responsible for the original idea, believed that for the Centre to be responsive, flexible and open to everybody, it needed to have a catchment area so that it wasn't overwhelmed. We still retain the catchment area and it is, in Jack Tizard's phase, within pram-pushing distance of the families who use it.

One third of the places are taken by children and families who have been referred to us either by social services or health, so there is a good mix. The hours the children attend are decided through negotiation with the family and with social services, health or other referrers. The decision is based, as far as possible, on the needs of the child and the parent, though inevitably we have requests for far longer hours than we can accommodate.

As I have said, the original idea behind the Centre was very much that of Professor

Jack Tizard. He had a very strong belief that early intervention was the way forward, and this is way back at the end of the 1960s, and the beginning of the 70s. So it's nice that his ideas are now finally coming into common practice. He believed that, if you were responsive to a community and you involved all parents and carers from the beginning, you could prevent a lot of problems occurring in the first place. He was particularly concerned about the isolation of women. The area we are in has a high rate of depression. People often don't have families around them, so Tizard was particularly concerned about the effects of maternal depression on children's development, as well as on the family structure. If the Centre didn't prevent problems occurring in the first place, it could minimise the difficulties that occurred, and that is borne out in practice. Tizard also had a view that having a genuine mix of the local community, rather than having a service that targeted high-priority families, was a way of getting communities working together and offering a focus for support. That has proved to be true.

One of the most interesting cases was a family that was referred to us through social services, where there was a great deal of concern about whether the children could remain in the family, particularly the youngest child. At almost one year she showed no signs of communication, didn't make eye contact, and if she was sat somewhere, she remained there until she was moved to the next place. The mother was very depressed. A year later, at two years old, the child was operating at two-and-a half year old level, she was extremely gregarious and confident and her mother was a changed women. So the social worker and I sat down, feeling a glow of satisfaction about the good work we had all done, and we were asking the mother about what had changed. The mother was very kind to us, and very gentle, and said: 'It was great having the support of yourselves, but actually, what changed was being involved in groups with other mothers. The thing I realised, as I sat with mothers who had everything, they had their own house, they had partners, they had money and they were still miserable. And what it had made me realise was the decision, about whether life was going to change, was mine. I could either sit there and continue to be miserable, or I could make use of the resources and facilities.' So as professionals, one always needs to keep a slightly humble note.

We act as facilitators, we are there as a resource for the community, to be used by the community in the way that they wish. It is the community that changes things, not us. And I think it's very important to remember that. Our role is to help that process, we're not god-like people that go in and do it. The mother I referred to above is now working as a social worker and I imagine she is highly successful because she can certainly say: 'I've been there.' Her children are also doing extremely well. So that's very much the philosophy that the Centre was built on.

We are funded by education and social services and education is the lead agency. Westminster is in the process of moving all its under-eights services over into education. We have a service level agreement with the authority, which outlines the range and quality of the service we offer, and that's related to the funds we receive. The budget from both departments is delegated to the Centre using a formula based on core funding and the number of places that we offer. We also attract some monies from charities. Interestingly, when the Centre was going through difficulties, it couldn't get money from charities for love or money. As soon as it was successful, people were ringing us up and saying did we want money. We now have money from the DfEE as well.

The Centre is managed by a multi-agency management committee, and it consists of representatives of all the stakeholders involved. It has members from the Mulberry Trust, which was the charity that gifted the Centre to Westminster in the first place. It has parent representation, it has staff representation, it has representation from social services, education, the local community and from the local authority. The committee has about 20 people. When we show visitors round and I talk about the management committee of 20, people look horror-struck. From my experience, if you can get those 20 peope to agree, a very sound decision is reached. Getting everybody in one room who has an interest in the Centre, to discuss what happens to it and how it develops, is a powerful management tool.

We are staffed by a multi-disciplinary team and staff have different roles and responsibilities. I would argue strongly that, in a multi-agency, multi-function centre, it is highly unlikely you will get one particular qualification or path of experience that will enable staff to do all the things we need. We don't need multi-ability people, we need a multi-ability team. If you try to squeeze into one person all the different skills you need – work with parents, work with children, work with other agencies, management, running groups – you end up with a very superficial person. Having a multi-ability team, with people coming from different disciplines, and each working together to contribute their discipline is a better model. We would argue that, while people have different roles and responsibilities and we are very clear about that and why it is necessary, all roles are equally essential to the running of the Centre, so each role is equally valuable.

Now the provision. We have a nursery for children from one to five and that has 65 full-time equivalent children in it. We have a drop-in for parents and carers from birth. I couldn't stress enough the importance of drop-ins where families – parents, carers, uncles, aunts, childminders, nannies and anyone else – are free to come in. The preventtive work that is done, and the number of cases that have been picked up and can be referred on to the appropriate agency, is immeasurable. To have the privilege of working in partnership with parents, from when their children are tiny babies until they are five years old, means you can build a real relationship and you can get in-depth sharing of views and ideas. I feel very sorry for colleagues who are in nursery classes where they have all the children in for one year. By the time they've got to Christmas, they've just about got to know everybody, they then have the spring term when they can do something and in the summer term they are preparing them to go on to the next thing. Compare that to a place where we often have children for four-and-a-half years, and the ability that gives you to work with the children and families. We now have a play scheme for three to five year olds from the local community, many of whom are ex-pupils of the Centre. We were always worried that children will get bored coming back. One of our ex-pupils, Scott, was asked whether he was bored coming back to the Centre. He pointed out: 'You do a lot of things in school but you don't have a lot of time to do them.' I hadn't realised that children at Key Stage 1 probably needed a refuge from the national curriculum for part of the year. Whatever else we did in terms of supporting parents, according to Scott we were offering a therapy for hard-pressed children under stress from Key Stage 1.

We also run a toy library, which is run by the parents themselves. We have a variety of support groups. We take the view that the people who are best able to decide what they need are the parents and carers themselves. We did not decide that we would run a pre-set parenting skills course over ten weeks, by the end of which presumably you're given a certificate that qualifies you to be a parent. I have great doubts about parenting skills courses. I don't think parenting is so much a skill as an art form and it evolves and develops and it's not about going through a series of packages. We act as a facilitator for parents, organising the groups and classes they think are going to be most useful for them at that time, and being prepared to change as parents need to change. That's why we run a variety of different classes: it depends on what the parents have identified. We also do some individual work and support for parents and carers.

We have a speech therapist based with us, a childminder network based with us, which again I think is another unrecognised asset. We don't have any under-ones in the nursery, they're with childminders, and the quality of work that can go on from well-supported, well-motivated childminders, is immense. The original idea was for the children to come into nursery provision at the age of one but a large number of parents are choosing for the children to stay with childminders, often up to three years old, because of the relationship they have built and the quality of the care they are getting. One of the nicest things was at a recent meeting of the Early Years Development Partnership, where the childminders were asked where they came from and they said Dorothy Gardner. They see themselves as part of the staff team at Dorothy Gardner and would describe themselves as professional childminders.

We are also an NVQ centre for qualifications for childcare and education and we offer a number of student placements. We now offer more advice and support to other providers and have links with a number of other agencies. Where we are in Westminster, we are blessed with being surrounded by some wonderful groups and organisations. I would say very strongly, there is no point setting up an early excellence centre that's duplicating good work going on elsewhere. Apart from causing resentment before you've even got your front door open, what's the point of reinventing the wheel? So we have links with educational psychology, the paediatric and child development team at St Mary's Hospital, the health visiting service, social workers and family therapy units. We have close links with the adult education service, which runs a number of groups at the Centre. Again, there are great advantages: the younger children are supported in a crèche where they already know the staff, the courses are run in the way the parents want, and to the parents' agenda, and break down the barriers that often occur when people feel that higher or further education isn't for them.

Our aim is to work in close partnership with carers, parents and the local community. We take as our starting point, that parents – all parents – want what is best for their children. They may be in circumstances which means they can't provide it at that moment, but that doesn't stop them wanting what's best for their child. It is a partnership. We have expert knowledge of children at this age and stage of development but parents have specialist knowledge of their child. If you can bring both those sets of skills and knowledge together, then we can genuinely do the best for each child. I was very interested in the speaker's comments this morning around children's self esteem and development. Very often, in English nursery education, there has been an emphasis on the individual child's development but not so much on their relationship as part of a group. A lot of the work on self esteem and their disposition towards learning happens between the children themselves, and in the dynamics within those groups. I am sure with us that occurs because they've often known each other since they were four months old and have developed alongside each other, so their relationships are very close.

We use Westminster's *Great Expectations curriculum guidelines.* We have a system of daily, weekly and termly evaluation in place and Ofsted is happy with this at the moment. We have Chris Woodhead's Oscar to prove it. The feedback from primary schools, in terms of the children's achievements as they move on, has been very positive. The view, from both Ofsted and from the local primary heads, is that the children coming from Dorothy Gardner, in comparison with children coming from other establishments in the same area, are doing much better, and they are doing as well as their more advantaged peers in other parts of Westminster and other parts of the country. That is one of the things that we and the parents would say is very important: parents want their children to have a good education, particularly parents that didn't have that themselves. They're keen that the children do well academically, as well as in every other way, and the feedback from schools is very supportive of that. At the end of 1997 we became an Early Excellence Centre, and our aim now is to share our work with other people. The grant we've got through the DfEE is to develop the NVQ assessment centre and to introduce a partnership teacher to work with a network of staff in other settings near the Centre and to expand our consultancy and advice services.

There's never enough time to do all the things we want to do as a Centre. When you ask the staff group, 'What are the constraints?', they say 'time and space'. Interestingly, terms and conditions are an issue, but they're a national issue and you do the best you can. In a multi-functional centre, the fact that you will never know, especially as head, what is going on half the time, means you work on a system of trust. I work on an act of faith model: I'm convinced that everybody is doing their best.

To conclude, I'll leave you with three main points:

- There is no off-the-shelf model, there is no model for a centre that is suitable for every community. If the Dorothy Gardner Centre has been successful, it's because it's been responsive to a particular community at particular times.
- The centre can't be all things to all people. You need to have a clear view about what the centre is best equipped to do, and how it links with other related services in the community.
- A centre needs the support of all those involved. Dorothy Gardner has taken time to evolve and Westminster has given us the freedom to do that. You can't set a centre up in isolation.

Discussion

What effect does the Centre's duty to refer a child to the statutory services, for instance if they noticed bruising, have on other children and parents?

Bernadette Duffy said staff talked to parents about this issue from the beginning and made clear that they would always put the child's interest first, and make referrals, even at the risk of offending parents. This policy applied both ways, so if a child went home with a bump or a bruise parents had the right to come in and be given an explanation. Ms Duffy said she had not found a way of referring children without everyone getting upset. However, despite this, parents had kept their children at the Centre following child protection investigations, both in cases where abuse was proved and in cases where it wasn't.

Another questioner asked how Bernadette Duffy would want other services, particularly health, to work within the Centre, if time and space allowed.

Ms Duffy said it would be great to have enough space to allow health visitors to work from the Centre. Health visitors currently run groups but they were finding it increasingly hard to justify doing centre-based work – which is what the families want – because of their new obligations to the GPs they are attached to.

Virgina Makins said some health visitors she had spoken to were squeezing in working at centres, often at the expense of their own time and without confessing to the GPs how much time they were spending, because centres were such wonderful places to run clinics and work with patients.

A delegate suggested that someone from the Centre could be part of the new primary care teams proposed in the Government's White Paper, as a way of legitimising the involvement of health services in the centres.

A health visitor said her experience of setting up a centre similar to Dorothy Gardner had showed that attitudes changed once you educated health managers about the nature of the work done in family centres. Her centre had a lot of health in-put – although, due to cuts, speech therapy was not represented.

Getting families in focus: lessons from the Refocusing Children's Services Initiative

Workshops chaired by Dorothy Blatcher, Social Services Policy Officer, Local Government Association

11 The Refocusing Children's Service Initiative: an overview of practice

Diana Robbins, social welfare policy and practice research consultant

The Refocusing Children's Service Initiative of the Department of Health was not like the major long-term studies which have been discussed earlier. The projects were quite small-scale bits of work and my evaluation was fairly low key but important evidence did emerge from it. The special thing about the projects is how concrete and how in touch with the real problems they were. Often they were dealing with very small groups of people but, because of the reporting relationship we developed, we were able to extract very practical lessons from them.

The Initiative

The Initiative was announced by the Department in September 1996. Projects were invited to bid for money for pieces of work which would contribute to one of the objectives. All of them were able to demonstrate that their work did contribute to at least one of the objectives, and most of them were able to show that they contributed to a number of them. That is one of the important features of the projects. They weren't just about control, intervention or anti-social behaviour. They were about looking at families as a whole. They were about supporting families and answering all the 'yes, but ... ' questions. 'We need child care so that parents can get back to work.' 'Yes, but ... what does that mean for the children, what does that mean for the family as a whole?' Projects were of that kind.

The whole initiative cost £700,000 for England, and that covered the costs of the projects, my evaluation, and a conference that we held. The range of funding was from £500 to the upper limit of £25,000. The funding period was variable. Some projects believed that they had to spend all the money by March 1997. Projects from organisations that were slightly more familiar with the funding business negotiated longer periods, and some of the projects weren't due to end until the end of March 1998. Forty lead organisations were successful in bidding, producing between 43 and 45 pieces of work, as some projects had several components.

The evaluation

The evaluation was developed after the projects were selected, and began after the projects had begun their work. I was working with the projects for the whole of 1997. We established that each project would answer a questionnaire, which provided basic data about the sort of work they were involved in, and each would provide a final report, according to a common format which emphasised outcomes. Most of the projects had no idea that they were going to be involved in something as elaborate as this, when they accepted the funding. Some were very small and it was a challenge for them, given that their time was over-stretched. But we got a remarkable degree of co-operation from everybody and that made it possible to extract the messages from the work.

The lead organisations were in almost every case voluntary organisations, ranging from big national organisations to a group of volunteers who happened to have heard about this initiative from their CVS, put in a bid for £500 and got it. There were some pre-existing multi-agency fora that bid successfully, and there were some new partnerships which were generated as a direct result of the availability of funding.

The organisations, by definition, had to engage in partnerships to secure funding. Partnership, like motherhood, is a universal good; but it can mean a great many different things. Half the projects said that the social services department was a partner in their project. In a few cases that meant matching funding, a high profile presence on steering groups, active and enthusiastic collaboration in development and support for the continuing work of the project. For many it meant a letter of support at the beginning, perhaps a burst of enthusiasm while the money was being generated, but quite difficult relationships subsequently in terms of getting referrals to the service that had been set up with the money. Health agencies were partners in 30 per cent of the projects and other agencies were mentioned by a few – police, probation, education. Projects were frequently disappointed that they couldn't get into closer contact with education colleagues.

Partnerships came and went during the life of the projects. You couldn't say 'the social services department is my partner and they'll stay so for the eight months of the funding'. Personnel came and went, obviously, but also the priority which agencies were prepared to give to the projects came and went, and this caused problems for some of them.

Location

A third of the projects were in London, a third of them were rural, or predominantly operated in rural contexts, and a third of them were in other urban contexts. This showed what was happening to the notion of children in need in a whole range of settings and what sort of services were important for the particular kinds of social exclusion which develop in inner city areas, in rural areas and urban areas. I think evidence about the nature of social exclusion in rural areas is part of what makes the initiative important. Almost all the projects felt that they were concerned with children in need, but that the local definition of 'in need', and where the project fitted in to that, varied tremendously according to location.

Target groups

Women were over-represented among the paid full-time staff and the part-time staff of projects – paid staff were in tiny numbers in almost every project. Women were heavily over-represented among volunteers, which I think raises a question about some of the good ideas being floated about parents helping parents. Is it always going to be mothers helping mothers, and is the system going to depend on the unpaid labour of women? Projects asked these questions about a number of the voluntary systems they were able to set up. Women were heavily over-represented among parents as well, perhaps predictably; but a few projects succeeded in doing more work for and with fathers. Boys were over-represented amongst disabled children but, otherwise, there was a fairly equal spread of boys and girls among the children who were worked with. There was an interesting difficulty in filling in the questionnaire, about whether the project was working with parents or children, when it came to teenage parents. The parenting needs were uppermost for the projects in most of these cases.

I do not have time to talk here in detail about the policy issues or the range of methods used by the projects. But one method used that we haven't heard about today is community development. This was used as a means of developing family support in partnership with the community, not as a form of intervention that imposes a set of norms on the community.

The successes

Projects did provide evidence of a range of kinds including evidence about outcomes, but it's a tall order to expect a voluntary group given four months funding to trace concrete outcomes in any great detail at the end of that time. It's remarkable that a number of them managed it. They developed proxy indicators for what they were aiming for, and were able to provide systematic evidence that they had achieved some of what they set out to do. These were not outcomes in the sense of the prospect of abuse receding, in a family where that abuse had been imminent. They were more in terms of the relationships that were developed with professionals, how to approach professionals, how to get them into partnership, how to approach parents. The evidence the projects provided, about **what works, or not, in getting through to parents,** is as important as any evidence about the outcome for individual parents from that project. There was one project, for example, which had an idea, gained funding for it, set off down that track and found it just didn't work.

One of the successes was the degree of creativity the projects brought to the process, and one element in that was their willingness to engage in self-evaluation. The really good ones were constantly reflecting on what they were doing, however small scale, and feeding the lessons back into their practice. I found that impressive, given the scale of some of the activities. They achieved outcomes out of all proportion to the amount of money that was put in to them. They did that by this emphasis on partnership, which they worked very hard at, and by the synergy they created, by bringing the goodwill and enthusiasm of voluntary organisations, statutory agencies, users, parents and sometimes children together in developing the work.

Transferability

One of the criteria, against which we decided we would judge how effective a project had been, was the extent to which it managed to develop a model which could be transferred to other contexts. Over half the projects could provide evidence at the end of the period of funding that somebody had taken their idea up, or their leaflets or were working with them to develop a similar kind of service.

Obstacles

Projects would say to me: 'These initiatives come and go and we carry on doing our work. We dress up pieces of work, that for years we've known to be effective, in order to get the money. We get the money for maybe six months and then we look around for the next pot of money. What we need is for people to take the evidence we've provided and implement it.' They said that there wasn't enough time to develop the work, particularly in areas where they were trying to change behaviour. It was ludicrous to suppose that they could change behaviour in any significant way in such a short period, and they didn't have time, either, to follow up people to see the extent to which those behaviour changes stuck. Projects had problems finding good staff, who they could employ for such short periods. They had problems with police checks, and generally getting staff into posts quickly enough to get the whole thing off the ground. Local government reorganisation caused chaos for some partnerships. Inter-agency relations were to some extent an obstacle. Some projects under-estimated what they were up against in trying to get agencies not just to work with them, but to work with each other, and that caused delays in some of the work getting going. I can't think of any project that would say they were wholly successful in getting what they regarded as a priority – prevention – to the top of the agenda for the agencies they were working with. Any kind of crisis in the agencies activities and prevention dropped lower down the agenda again. And all of them were starting to look for their next batch of funding, the minute the initiative started. They had good ideas, they did good work, they didn't need to pilot it, they knew it was effective, but they hadn't got continuous funding and all of them were looking for that.

Three things were special about these projects. They were all concerned about prevention and were able to put it into effect. One big bonus of the initiative was that it shifted the balance of power to the voluntary sector, and therefore to users, because the voluntary sector in some cases was more in touch with what users wanted. They were able to say, 'No, we've got the money and we say the service needed is X.' The second thing was they were working with whole families, they were answering the 'yes, but ...' questions: they were looking at families in the round. And thirdly, they were working on ways of getting towards user-led service provision. One project in particular used the personal testimony of users to turn around service provision in a local authority area. Some canvassed the views of parents as a group in a locality, some worked with the views of children to see what was required. For many, if not most of them, the views of the people concerned were basic to what they tried to do.

12 Developing new partnerships with families and other agencies

Sue Blake and Melanie Dopson,
Ormiston Children and Families Trust,
East Anglia

Ormiston is a family support agency working in East Anglia and aiming not only to provide direct services for families, but also to give families a voice with other agencies. The Refocusing Initiative was meat and drink to us: it is what we try to do. We decided to apply for refocusing funding for three of our pieces of work. Melanie Dopson and I are going to talk to you about two of them.

The city of Peterborough is a combination of an old cathedral city and a lot of new satellite communities, added in the new town initiatives over the last few decades. The families who came to Peterborough came predominantly with young children. They came to full employment, good jobs, good houses. Now there are many older children. The housing is still okay, but can be difficult to heat and run. The jobs aren't there any more. What's been created on the edge of Peterborough is a series of new town environments which are showing their age. There is a massive drugs problem, particularly for young children on the housing estates. There are a lot of un-policed areas, because most of it is pedestrianised. It is extremely difficult for the police and other agencies to work in environments where much of what goes on is hidden from the main roads.

We have had a family centre in the Ortons, which is one of the townships of Peterborough, since the early 1980s. We know the community we are working with. When the initiative came on the scene, we already had anecdotal evidence that services were being provided for young children and their families, and to some extent for teenagers and their families, though services are never as good as they could be. In the middle, the 11 to 14 year olds were missing out. Their young siblings and their parents told us about this when they used our family centre, and we knew from our own observations on the streets that these children were having a difficult time. One of the important things for us was that many of the 11 to 14 year olds had used our project in the past. I want to emphasise the importance of sticking around. So often, initiatives create projects which are short-term in nature. Not only do you then not gather the evidence that Diana was talking about, but you're not there to go back to the families and see what's happening to them, face to face. Very often they'll tell us things that they won't tell a researcher, because they know us and they consider that we've helped them in the past.

So what did we do? We decided that we had to find out more about what was happening to the 11 to 14 year olds in Orton. Secondly, we needed to test whether there was anything that we, Ormiston, could do to meet any need which emerged. We set up a group, because that's what our family centre does, and we used all the mechanisms that we had used for other kinds of groups, like parenting groups or groups for young children. We put out flyers, we publicised what we wanted to do – an after-school group for 11 to 14 year olds. Then our two workers sat and worried because nobody came.

It became obvious that we hadn't done something crucial, and our first lesson was learnt – that 11 to 14 year olds have different needs from other age groups. What we did about it was to persuade a 13 year old, who hadn't used the new group but whose younger siblings and parents were using the centre, to talk to us. She told us about the realities of her life and that of her peers. She told us of the necessity to have street credibility for groups in this age range. She told us how communication works in schools, as opposed to the way that we thought it worked. She gave us clues about re-launching the group. The next week we had between 30 and 35 eleven to fourteen year olds. This was too many for us to do effectively what we wanted to do. So we took another deep breath.

We devised various ways of splitting up that large group of children, and getting them to talk to us about the things that they wanted. We threw away most of our plans about the structured activities we could do together, children and staff, because what the young people wanted to do was to talk. They wanted to unload, they wanted somewhere to be. They told us that they wanted activities, but at their discretion. They wanted the ability, when they felt like it, to have some individual time with the worker, or to have some time in small groups of two or three of them with the worker. That's a nightmare for staffing and funding. But it's no good denying that that is what those young people wanted. The other practical thing we discovered was that our centre was, in their eyes, clearly somewhere that had been designed for families and young children. They felt like lodgers in a day nursery and, although we felt we'd gone to enormous trouble to try and overcome that, we clearly had not succeeded. Our house has a particular niche in the local community and wasn't the right place for 11 to 14 year olds.

That gives, I hope, a brief and graphic description of the first stage. We held that group for the number of weeks that we had planned to under the initiative, and then we set about trying to draw the lessons from it. The first lesson, as I've already indicated, was that Ormiston wasn't going to be able to solve this alone. We had neither the premises nor the staff group, nor necessarily the staff skills I think, for this particular age group. One of the first things we did was to look around locally to see whether anybody else did. We discovered there was the potential for some lottery funding in the community education area, which could be used for this particular age group. So we began to talk to community education and, more importantly, we began to encourage the children and parents to put their needs directly to community education. I wish I could stand here and say that the group was now up and running. What I can say is that, in principle, community education have seen the need. In practice, recruiting good quality staff, for a period between half past four and six o'clock at night, is almost impossible, in Peterborough. So there are lots of difficulties. We were, however, able to convince other agencies of the need, and the fact that we couldn't meet it ourselves. We feel that, in partnership, we could meet some of the need. Once a group is up and running, we could provide a more intensive service for small, self-selecting groups, of 11 to 14 year olds, who want to come to our project house. This is the bit we know we do well, working with children and families to promote long-term change in their lives.

That's just a small example of partnership. The biggest outcome of the initiative has been more about method than about a specific achievement. We decided to adopt the same method to approach the local schools and we've created something which **is** up and flourishing – the Bridge – which addresses what the speakers this morning were talking about. It's very hard for parents, who don't feel that they're well equipped, to approach schools and talk about the difficulties that their children are having. Similarly, it's difficult for children to go into school and talk about their experiences, because they don't feel that they can have an equal conversation. We've created a Bridge which involves our staff following families and children through into the local schools to try to do just that – to start the sort of conversations that we've heard of from speakers today. That is going to be a permanent outcome of the Refocusing Initiative. It is low cost and I hope to be here in a couple of years time, to say it has also been effective.

Melanie Dopson

I called this Getting Families in Focus in March and then I realised that, for most of you, March is a month but, for us in the Fens, it's a town. The Fens are flat, but they also have a considerable isolation problem. Communities may be separated by only a few hundred feet, but you have to travel a long distance to get to the next community, because you have to travel round the dikes rather than across them. March and the surrounding villages have few amenities. There's no cinema or entertainment complex, and public transport is scarce or pretty well non-existent. Much of the area has been recognised as a rural development area. Ormiston Trust, as part of the Refocusing Initiative and with joint funding from social services, commissioned a report to find out what was needed in that part of Fenland. The consultative document, *Views on the future for families with young children in Fenland* took into account the views of parents and professionals about what services they wanted to see in their communities. As a result of that, further funding was obtained. I'm another outcome, because I was employed to take the initiative forward, and deliver the services that parents said that they wanted, and professionals said were needed, in the area. That process of consultation has continued. One of the things that people said they wanted was information as to what services were available: where the parent–toddler group was, what to do about choosing a school, when you have to apply. I've worked in collaboration with the local Community Forum for Under-Eights and we're currently producing an information pack for parents. I've had a lot of consultation with parents as to how they want that to look, and how it should be produced. They are part of the sub-group that are getting that together.

I get the views of parents, not by asking them to come to me at my small office base at the local community education centre, but by going out to meet them in health visitor clinics, parent–toddler groups, and on the street. In March I travel round on my bike, so I'm visible to members of the local community. I don't travel out to the surrounding villages by bike, that has to be done by car, but I still get out and meet people where they are. The other thing that has come out of talking to people, and the continuing consultative process, is that parents not only want to make life better for their children – better play activities, safer places to play – they also want things for themselves. They want parenting skills and access to training. So we've recently appointed somebody to take on that area of work, to allow parents to access the things that they need.

I also do individual work with families. We take referrals from anybody in the community. Within the local social services area, the local practice manager set up a resource forum, where voluntary organisations and statutory bodies meet together to discuss families, with their consent, and look at the best way of providing services for those families. Home-Start, Portage, health visitors, education, social services and I form part of that group. It may be that people need to know what's going on, they need somebody just to go and talk to them, perhaps they need to go to a parent–toddler group but haven't got the confidence. That's the sort of work that I do on an individual, one to one basis with families. I meet a family, talk to them about what's available and say, 'Perhaps I can come along on Wednesday afternoon and we'll go to the group together,' so they can access what's already there. A lot of the time I'm holding their hand, to bridge them in to existing services, but I'm also talking with them to find out what they would like enhanced and what new services they would like developed. And I'm meeting with professionals as well, so that I can feed that information back. I'm trying to deal with people who are not in a crisis, but at the early intervention stage, so that people do not end up with their children on the child protection register or with the disruptive behaviours that we've heard so much about this morning. That is the key to all of the work that we're doing in March: to continue to talk to the people who use the services, and take their views into account, before we start saying we know best.

Discussion

An audience member asked for more details about learning how not to approach parents.

Diana Robbins said the lessons from her evaluation were varied, on approaching parents but also professionals – and children. One project decided parents needed information and set up a focus group to tell them what kind of information could most usefully be put together in a pack. Some weeks into the project, they found the parents didn't want a focus group on top of everything else they'd got to do. The mistake was the result, repeated in several other projects, of transferring successful techniques from other work, only to find that it didn't replicate, she said. However the initiative allowed projects to learn the lessons, because opportunities for reflection and development were built into the project. Important issues came up about involving professionals in training sessions: whether to go in at the top or lower down the organisation, using personal testimony of users to prod professionals into taking up the offer of training, integrating users into the professionals' training. On the question of finding out children's views, Ormiston was one of a tiny minority of projects that even came close to doing this, although virtually all wanted to, she said.

Sue Blake said it was difficult for parents, and children, to tell you what they wanted if they didn't know what was on offer. It was important to present alternatives rather than wasting their time by getting them suggest things they could not have. She added a note of caution about Ormiston's success in communicating with children, based on an evaluation they had commissioned. 'Getting in touch with children is an incredibly complex and skilled area, and we are by no means there yet,' she said.

Another questioner asked Diana Robbins whether she felt the Department of Health would think about refocusing and creating a bridge between the voluntary sector and the statutory sector, and whether it might re-visit the idea of community social workers, who were statutory workers who thought beyond their statutory responsibilities and engaged in preventive work. Was the Department of Health going to fund the voluntary sector, rather than relying on local authorities?

Dr Bob Jezzard from Women's and Children's Health Services in the Department of Health said he and colleagues would take that message back to the Department. He hoped the consultation on core funding would be helpful.

Diana Robbins said the message coming from the projects was, 'We know what to do, now let's have the money to do it.' She believed there were now political opportunities that could be used. For instance, was the national childcare strategy just going to be about women getting back to work or was it going to be something good for children?

Another participant said there were problems with core funding, when many different agencies were involved, and that strategic management of the effort was needed.

Diana Robbins agreed, saying that genuinely collaborative inter-agency teams, while difficult to put together, were more successful than others in dealing with all the facets of the needs of the families.

Sue Blake said the relationship between the voluntary sector and the funding authorities needed to be looked at. One of the strengths of Ormiston, for example, was that about one third of the funding did not come from the local authorities, so they were not acting merely as agents. Giving too much money to particular organisations, rather than developing genuine partnerships, could end up defeating the object of the exercise, she warned.

Zena Peatfield from the Social Exclusion Unit, said the Unit was thinking along these lines in looking at a holistic approach to disadvantaged neighbourhoods. It was starting from the Single Regeneration Budget type model, which was housing and employment focused, but was bringing in issues about family policy and childcare. 'Prevention, alongside the issue of how you can get people working together more effectively, is a key underlying theme to that work.' she said.

Healthy living initiatives

Workshops chaired by Dr Bob Jezzard, Women and Children's Health Services, Department of Health

13 Evaluating early interventions in children's mental health: the case of parent advisers

Professor Hilton Davis, Guy's Hospital, London

The aim of my presentation is to talk about the Parent Adviser Service which we've been running in Southwark and Lewisham, staffed by health visitors and community doctors (CMOs). It's a complex project with many people involved – the families, the parent advisers, the steering group. It's been funded by a number of people. This isn't just my work, it's very much a co-operative effort of Lewisham and Guys Mental Health Trust and other agencies.

We are working in one of the most deprived areas in the UK. It is characterised by enormous need – socially, educationally and in health. From the epidemiological literature, one might argue that something like 25 per cent of the children in that area might have psychological, or psychiatric disorders.

To illustrate the extent of the need, we did our own study in Southwark recently. We haven't published this yet, and we're still working on the data, but we interviewed a random sample of 253 parents, taken from GP lists in the local area in which we were going to work. We asked the parents about the problems they had with their children, and about the problems that there might be in the families, that is the risk factors for child mental health difficulties. We found that 72 per cent of these children had at least one moderate to severe psychological or social problem. Something like 37 per cent of them had three or more such problems. We also asked the family about other difficulties, which included mental health or physical difficulties in the parents, marital difficulties, and so on. In this sample, 15 per cent had no risk factors. Eighty-five per cent of them had at least one risk factor, of the type that we were looking for, and almost half had three or more. Our evidence is that we were probably failing to pick up quite a lot of difficulties. There was some denial of certain problems that were likely to be there, considering the evidence from other studies.

Now, given the worrying level of need, resources to meet the need are severely limited. Not all of these families turn up to services. Something like a quarter of them said they needed help. But even if you took just a quarter, you would still have a lot more people than are ever dealt with.

There are long waiting lists and specialist services estimate that they see only about

10 to 20 per cent of those in need. So there's real need and there are serious resource limitations. What we've been trying to do is to develop services, so that we might meet that level of need more effectively. We've been developing a tiered model of service, similar to that suggested by the HAS Report, with tiers one and two based in the community, not in mental health centres, for example. The Parent Adviser Service is one of our attempts to develop a community tier, enabling non-mental health professionals to work more effectively in dealing with the psychological and social problems of children and families. Our notion is to increase available resources and expertise, using professionals who happen to be in the community, by training them, supervising their work and then developing systems that enable them to work effectively in the area of child mental health.

We've also been trying to evaluate the work. Our resources have always been limited and evaluation is difficult, but we've been trying to evaluate the different services we're developing. I'm first going to present the service, and then talk about the evaluation which isn't a perfect study but is, I think, quite robust.

The service is based on explicit theory. We've trained health visitors and CMOs in the skills of basic parent counselling, which is not unrelated to cognitive-behavioural work. The process is seen as one of setting up a partnership between the parent adviser, (the health visitor or the CMO) and the parent or parents. The notion of a respectful partnership we think has value in itself. By according respect to parents, they may well respect themselves more, their self-esteem may well increase and therefore they are likely to be more effective in dealing with the issues around them, whether or not these are to do with children.

Setting up that kind of relationship is not easy to do necessarily, but it gives parents the opportunity to explore the difficulties they're facing, to explore themselves in relation to those difficulties and, we hope, to derive a measure of clarity which will enable them to pursue ways of coping with them. On the basis of this clarity, they may be able to engage in a process of goal setting, careful strategy planning, if necessary, and then implementing strategies to deal with their problems, whether child or other difficulties.

Our fundamental aim is to help parents feel more confident and to understand and manage the problems they are facing. The delivery of the service is by four health visitors and two community doctors. We trained them in basic parent counselling skills, in issues to do with parenting and, to some extent, in child behavioural management skills.

The course was designed specifically for this purpose. Those trained were then based in two separate health centres, one in north Southwark and one in Lewisham. There are two health visitors and a CMO in each place, where they each have a day dedicated to acting as parent advisers. In each health centre, there are then three parent adviser days available per week. They take referrals from the local geographical area, an area which includes an estimated 4,500 pre-school children. The referral criteria were originally very broad for a number of reasons. They included all emotional behavioural problems in the under-fives, parenting problems or problems in the parents. An exclusion criteria was evidence of abuse. If the problem was that severe, then a different approach is needed and the families should be referred on to the second tier of service (the social services and multi-disciplinary teams).

A total of 87 families were referred from June 1994 to the end of May 1995, 72 per cent by health visitors, 15 per cent self-referral, 7 per cent by GPs and some from a nursery. Approximately 57 per cent of the children were white, 54 per cent were boys, and the average age was 2.3 years.

The service was by home visiting. Once the referral was made, the parent advisers would visit the homes of the people they were seeing for an hour, and continue to do so as necessary. The frequency was normally weekly to start with, then at longer intervals as the relationship was established, and finally tailing off.

The management of the service was initially in the hands of a full-time clinical psychologist, then a social worker. The notion is that the service should be in the hands of a trained child mental health specialist. Supervision was provided for each person individually, once every two weeks and then in groups, once every four to six weeks. Supervision of that sort is absolutely crucial. There's no question in our minds that the training on its own was inadequate. We don't just train people for that sort of short length of time and throw them into very difficult situations. They need regular supervision, which is often not available to a lot of people working in the community, such as health visitors.

We had independent researchers doing the evaluation and they saw families before the intervention and then four months later, whether the intervention was finished or not, because we had to fit the study into two years. We compared intervention families with a group of families from a neighbouring area, who had the same kinds of problems. In most of the measures we took of the families, there were no significant differences between the comparison group and the group who had the intervention at the beginning of the study. The full details of the intervention research can be found in Davis, *et al.* (1997) and Davis and Spurr (1998).

The sample we took includes 60 families – those who had had at least two intervention sessions. There were some families who were seen by the researchers but who, for various reasons, were never seen by the parent advisers, and there were some who only had one session, who were excluded from the results. About 25 per cent were excluded on that basis.

These families could not be considered to have simple problems. For example, most of the children had multiple problems not just simple tantrum or sleep problems. Parent–child relationship problems were the most frequent, and then aggressive behaviour, non-compliance, sleep problems, tantrums, over-activity, and speech delay and disorder. They also had difficulties including physical health problems, peer relationships. 15 per cent of children had a learning disability and some had serious problems of self-injury.

The parents also had considerable problems themselves. For example, 41 per cent were judged by the parent advisers and supervisors to have depression, mood swings and anxiety. Many of the parents had been abused themselves and social isolation was another problem. Nearly a quarter of them were judged to be socially isolated. There's also the context of poor housing, housing problems, financial problems, and 35 per cent were lone parents. Marital and parental relationship difficulties were judged to be present in about 60 per cent of families and, in 30 per cent, we had evidence of violence going on between the partners. These were not easy families and we were asking health visitors and CMOs, trained on a short course, to see what they could do to help.

The research took measures before and after intevention. Most of the variables we took were chosen on the basis of *a priori* hypotheses about what we expected to find, if the intervention was working. For example, we expected increases in maternal self-esteem and changes in the child. Before intervention, the groups were evenly matched on a measure of the mothers' ratings of the severity of the problems in the child. Four months after the interventions began, there was a significant decrease in the severity of the child's problem in the intervention group, with no change in the comparison group, and that change is statistically significant. We used a discrepancy measure to assess maternal self-esteem. We asked mothers to rate themselves on a number of scales, and then how they would like to be. The more similar the self is to ideal self, the greater the self-esteem. There was an improvement in maternal self-esteem and again, it was a significant improvement in the intervention group only.

Parenting stress was measured by the short form of the Parenting Stress Index. After the intervention, there was a significant decrease in stress levels in the families in the intervention group, with no change in the comparison group. The post-intervention mean for the intervention group reduced to below the clinical cut-off point which is the point at which people are judged to need help. We also used the GHQ, which is a measure of parental anxiety and depression, and similar results occurred with decreases in anxiety and depression only in the intervention group.

We didn't get significant changes in everything. There were no differences to begin with in the measure of the marital relationship. There was an improvement in the intervention group. However, in the comparison group, the relationships seemed to have got worse over the period suggesting a possible prevention effect.

The discrepancy between the mothers' ratings of their child and ideal child was taken as an indication of the mother's positiveness towards the child. There were no significant differences between the two groups at the beginning, but positiveness towards the child increased significantly in the intervention group and not in the comparison group.

Most of these measures are based on the reports of mothers, but we also looked at the home environment, using the HOME inventory. This is a measure of the extent to which the mother and home are geared towards the child, and optimising the child's development. We found no differences to start with. Four months later, there had been a significant improvement in the intervention group, but no change in the comparison group.

Similarly, and not surprisingly, we measured child behavioural problems using the Achenbach. At the beginning of the intervention, the mean for children in both groups was above the clinical cut-off point for severe problems. After four months, the mean for the intervention group had decreased significantly and was below the cut-off point, whereas there had been no change in the comparison group.

Lastly, as an independent measure, we looked at the number of contacts between the family and health visitors and GPs. What we found was a significant decrease in the number of contacts in the intervention group but, interestingly, a significant increase in the number of contact in the comparison group. I'm not sure how we would explain that.

We also asked mothers how they felt about the intervention and the findings were extremely positive. One of the questions was, 'How well respected did you feel as a result of the interventions?' and the results were very high. We also asked referrers to evaluate the system and they judged 87.5 per cent of the families to have benefited. So although our measures are very much based on maternal self-report, there is independent evidence to suggest that there had been significant changes over the period of the intervention.

References

Davis, H. *et al.* (1997). A description and evaluation of a community child mental health service. *Clinical Child Psychology and Psychiatry,* 2, 221–238.

Davis, H. and Spurr, P. (1998). Parent counselling. *Journal of Child Psychology and Psychology,* 39, 365–376.

14 The WellFamily Service: family support in general practice

Lonica Vanclay with Alice Cook, Family Welfare Association

The healthy living initiative that I'm going to describe for you is not about a particular centre but it's very much about working across existing organisations, with a view to providing family support services from primary care settings, and developing different models for doing that.

The aim is to promote healthy living in the broad sense of physical, mental, emotional and social well-being by:

- listening to people;
- offering help and support;
- working with them to identify from their perspective, the particular issues and concerns that they want to deal with;
- helping them think about how to address those concerns.

The idea for this grew from a study that was done by the Family Welfare Association, in partnership with the University of East London, with Department of Health funding in celebration of the International Year of the Family in 1994. It looked at how people kept well, by asking 202 individuals, who visited a GP practice in North London over a two week period. Some of the professionals were interviewed as well.

This study, like others before it, found that family members did cope with quite a lot themselves. They felt less able to cope with needs, stresses and feelings of not being well when there was a lot of change or when they lacked social or family support networks. Many expressed a wish to have open access to a family adviser, who could listen to them and work with them. So, with Department of Health funding, FWA established the first WellFamily Service in Hackney in September 1996.

The idea was that the family support co-ordinator would be based in the practice. Earlier reports, looking at how to encourage health and social care professionals to work together, often concluded that being based under the same roof, having opportunities to develop working relationships and to communicate informally, were very important factors in encouraging people to work together.

About one-third of the families that Alice Cook, the family support co-ordinator, works with, she sees once, slightly more than a third have been seen two to five times, and slightly less than a third have been seen six times or more.

Most of the families have been referred to her by the general practitioners in the practice, although about a fifth of the families contact Alice directly themselves. Families come with a very wide range of concerns, and the concerns that they want to talk about are not always the same as those that the referrer has identified. Undoubtedly, the main areas that people want to talk about are parenting and relationships. The focus with all families is on identifying and building on their strengths and a solution-focused approach is adopted. It's very much about building people's own confidence and self-esteem, and enhancing their coping capacity.

The work Alice does is often with children in need and always about early support and intervention. The families seem to fall into three main groups. There are those who consult GPs frequently, often with continuing and complex problems, sometimes unnecessarily or inappropriately so, at least from the GP's perspective. Many of these families are already in touch with social services but perhaps feel antagonistic or wary towards them. They are sometimes dissatisfied with the service that they've been receiving.

The second group are those who have slipped through the service net. The GP may have been seeing the family for a while and may be conscious that something is not quite right, but hasn't been able to put a finger on it. It's easy to go to the GP and ask for support. It's much more difficult to go to social services or any other formal helping agency because of the associated stigma. These families are readily referred by the GP to Alice down the corridor. They may need to be in contact with social services, because there are child protection concerns that haven't been identified. These families often identify safe, practical reasons at first and it may take some time, having built up a trusting relationship, before the real needs are identified.

The third group are those whose problems, although serious, are perhaps short term or new, and don't warrant referral to social services, given the increasingly tight eligibility criteria that many social services departments have these days.

The outcome of the service varies according to particular individuals. Some of the outcomes for professionals include a reduction in inappropriate, frequent consultations with GPs. In some situations, social services have been able to close cases, knowing that the WellFamily worker was in touch with the particular family concerned. But reduced statutory involvement isn't always the outcome, because sometimes the service identifies families who need a particular service, and haven't had it before.

A qualitative study of the Hackney WellFamily Service is being undertaken at the moment and is nearing completion. Preliminary findings suggest that the users value the accessibility and personal feel of the service, which they attribute to its location in general practice. We all go to the doctor, it's a non-stigmatising setting and people value that. They also value its independence and this independence, coupled with the familiarity of general practice, enables trusting, helping relationships to develop quickly.

With some funding from the National Lottery Charities Board, we're now in the process of developing several more WellFamily services in different locations. We identified a number of areas that met the range of criteria we identified. We wanted to ensure that there was a rural area, an inner urban area and a town, in different parts of south east England and that different forms of general practice organisation were involved.

We contacted the Directors of Social Services and Directors of Primary Care in the health authorities, asking them to identify a particular patch of need. We then approached the GPs in that patch. This was a slow but vital development process. We didn't want to just go in and set up the service, without having the support and involvement of the key players beforehand, because they'll be the organisations who'll need to be involved in continuing this service after the pilot period.

The service pattern will obviously develop in response to particular local needs and situations but, in each service, there will be a mix of case work, group work, information and advice, liaison and community work, working with people according to their particular needs and interests. The services include facilitating mutual support and volunteering with groups of people within each practice.

All of these services will be evaluated, in partnership with the University of Manchester and the National Primary Care Research and Development Centre, over the three years, and we will be looking to suggest some models for family support in primary care, based on this experience. We're hoping that the evaluation will be outcome focused, looking at the outcomes from the perspective of the difference the service has made to individuals and families, as well as to the professionals and other organisations in the patch

The particular features of this approach to providing family support services that make it interesting, and perhaps unique, are:

- The accessibility, because of the primary care base, and the non-stigmatising setting.
- The service is open to all people in the patch who are registered with the GP. They can phone up or be referred and can usually drop in and be seen within the next two days.
- It's holistic, in the sense that it works with the whole family and with all aspects of their concerns. Families don't have to go to one agency for housing advice, another for welfare rights, for social services or something else. Concerns can all be addressed at the same time, within the same setting.
- The service offers a supportive, consistent and flexible approach to working with families, which is very important. The family support co-ordinator is somebody who becomes known and trusted, like the doctor. We know from research that having a consistent, non-judgmental person can make a big difference. Families don't like having to tell their story over and over to different people. It's important to them that, when they need support, they can go to somebody they know who can provide it.
- People appreciate a service that can adapt and respond to their particular needs. Users of the Hackney service have said that they don't like going to social services as they feel social services staff follow procedures and treat them the same as everybody else. There's no recognition of the particular aspects of their situation, or of themselves.
- And finally, the service is independent and complementary to other services. Given the complexity of the situations that many people are dealing with and the multi-causation of many problems, it's not possible for any one profession to

> provide an adequate response on their own. It's important that different people work together. An independent neutral person, based in a practice, can play an important role in facilitating the discussions and joint working, between the various people who need to work together.

So what's the potential then for the WellFamily Service and what are the issues that the service picks up on?

Widening the partners

There's scope for planning together and more pro-active forging of links between services. Joint working isn't just about referring backwards and forwards, important though that is. Including some of the other service delivery agencies – education, housing, arts and leisure, youth services, adult education and training – in the group of people who can work together to address a particular situation, and provide early support for a family, is very important.

Links with professionals

There are some areas of link and overlap with other professionals, particularly health visitors and counsellors. Sometimes these professionals have felt uncertain about somebody called a family support co-ordinator, coming into a situation and perhaps working in areas which they felt to be part of their area of work, and they've felt encroached upon. We see the role as complementing, rather than duplicating the role of other professions, and it's important to think about the particular influence of the employing agencies of different professions as well.

Long-term work

Supporting and changing families, their behaviour patterns and coping mechanisms, is a long-term process, especially when the stresses have been quite severe and people have been frequent service users for a long time. Change doesn't happen overnight. But the Hackney WellFamily service is already beginning to show that small changes in people's confidence have resulted, that people feel more able to cope positively themselves. This often results in quite large savings in terms of the time and money expended by other professionals and other agencies.

Future funding

Services like this fit well within the joint commissioning possibilities and plans for primary care groups, that will be developing over the next year or two, with a local focus on joint health and social care commissioning of front-line health services. There will be a lot of scope for thinking much more about how we can provide comprehensive, accessible, non-stigmatising, early support services within primary care settings.

Discussion

Professor Davis was asked how the training for the intervention affected health visitors and CMOs in their other work.

He said there was no hard evidence on this, but the informal feedback was that many people had been feeling demoralised and might have moved elsewhere, if it hadn't been for the training. They said the intervention had made enormous differences to their work and gave them the opportunity to be with families in a way that they'd never been able to be before. It seems that they were able to use what they learned with all families, including their own!

How could the intervention be sustained, asked one delegate, suggesting that setting up a group might be a possibility.

Professor Davis said that there had not been a long-term follow up, and agreed that setting up a group to provide peer support might be the way to maintain effects. A project with families of children with disabilities in Tower Hamlets had done this, starting by engaging deprived families individually and then bringing them into a group. The Bangladeshi Mothers Group had just celebrated its 10th anniversary with 250 mothers and their families attending.

How long is the period of training?

Professor Davis said the sessions lasted three and a half hours, weekly over 15 to 17 weeks. Sessions were skills based, with discussion and small groups to practice basic listening skills. There was also homework – reading and observational work – which amounted to about two hours extra.

Is everyone able to do the work?

Professor Davis said some people did not reach the required levels of competence. He thought the major characteristics required by parent advisers were respect for parents, empathy, genuinness, humility and quiet enthusiasm. Most participants started the course with these characteristics to some degree and the evidence was that they developed them further. However, some people are unable to respect others and attempted to take over from them and these people are unlikely to be successful in the role, which requires a close partnership with parents.

Lonica Vanclay was asked what the distinguishing features of a family support worker would be, in relation to health visitors, social workers or other professionals?

Lonica Vanclay said one of the features was the breadth of focus. Professionals working in child protection, mental health or community care often had to focus on particular aspects of people's needs. 'The distinguishing aspect of this is trying to get away from those boundaries and work with the family as a whole, in one situation'. The family support co-ordinator role was not restricted to people with a particular professional qualification. People had come into posts from social work, nursing, play therapy. What was important was respecting the family, working with their strengths, helping build their confidence but also being able to respect and work with the other professionals.

The speakers were asked about child protection issues, given the positive approach embodied in the name 'WellFamily Service'.

Lonica Vanclay said it was important that the service doesn't have a statutory responsibility. If the family support co-ordinator identified a child protection case, they would discuss with the family the fact that a referral would be made. Occasionally there was an advocacy role as well, if families were in touch with social services but were dissatisfied with the response and wanted to talk to somebody outside the system. Sometimes the co-ordinator worked as a kind of a key worker, linking other services through the statutory agencies, and improving communication between agencies.

Another participant asked whether there was a danger that this broad approach might become a panacea, whereas research evidence suggested that offering a general approach to everybody, sometimes finished up not clarifying their focus for anyone.

Lonica Vanclay said the approach was general in the sense of working with the family to identify their main problems or concerns and how they wished to address them. 'The service doesn't deal with crisis or very severe situations. It's a preventive, early intervention service.' Referrals were made if specialist help was needed with particular families. Often families had various services involved but felt they were not relevant. Good referrals, to agencies that families would work with, were valuable for these families.

The questioner said the issue was not the specialists, but specialised work.

Lonica Vanclay said the work was divided into three distinct sections. First, basic information, usually through single sessions, to put people in touch with other services. Then short-term work, largely parents with parenting difficulties, behaviour problems, self-esteem. The other group is long-term support work, where a general practice base, that is accepting of the families and doesn't depend on making appointments, appeared to be ideal.

A delegate said many people rang their organisation's helpline because they felt the GP or health visitor hadn't picked up the complexity of what was happening in that particular family. Long term, easy access within the setting of general practice was precisely what such people were looking for.

15 Panel discussion

Chaired by Rita Stringfellow, Chair of the Local Government Association Social Affairs and Health Committee and leader of North Tyneside Council

Elizabeth Johnson, Department of Health, with responsibility for social services issues

Rob Smith, Department for Education and Employment

Jon Bright, Social Exclusion Unit

Norman Glass, HM Treasury

Georgina Fletcher-Cooke, Department of Health with responsibility for women's and children's health

Mark Perfect, Home Office

Interdepartmental co-operation and multi-agency working are very much the theme of the moment and clearly if early intervention is to work effectively we are all going to have to collaborate and work together across various divides, whether this be central and local government, the statutory and voluntary sectors, health, social services and education, or whatever. It won't surprise you that I see local government as the key player to bring all of these strands together, not always as the paternalistic provider but with a new and challenging role. However we also need to feel that there is genuine collaboration among the key central government departments.

We therefore close today's conference with a most unusual panel from central government. Representatives from the main departments currently working with families with children have been asked to put themselves in the hot seat and to respond as a panel to your questions. This is an opportunity for you to quiz them and find out how much joined-up thinking there really is.

I want to take as many questions as possible, and so will not ask everyone on the panel to speak on every question. Even so, I hope everyone will get a chance to put their point of view. The first question please.

How will we 'out in the field' know that you have all succeeded in working jointly across departments? What will be different for families?

Jon Bright: The Social Exclusion Unit is focusing on three priorities: truancy and exclusions from school, disadvantaged neighbourhoods and rough sleepers. All of those topics involve inter-departmental working. When we present our reports to ministers, there will be outcomes linked to the recommendations that we make, and we will be judged on the extent to which those outcomes are achieved. That will in itself reflect good inter-departmental working. As to what will be different for families, I would like to see much wider replication of proven preventive programmes, that work in terms of supporting families under stress and preventing negative outcomes for their children.
Rob Smith: One of the measures of success in this field will be when those both in receipt of, and delivering, services – for example parents and head teachers – are able to access what they need quickly and from one source. Dealing with cases from parents of children with special needs, I know how easy it is for them to be passed from one reference point to another, without finding someone who can help them. Head teachers trying to arrange support for pupils find it hard to know the right person to go to, who will successfully bring that support. That's one way we should be judged on whether we've got our act together.

There has been a lot of talk about measuring outcomes, but when we are aiming to improve the health of the whole community in its broadest sense, how do we measure that? This is especially pertinent, given that improving the health of a whole community will take considerably longer than the four years in office of each government.

Elizabeth Johnson: There has been a great lack of outcome measures in these areas, which makes it difficult often to know whether things are succeeding. We heard some anecdotal stories about things that are succeeding, but the challenge is how then to apply that and to convince people at the centre that it is worth replicating. We talk a lot about outcomes but we have to stop talking about them generally and start suggesting one or two outcomes that we can all start to measure. At that stage, people will say, 'Were they too simple?' and 'That doesn't fairly reflect this'. I think that's inevitable. We have to look for one or two measures that most of us would expect to find in a healthy community. Perhaps the educational achievement of children is a good starting point because it is difficult for them to achieve unless they've got good health. You can pull other things in its wake, provided you pick the right outcome measures.
Georgina Fletcher-Cooke: One of the problems with the health service over recent years is that we've been focused on the inputs, rather than on what we're trying to achieve.

The key to working jointly at a local level is for agencies to agree outcome measures, locally, that they will all work towards. We're thinking of developing a list and you can obviously argue about what should be on it. One element of a composite measure on parenting, for instance, could be whether parenting programmes result in more children attending school, not just because they're not excluded any longer but because they are not truanting and they're not 'sick'. You could also use measures like the amount of juvenile crime or the number of children taken into the care of the local authority, which are not health specific in the way that we've thought of them in the past. They are indicators of community well-being.

Mark Perfect: I was going to speak on the same lines, taking the phrase 'health of the community' in the wide sense. Fear of crime and juvenile disorder are things that do concern a lot of people. There are specific health issues which have been correlated with drug and alcohol abuse, and possibly even teenage pregnancies because of the life cycle. As for the earlier question, one measure of whether or not we're succeeding in working together is whether we use the same language. At this moment, we are speaking in similar terms.

Norman Glass: I have been particularly concerned over the past few months with early years programmes and early years development. There seems to be a consensus that a good measure of whether the range of early years services are working is early educational performance. In particular, one would want to see an increase in the educational performance of those who are performing particularly badly now, concentrating on raising the bottom end of the performance range. That does seem to be a good indicator of both how well services are working and a good predictor of subsequent performance in school, the workplace and the wider social context.

With the competition that occurs within and between the local statutory agencies – health authorities, trusts, local government, social services, education departments – should the development and funding of early intervention initiatives be the responsibility of joint commissioning forums?

Georgina Fletcher-Cooke: It depends on what you mean by joint commissioning. As I said earlier, the key to joint working is for the objectives of that work to be agreed between all the agencies concerned. Once you've got over that step, you can say, *'What are the inputs that we are able to make towards those mutual objectives?'* When you've worked that out, the service interaction should flow from that. You don't necessarily need to commission the services jointly – that's what we've been finding in adult services for the elderly in the Department of Health. The commissioning issue is difficult and it partly stems from each agency focusing on its own target. Children's health, for example, is a huge area. There are things like immunisation, which is clearly the responsibility of the health services alone, and the danger is that people focus on that aspect of their work and less on those working towards the joint outcomes that all the agencies must own.

Norman Glass: If one has a shared vision of what one is trying to achieve, there are a number of ways to get there. Some of them will be successful, and some won't be. You can disseminate good practice, introduce joint planning, do things together in a more integrated way. You can have financial incentives of some kind that will make people work across boundaries and try to submerge professional differences. I wouldn't like to

think of it as just being a one club policy. It might be interesting to see, on an experimental basis, whether you could get a joint commissioning, single purchaser arrangement. Could you imagine at local level an early years programme which stretched, not just across the local authority, which might be easy to achieve, but across health authorities and other sorts of agencies in an effective way? It might be worth having a trial to see whether it gave you better outcomes, and was a more effective way of implementing the joint vision of what you are going to purchase.
Rita Stringfellow: If we had the shared vision, that ought to take us to where we need to be. From the point of view of local government, sometimes the separating out of purchasing and providing isn't the most effective way of doing things.

We've heard a lot today about the importance of children and parents in need experiencing a consistent, quality, one to one relationship that enables the children to build trust in others and faith in themselves. Might we conclude that schools, particularly primary schools, fall down in delivering that kind of relationship and could we not adjust the traditional organisation to facilitate this?

Rob Smith: We will see a continuing trend towards much closer relationships both at secondary, but particularly at primary level, between the school, the parent and other adults who have an interest in the child. This is already being developed through a range of initiatives including the CEDC 'Share' initiative, which acknowledges the parent's role as first teacher for the child, and the need for support for the parents in fulfilling that role. That involves ongoing relationships between the primary school and the parent, the development of parental and family learning and changing school structures, so many more different sorts of adults will be in the school.
Norman Glass: It's becoming clearer that the role of the parents is absolutely crucial, in terms of under-achievers. Schools reaching out to parents seems to be an effective way of overcoming some of these difficulties. We have not traditionally tended to think in that way. We need to establish relationships between parents and schools which are two-way, not one-way, relationships.
Jon Bright: The research draws our attention to the importance of the connection between parents and schools at pre-school, primary and secondary levels. We've got to come up with some new and imaginative ways of making this happen more frequently, and in a better way which involves more parents. There are all sorts of ideas around that which will break down the barriers between schools and parents, and schools and the community, which will have a positive knock-on effect in terms of children's educational performance.

Given the Government's commitment to preventive strategies and early intervention, it seems likely that this will only be universally funded by a top slicing of the more specialist health, social services and education budgets. How is this budgetary problem to be managed, particularly in the context of imminent health changes?

Norman Glass: It may be necessary to think in terms of some kind of pooling of budgets. If we do go that way, we ought to be sure that we have tried joint planning first.

Coming from the Treasury, I think money matters. People do things more readily when they can see a financial incentive. Otherwise, no matter how well-meaning everyone is, you are simply exhorting them to behave in a way which in some case comes into conflict with their own functional or professional interests. So I would not want to rule out the notion of top-sliced budgets, or pooled budgets, or something of that kind to encourage people to work across boundaries. However, I'd want to see how it would work and what it would mean in practice, at a local level.
Rob Smith: One needs to be a bit careful about the operation of a pooled budget. The first thing you're doing by pooling that budget is allowing for the possibility that one of the partners will spend more of the resources than they otherwise would have done. Given the wide range of views about the right way to spend money, people might be unhappy if it all went to one agency. Secondly, if there isn't enough money to do the job, pooling the budget won't make there be enough. And then you have to look at some difficult issues about getting the money out of the pooled budget, at the end of the process.
Georgina Fletcher-Cooke: For the NHS the first issue is whether the priorities are right. It's going to be difficult for the NHS to put money into preventive services, given the other things it has to do: waiting lists, paediatric intensive care, dealing with children with life-threatening conditions who want to be, or need to be, at home. This conference has shown that perhaps some of our priorities are not right. We need them to be more towards the front end, the preventive end. The issue about children and young people's mental health services is complex. It's about the ability to recruit people and whether the service is being provided by the right people at each level.

How can government best ensure that support to families is well advertised and regarded as socially acceptable?

Elizabeth Johnson: The answer has to be at the local level. It's got to be community-based, and part of building strong local communities. If these services are seen as bubbling up from the community, or part of what the community wants, and are tied in with initiatives by people themselves, you won't get a patronising attitude which people find stigmatising. The question about advertising is interesting because we often have problems about the supply of information. If I have a worry about all the zones and action areas we are creating, it is that there is going to be inconsistency. People may hear about a service somewhere and then find it isn't provided for them. We have to manage those kind of expectations, so people realise that you can't have local innovative projects without also having a measure of inconsistency. The challenge for us at central government, which we're beginning to address, is thinking what the basic standards should be.
Jon Bright: Open access family centres are probably the best way of providing support services to families in disadvantaged neighbourhoods. To provide services in a socially acceptable way, it probably helps if they are managed or partially managed by the users. But from the preventive angle, it's important to make sure that the families that would most benefit from preventive support services are encouraged to use them. We need to think through different ways of providing outreach from these centres. I've seen some outreach services which were absolutely excellent in reaching out to those

families, who would never have come to the family centres under their own steam.
Mark Perfect: Good practice is the most persuasive way of promoting these things. Some of the Audit Commission reports have been fairly useful in spreading good practice but there's more that we could do. One of the difficulties in doing that sort of report is getting the evidence to show other people that what these projects are doing is effective. With good evaluation, we can make progress.
Georgina Fletcher-Cooke: The message we want to put across with parent support is that the need for support is completely normal. It is not about class or social deprivation. Everybody has problems at some time with their children. Recognising that means that we make it socially acceptable. We've got to avoid targeting particular groups. The evidence shows that the majority of children have behaviour disorders, if we can call them that, regardless of social class.
Rob Smith: We start from a fairly low base on this and there is plenty of scope for a major change, making people more aware by using advertising outlets like the schools. I seldom walk into a primary school and find an array of leaflets about family support, but I think in about two or three years we will find them.
Norman Glass: The 'well advertised' question is the one that I struggle with. I was down last week in a pre-school playgroup just outside Bath, in a rather run down area, and it was heavily over-subscribed. What came out in discussion was that, if it's working well, word of mouth will get round. People will know what is good and what is not good. If you have to advertise it, there's probably something wrong with it in the first place.

Much of today has focused on the inclusion rather than exclusion of children in need. Paul Boateng chillingly commented that the state has so far failed as a parent. How then can we justify and support the policy of school exclusion for so many children, and how can we implement policies to combat this on the ground, when current guidelines almost encourage it as a resource?

Mark Perfect: I don't think any of us would want to justify a policy of exclusion. When I was at the Audit Commission, I interviewed 30 or 40 people on supervision orders. An awful lot of them were not in school and for most of the time they did nothing. When they did do something, often it was an offence. Looking from the point of view of society as a whole, we can't just exclude children from school and offer them nothing. Something else has to be put in place.
Rob Smith: It is an accepted government priority to do something about children whom the education system is failing. There are statistics which show that looked-after children have a very rough deal in this respect. You've got to have a whole range of policies in place. Some of them are nuts and bolts things, like schools having better information about the backgrounds of children. There needs to be more easily available support when things begin to wrong, rather than at the end of the process. We need to look at the sort of processes which are gone through when circumstances arise which could lead to exclusion. We need to look at some of the good practice around the country in behaviour support, which can include pastoral and other help for the child, the teacher, and the parent as soon as a problem arises. It can include some withdrawal of that

child, provided the withdrawal involves proper educational coverage and a constructive solution for getting the child back into the mainstream school. It is possible to have arrangements which allow for some cooling off without going through the exclusion process. Lastly, I hope the Government will very soon come to a view about tackling the quality of education provided if children are out of school for any reason.

Jon Bright: One of the first tasks of the Social Exclusion Unit is to consult people, including other government departments, and come up with some ideas about reducing exclusions from school quite dramatically, and making sure that there is proper provision for those young people who do have to be excluded. I can't say much about that as we are going to report on it soon. There are some good projects on helping schools reduce the risk of excluding those young people who are most likely to be excluded.

Rita Stringfellow: If all of us in our various professional disciplines applied best value to children, and had a lateral think about what we are doing, I think that we would come up with a different way of approaching some of the challenges we have at present. There is a lot of good practice. The Local Government Association is certainly going to be disseminating good practice, along with government departments, in terms of Health Action Zones and best value. May I suggest that we all indulge in joined up thinking? We've had a lot spoken about joint planning, we've got government departments indulging in joined-up thinking. If we do that at the local level too, maybe there can be some real success and in four or five years time we'll be back here talking about children, but the starting point will be very different. I hope that my optimism is well founded. Meanwhile, my thanks to the questioners for some very pertinent questions, and to the panellists for their helpful responses.

A1 About the speakers

Sue BLAKE, Ormiston Children and Families Trust

Sue Blake is the founder Director of Ormiston Children and Families Trust. She joined the Trust in 1981 just as it became operational. The Trust's first project was a family centre in Ipswich and Sue became its manager following a period in the statutory social services and the voluntary sector. Over the intervening 17 years Sue has assisted the Trustees to grow the organisation to the point where it now has 14 projects in East Anglia and a strong research and issue promotion area. She is a qualified social worker and a member of the Institute of Management.

Paul BOATENG, MP, Department of Health

Paul Boateng, aged 45, has been a member of the Labour Party since the age of 15. Educated at Bristol University (where he was President of the Debating Union) and a Barrister by profession, Mr Boateng has since 1987 been the Member of Parliament for Brent South, a strongly pro-Labour consistency in inner city London.

Mr Boateng was born in Hackney, London but spent much of his childhood in Ghana, West Africa, and was the first person of African descent to be elected to the British Parliament. Prior to entering Parliament Mr Boateng held elected office as a Member of the Greater London Council between 1981 and 1986, when the Council was abolished. During his time on the Council Mr Boateng was Chairman of the Police Committee and Vice-Chairman of the Ethnic Minorities Committee.

Since becoming an MP, Mr Boateng has served on the Select Committee on the Environment, taking a special interest in housing policy and homelessness. In 1989 he was appointed to the Labour Front Bench as a member of the late John Smith's Shadow Treasury Team, a post he held until 1992 when he was appointed as Front Bench Spokesman on Legal Affairs. Following the General Election in 1997 he was appointed to his current post as Parliamentary Under Secretary of State at the Department of Health with responsibility for social services and mental health.

Mr Boateng is a Methodist Lay Preacher and a former Vice-Moderator of the World Council of Churches Programme to Combat Racism. He is a member of the World Development Movement and holds a Woodrow Wilson Fellowship. In 1988 Mr Boateng was the recipient of the Martin Luther King Memorial Prize for his contributions to the field of social, economic and racial justice at home and abroad. During the historic 1994 South African general elections he was a participant in the delegation sent by the Association of Western European Parliaments Against Apartheid (AWEPA) to monitor the elections.

Mr Boateng is a prolific broadcaster and has written and presented his own television and radio programmes, most recently the series *Looking Forward to the Past* (Radio 4) and *Nothing But the Truth* (Channel 4). His most recent publications include a chapter in *Reclaiming the Ground,* with Tony Blair and the late John Smith amongst others, published by the CSM, and the foreword to *Sense and Sensibility* by Jane Austen (Harper Collins collected works). His recreations include his family, swimming and music. He serves as a Member of the Board of the English National Opera. Mr Boateng is married to Janet and they have five children.

In October 1998 he became Minister of State at the Home Office.

Jon BRIGHT, Social Exclusion Unit

A member of the Government's Social Exclusion Unit (part-time) Jon is also Director of Field Operations, Crime Concern and so is responsible for Crime Concern's project management, consultancy, training and policy work. In addition to substantial experience of supporting local crime prevention initiatives, he has worked closely with central government and has prepared guidance issued by the Department of the Environment (1991) and the Home Office (1993). In 1990/91, he was awarded a Harkness Fellowship to study crime prevention and urban safety in the USA. Since 1994, he has advised State Governments in Australia and in 1996 was elected an Associate Fellow of the Australian Institute of Criminology. He has written extensively on the subject of crime and its prevention including a book – *'Turning the Tide: Crime, Community and Prevention'* published by Demos in 1997.

Martin CRAIG, Waterville Projects for Children and Young People

Co-founder and Director of the Waterville Projects, he has been employed as Project Leader for Meadow Well Health Project since 1989.

Hilton DAVIS, Professor of Child Health Psychology, Guy's Hospital

Hilton Davis, BA, DipClinPsych, PhD, Cpsychol, FBPS is Professor of Child Health Psychology at UMDS at Guy's Hospital (London University) and Head of Child and Adolescent Psychology for the Lewisham and Guy's Mental Health NHS Trust. He previously worked as a Reader at the London Hospital Medical College.

He qualified as a clinical psychologist in 1972 and was awarded his PhD at London University in 1980 for research in the area of parent-child interaction. He became a fellow of the British Psychological Society in 1988.

He has had extensive experience of clinical and research work with children and their families since 1973. This has occurred in a variety of contexts involving early intervention and prevention for families of children with disabilities, chronic illness, and emotional/behavioural problems. He had developed a number of training courses for all health care, education, and social services professions in relation to counselling and communication skills and child management. These have been used internationally to develop various family intervention systems (eg. Parent Adviser Service). He has conducted several major research projects in relation to the development and evaluation of different community support systems for families, with funding from, for example, the Department of Health, Mental Health Foundation, Joseph Rowntree Foundation and Gatsby Charitable Foundation. He has collaborated on several international projects and is currently involved in a major European prevention/promotional project.

Melanie DOPSON, Ormiston Children and Families Trust

Melanie Dopson joined Ormiston in 1997 to become Project Leader for work in the town of March in Cambridgeshire. Melanie has a background in adult education and youth work. She has also worked in family centres and as a foster parent.

Bernadette DUFFY, The Dorothy Gardner Centre

Bernadette Duffy is Head of the Dorothy Gardner Centre in Westminster. Dorothy Gardner offers fully integrated care and education for children from birth to five years, groups and classes for parents and carers, and is also an NVQ Assessment Centre for Qualifications in Child Care and Education. A recent OFSTED report described the Centre as a 'beacon of excellence'.

She is also Chair of the National Association of Nursery Centres (NANC). The Association supports institutions and individuals who are seeking to integrate care and education, and work in partnership with parents and carers.

Bernadette has contributed to a number of publications, including *Great Expectations – a Curriculum for the Under Fives* (Westminster Guidelines). She is currently writing a book on promoting creativity and imagination in young children for the Open University Press.

Graham EVANS, Principal, Minsthorpe Community College

Graham Evans has taught in comprehensive schools and further education colleges in Berkshire, Shropshire, Merseyside and Yorkshire. In 1987 he became the Headteacher of Herries Comprehensive School in Sheffield. He became Principal of Minsthorpe Community College in January 1993. Minsthorpe Community College is located in the village of South Elmsall which is near Pontefract in West Yorkshire. In July 1996 Her Majesty's Chief Inspector of Schools recognised Minsthorpe Community College as 'a good and improving school'.

Georgina FLETCHER-COOKE, Department of Health

Branch Head in the NHS Executive dealing with health services for women and child-ren. Particularly concerned at present with factors that can lead to improved inter-agency working to the benefit of children, and with ways in which the health service can help to prevent social exclusion. Previous posts within the Department of Health include work on food safety and on social services finance. She has also worked in the Department of Social Security and in the Department of the Environment.

Norman GLASS, HM Treasury

Norman Glass is a Deputy Director in the Treasury Spending Directorate. He is currently chairing the Cross-Departmental Review of Services for Young Children.

Colin HOLT, Lawrence Weston Family Centre

Colin Holt has 20 post qualifying experience as a social worker and has carried out direct work with fathers for 15 years. Colin undertook a four month fellowship at Bristol University on engaging and working with fathers within Family Centres. His dissertation is published by Barnardo's.

Colin is currently a Senior Practitioner at Lawrence Weston Family Centre where he initiated and has run the work with fathers over the last eight years. Colin is married to Anne and has two sons, Jacob 12 years and Reuben 10 years who remain the most important teachers about being a father.

Elizabeth JOHNSON, Head of Children's Services, Department of Health

Elizabeth Johnson is currently Head of Children's Services in the Department of Health's Social Care Group. Her particular responsibilities include the Children Act, child protection, family support services and adoption. In over twenty years in the Civil Service she has worked in a wide variety of areas including implementing the Mental Health Act 1983, setting up the financial regime for NHS Trusts and being Deputy Director of the Citizen's Charter Unit in the Cabinet Office.

Michael LITTLE, Dartington Social Research Unit

Michael Little is a researcher at the Dartingon Social Research Unit, a Department of Health centre for the study of children in need. The Dartington Unit aims to produce evidence of the highest scientific standard and also to communicate this effectively to policy makers and clinicians.

Virginia MAKINS

Virginia Makins is a former deputy editor of the *Times Educational Supplement*. She is the author of *The Invisible Children: nipping failure in the bud* (David Fulton, 1997) and *Not just a nursery: multi-agency early years centres in action* (National Children's Bureau, 1997).

Dagmar McGILL, International Director, Big Brothers Big Sisters of America

Dagmar has worked with Big Brothers Big Sisters of America since 1985 and now leads their international division. Previously she had responsibility for the national organisation's programme development, planning, training and education and programme evaluation. A representative and a member of many professional organisations and currently co-Chair of the Executive Committee, Parenting Initiative for Education and Society and President of National and Community Service Coalition Board of Directors, Dagmar has presented programmes and papers extensively in North America, Europe and elsewhere, and her programmes initiatives have been widely reported. Her most recent publication is *Blueprints for Violence Prevention: Big Brothers Big Sisters of America* (1997).

Mark PERFECT, Home Office

Mark Perfect is Secretary to the Task Force on Youth Justice. Mark began his career in the Treasury working on international finance and public expenditure planning and control. In 1995-96 he went on secondment to the Audit Commission where he co-authored *Misspent Youth: a study of the youth justice system and services to prevent crime*. In 1997 he returned briefly to the Treasury to advise on social exclusion before taking up his current post in May 1997.

Diana ROBBINS, Social Welfare Policy and Practice Research Consultant

Diana Robbins is a freelance social policy analyst and evaluator who has just completed an evaluation of the 41 projects funded under the Refocusing Children's Services Initiative for the Department of Health. She has worked on evaluations of poverty and equal opportunities projects funded under European Programmes for the European Commission, and of Charity Know-How projects for the Joint Assistance Unit of the FCO. Between 1989 and 1994, she was the UK representative on the European Observatory on National Policies to Combat Social Exclusion. She has also completed a series of research and writing projects for DH and the Social Services Inspectorate over the past 12 years on both childcare and community care themes. She is currently working part-time as the evaluator in ANIMA, the Technical Assistance Unit managing the European Equal Opportunities Programme; and is also contributing to a short-term study of assessment in children's services for the SSI.

Professor Michael RUTTER, FRS, Professor of Child Psychiatry, University of London

Michael Rutter has been Professor of Child Psychiatry at the University of London since 1973 and he is currently also Honorary Director of the Medical Research Council Child Psychiatry Unit and of the Social, Genetic and Developmental Psychiatry Research Centre, at the Institute of Psychiatry, London. He has published some 36 books and 445 journal articles and book chapters. He was elected a fellow of The Royal Society in 1987, was a Founding Member of Academia Europaea in 1988 and is a member of many international academies in fields spanning science, medicine, education, and the arts. He is currently President of the International Society for Research in Child and Adolescent Psychiatry, and is President-Elect of the Society for Research in Child Development. His research has led to numerous international awards, one of the most recent being the prestigious Helmut Horten Award, given for his research on autism. His interests in the field of developmental psychopathology particularly focus on the use of genetic, epidemiological and longitudinal research strategies to study the interplay between nature and nurture.

Rob SMITH, Director for Pupils, Parents and Youth Group, Department for Education and Employment

Rob Smith joined the Department for Education in 1981 and worked first on higher education policy. He was then Principal Private Secretary to Sir Keith Joseph and Kenneth Baker before heading up the finance division dealing with local authority funding of education. In 1991 he became head of the division developing the grant maintained schools programme. In January 1994 he was promoted to Under Secretary to take charge of the Schools Branch dealing with pupil related matters, including special educational needs, health and safety of pupils, admissions, performance tables, attendance and discipline, pupil motivation, pupil welfare and independent schools. He became Director for Pupils, Parents and Youth in November 1995 following the creation of the new Department for Education and Employment.

Jon SNOW, ITN – Channel 4

Jon Snow is a presenter for Channel 4 News and has been since 1989. He is Chair of The New Horizon Youth Centre (teenage homeless) and has been since 1986. Trustee of the Noel Buxton Trust. Deputy Chair of the Media Trust and a primary school governor (Brecknock School, NW1).

Councillor Rita STRINGFELLOW, Leader of North Tyneside Council

Councillor for 22 years serving on numerous Council Committees and outside bodies. Past Chair of Council's Social Services and Social Affairs Committees.

Now Leader of North Tyneside Council and Chair of Policy and Resources Committee. Chair of the Local Government Association Social Affairs and Health Committee since its formation. Also the Chair of the Board of Newcastle International Airport.

Lonica VANCLAY, Family Welfare Association

Lonica Vanclay is a qualified social worker and has an MA. She worked in Australia in community development and social services. She came to the UK in 1982 and has worked in a refugee reception centre and with homeless families. She joined Family Welfare Association in July 1997 and manages, amongst other services, the WellFamily project which provides family support services in primary care. Prior to this she was Director of CAIPE, the UK Centre for the Advancement of Interprofessional Education.

Contributor to articles in journals and magazines on a range of social policy issues.

Carolyn WEBSTER-STRATTON

Dr Carolyn Webster-Stratton is Professor and Director of the Parenting Clinic at the University of Washington. She is a licensed clinical psychologist and nurse-practitioner and has published numerous scientific articles on conduct disordered children and parent training. She has had extensive clinical and research experience in helping families with conduct disordered children. She has developed and evaluated videotape-based training programmes for parents regarding effective parent management skills as well as communication, problem-solving and anger management. In addition she has developed a social skills and problem-solving curriculum (Dinosaur Curriculum) for training young children, ages 4-8 years. Currently she is conducting a study evaluating a partnership which combines teacher training with parent and child training for young children who are highly aggressive and non-compliant.

In recent years her interventions, originally designed for helping children who were diagnosed with conduct problems, have been used in efforts to reduce the occurrence of aggressive behaviour problems and to promote children's academic and social skills.

Work

Personal Lives and Social Policy

Edited by Gerry Mooney

This publication forms part of the Open University course DD305 *Personal Lives and Social Policy*. Details of this and other Open University courses can be obtained from the Course Information and Advice Centre, PO Box 724, The Open University, Milton Keynes MK7 6ZS, United Kingdom: tel. +44 (0)1908 653231; e-mail general-enquiries@open.ac.uk. Alternatively, you may visit the Open University website at http://www.open.ac.uk where you can learn more about the wide range of courses and packs offered at all levels by The Open University.

To purchase a selection of Open University course materials visit the webshop at www.ouw.co.uk, or contact Open University Worldwide, Michael Young Building, Walton Hall, Milton Keynes MK7 6AA, United Kingdom, for a brochure: tel. +44 (0)1908 858785; fax +44 (0)1908 858787; e-mail ouwenq@open.ac.uk

First published 2004 by The Policy Press in association with The Open University

The Open University
Walton Hall
Milton Keynes
MK7 6AA
United Kingdom
www.open.ac.uk

The Policy Press
Fourth Floor, Beacon House
Clifton
Bristol
BS8 1QU
United Kingdom
www.policypress.org.uk

British Library Cataloguing-in-Publication Data
A catalogue record for this book is available from the British Library.

Library of Congress Cataloguing-in-Publication Data
A catalogue record for this book has been requested.

Edited, designed and typeset by The Open University.

Printed and bound in Great Britain by The Bath Press, CPI Group.

ISBN 1 86134 520 8

1.1

Personal Lives and Social Policy

Personal Lives and Social Policy
Series Editor: Janet Fink

This book forms part of a series published by The Policy Press in association with The Open University. The complete list of books in the series is as follows:

Sexualities: Personal Lives and Social Policy, edited by Jean Carabine
Care: Personal Lives and Social Policy, edited by Janet Fink
Work: Personal Lives and Social Policy, edited by Gerry Mooney
Citizenship: Personal Lives and Social Policy, edited by Gail Lewis

Notes on contributors to *Work: Personal Lives and Social Policy*

Gerry Mooney is a Staff Tutor and Senior Lecturer in Social Policy in the Faculty of Social Sciences at The Open University (Scotland). He has written widely on different areas of social policy and urban studies. He is co-author of *Rethinking Welfare* (2002), and co-editor of *Unruly Cities?* (1999) and *Class Struggle and Social Welfare* (2002). His research interests include the development of social policies in post-devolutionary Scotland and New Labour's policies for disadvantaged communities.

Janet Newman is Professor of Social Policy at The Open University. Her research interests focus around new forms of governance and their implications for policy and practice. Her work has traced the impact of state restructuring on those working for the public sector and on the users of public services.

Beth Widdowson is a Staff Tutor in Social Policy at The Open University. She worked as an Associate Lecturer at The Open University for a number of years and has taught on a range of different social policy courses. Beth's PhD involved an exploration of gender (in)equality in the field of vocational education and training, and her earlier work turned on ethnographic research into violence and sexual harassment at work. Her current research interests are mapped around the area of age divisions and employment.

Ross Fergusson is a Senior Lecturer in Social Policy and a Staff Tutor in the Faculty of Social Sciences at The Open University. He contributes to courses in social policy and criminology, and his research interests are focused on the interface between young people's transitions to adulthood and the criminalization of social exclusion through welfare policies and juvenile justice.

Contents

Preface

Work: Personal Lives and Social Policy is the third of four books in a new series published by The Policy Press in association with The Open University. The series takes an interdisciplinary and theoretically informed approach to the study of social policy in order to examine the ways in which the two domains of *personal lives* and *social policy and welfare practice* are each partially shaped and given meaning by the other. This process of mutual constitution is explored in the books through core practices of the everyday. Such an approach is both exciting and innovative. It is also indicative of a growing recognition within the social sciences that 'the personal' is a valuable lens of analysis. More generally, the series is concerned not only with debates and questions that are highly visible in social policy, but also with those that tend to be marginalized or silenced and how these might be interpreted through the use of different theoretical perspectives, conceptual tools and research evidence. Overall, therefore, the books move beyond what are usually considered to be the parameters of social policy and its study.

The four books make up the core texts of an Open University course entitled *Personal Lives and Social Policy*. The first book, *Sexualities: Personal Lives and Social Policy*, considers why questions of sex and sexuality matter for the study of social policy and, in turn, illustrates how such questions provide important insights into the relationship between personal lives and social policy. Its concerns with the normative and taken-for-granted assumptions about sexuality, that inform social policy and welfare practices, establish the central interest of the series – the dynamics by which social policy and personal lives intersect and become entangled.

The second book, *Care: Personal Lives and Social Policy*, focuses on the meanings and definitions attributed to care and examines the norms and values associated with care relationships that are embedded in welfare policy and practice. The book illustrates the highly charged and often contradictory nature of care relations by exploring issues of power, conflict and control and considering the different spaces and places where questions about care have been lived out, debated and struggled over.

This third book, *Work: Personal Lives and Social Policy*, traces the central place that work has been afforded, historically, in policy-making and the extent to which it has remained an unproblematic category not only for policy-makers but also in the study of social policy. The book foregrounds the contingent relationship between work and welfare in order to examine the ways in which this arena of policy practices and discourses has developed around particular constructions of personal lives.

The fourth and final book, *Citizenship: Personal Lives and Social Policy*, looks at ideas and meanings associated with citizenship in order to broaden and problematize the term. In particular, it emphasizes the importance of moving away from associating citizenship with rights and obligations within nation-states towards recognizing how a consideration of multiple belongings and practices of the everyday opens up the study of social policy to new and challenging questions.

Although these books are edited volumes, each chapter has been specially written to contribute not only to the exploration of the mutual constitution of personal lives and social policy, but also to the process of student learning. The books have, therefore, been constructed as interactive teaching texts which encourage engagement with and further reflection on the themes, issues and arguments presented in the chapters. The process of interaction is organized around:

- *activities* – variously made up of exercises, tasks and questions, highlighted in colour, which have been designed to extend or consolidate understanding of particular aspects of the chapters;
- *comments* – interpretations and discussions of the activities, which provide opportunities for readers to compare their own responses with those of the author(s);
- *in-text questions* – short questions, again in colour, that build into the chapter opportunities for consideration of core points or arguments;
- *key words* – terms and concepts, highlighted in colour in the text and in the margins, which are central to the arguments, theoretical perspectives and research questions being used and interrogated by the author(s).

In addition, the opening chapter of each book has been written to provide a critical introduction to key issues, ideas, theories and concepts associated with the book's field of interest. The individual books are self-contained but there are references to other chapters and other books in the series. Such references help readers not only to make connections between the books, but also to understand and reflect on the themes and debates that run across the series overall.

The series has been shaped and informed by discussions within the Open University Course Team. Each member of the Team brought to these discussions their own interests, enthusiasms and fields of expertise, but never lost sight of the overall aims of the series and their commitment to those aims. The series is, therefore, the product of a genuinely interdisciplinary and collaborative process. This also means that contributions have been made to all the chapters of the books within this series by people who are not explicitly named as authors. The process of collaboration extends further, however, than the production of materials by academics. In writing chapters, the Course Team and consultant authors have been advised and guided by an external assessor, a tutor panel and a developmental testing panel. The wide-ranging involvement and assistance from the editors, designers and picture researchers have been invaluable in the production of these accessible and attractive texts. Course managers have used their knowledge and skills to resolve the many questions and difficulties that arose during the course's development. Secretaries brought their expertise to the styling and organization of seemingly endless manuscript drafts – and did so with admirable good humour. We thank them all for their work and support which are reflected throughout this book, the series and the course as a whole.

Janet Fink

CHAPTER I

Exploring the Dynamics of Work, Personal Lives and Social Policy

by Gerry Mooney

Contents

1 Introduction

All of us in different and unequal ways have a relationship with 'work': as employees or employers; as voluntary workers or benefit recipients. As mothers, fathers and carers we also engage in activity that can be considered 'work'. We may be involved with different forms of 'informal' or 'irregular' work (moonlighting), and school-age children may undertake some paid work. There are few areas of our day-to-day lives that are not affected by 'work', whether we ourselves are *formally* employed or not. This may revolve around a schedule that is governed by the time demands of shift work, by the hours that family, friends and colleagues work and/or by caring for children before and after school. Our lives are structured around diverse forms of work that have far reaching consequences for the other activities in which we are engaged. But, work is also often central to our life story, to our personal biography. It is a mark of who we are, how we are defined and seen by others: a key element in our identity. Asking new acquaintances if they are 'working' is a common method of establishing some knowledge of an individual. There is a widespread tendency to 'read' someone through the work that they do while for many of us our paid employment is a key marker of our social standing and position. Our work is, then, part of us; it helps to construct who we are and how we are defined, perceived and classified.

Through work we may also derive some meaning and fulfilment in our daily lives. As the US social commentator Studs Terkl (1980) notes in *American Dreams Lost and Found*:

> The job. Something more than Orwellian acceptance, something less than Luddite sabotage. Often the two impulses are fused in the same person ... It is about a search too, for daily meaning as well as daily bread, for recognition as well as cash, for astonishment rather than torpor; in short, for a sort of life rather than a Monday through Friday sort of dying.
>
> (Terkl quoted in Brown and Lauder, 2001, p.41)

Terkl highlights the central tension in work: the search for recognition against the disillusionment and despair that all too often characterizes work. He makes note of the search for personal 'meaning' and 'astonishment' on the one hand, against what he terms the 'sort of dying' that is part of the alienating working conditions that many of us experience daily. For many workers in the UK, the culture of long working hours, the increasing intensification of work, and 'anti-social' shift patterns have far-reaching negative consequences. Little wonder that people often say that they want to *work to live*, not *live to work*. It is, then, not surprising that the pursuit of 'family friendly' employment has become more evident since the late 1990s at government level in both the UK and through European Union (EU) legislation such as the Working Time Directive. Such policies, which appear to prioritize the organization of work around personal lives, are crucially about maximizing formal paid employment and in the process legitimizing particular forms of work.

The analysis of work has long occupied a privileged position within the social sciences. This reflects the centrality of work in contemporary societies. Work connects in a myriad of complex and diverse ways to other core concerns of the social sciences: to questions of power, inequality, social differentiation, globalization, social and economic change, the role of the state, and welfare provision among others. In social policy analysis work is also an ever present, even if it is often marginalized. Here work connects with issues of social security, health, education, housing and other key areas of social policy research. As we will soon discover, however, the study of work is characterized by conceptual and theoretical disputes, not least around the notion of 'work' itself. The boundaries between work and other areas of our lives are constantly shifting and being redrawn. Since the early to mid 1990s, for example, there has been a growth in what has been termed 'domestic outsourcing' (or perhaps more correctly 'insourcing'): replacing unpaid domestic labour with paid labour. Examples include the purchase of takeaway or ready-made meals (which in turn relies on the industrialization of food production and often assembly-line type labour in food factories) as a substitute for home-prepared food; and the purchase of 'external' labour for ironing, cleaning and a range of other domestic tasks.

In relation to social policy, paid work is a key factor that determines our entitlement to a diverse array of social benefits. Work is one of the main ways in which welfare policies help to construct our personal lives and define us as eligible for, or deserving of, benefits. It is a key vehicle through which social policy intervenes to regulate and shape 'the personal'. But 'the personal' also shapes and conditions work and our experiences of it. In other words, in this book, 'work' is to be understood and analysed as part of 'the personal': our personal encapsulates our work; it is not 'suspended' in the process of working. In the personal narrative that follows, a Birmingham steel worker talks about the pivotal role that his work has played in his life and in his family history:

> I started here in 1939, but I was called up for the army in 1940. I got demobbed in July 1946 and I started back here in August. I worked on the 28-inch mill. It was hard in those days, they hadn't any tilters or things like that to turn them over. I worked on the mills for about eight years, then I had pneumonia. I was labouring for a bit after that, but it got a bit too much for me. I'm not very tall and you had to use all muscle power then. You needed to be a big 'un with those steel barrows. Then I got a regular job on the old soaking pits, and when they closed them down I come up here. I've never wanted to work anywhere else. My father worked here. He died when he was 64 and he worked here for over 50 years. My grandfather worked here too. I don't remember this myself, but he used to be a shearer on the open plate mill. You can grumble about the money and the conditions we work in, but I suppose you're reared in it more or less. You know it's hard work in the mills and you know what to expect. I've had my ups and downs but I've not wanted to work anywhere else. You've worked your way up to get a job and you know what to expect. Those that have left they've been glad to get back. My daughter worked here in the office. That was the fourth generation.
>
> (Hedges and Beynon, 1982, pp.10–11)

When we enter paid work, or undertake voluntary and other forms of work, our personal is part of this activity. In other words, we carry our personal to work. As the quotation above shows, our personal is constructed relationally, not only in relation to close family members, but also to fellow employees and employers. If we are labelled as state 'dependent' we would be defined against people who are formally working, and our eligibility for benefits will be questioned as a result. But 'the personal' is in turn partly shaped by the work that we do. In the quotation above we get a strong sense of a male-dominated world of work: 'maleness' and masculinity are, in part, constructed through the work being performed and in the industry in which they are located.

Social policy as a field of academic study engages with work in many different ways, for instance in relation to income maintenance, employment policy, social care, family policy and urban regeneration programmes. This academic interest reflects the centrality of work in the development of social policy. From the New Poor Law of 1834 through to the social inclusion policies of the Labour Government in the late 1990s and early 2000s, successive policy-makers have privileged paid work, and in the process made a distinction between the 'deserving' and 'undeserving'. But, work also features in a range of other social policies. Following the Boer War (1899–1902), for instance, when a shortage of fit and healthy recruits for the army caused considerable political alarm, a Royal Commission on the Physical Deterioration of the Working Class was established. It was concerned not just with issues of military effectiveness, but also with economic efficiency in the face of growing competition from the USA and Germany. In the series of Liberal welfare reforms (1906–1914) that followed soon after, the development of a fitter and healthier workforce was a central goal. These reforms were premised on the notion that men were the primary breadwinners, while women were assumed to be, and constructed as, unpaid domestic workers, even though in 1900 some 5 million women were in employment, comprising 29 per cent of the total labour force (Lindsay, 2003, p.138).

Work has, then, long been central to social policy. In this book we explore some of the conceptions of work that are mobilized through different social policies. We examine the relationships between personal lives, work and social policy, highlighting the different ways in which they constitute each other. This involves much more than simply recognizing that work is intrinsically connected with social and welfare policies: 'the personal' matters in multiple and overlapping ways. Social policy has been premised on particular understandings of work, whereby work and 'the personal' are imagined to belong to different spheres of life: 'the personal' taking place 'outside' the process of labour exchange. Against this, the chapters that follow are concerned to explore the interconnections between personal lives, work and social policy, illuminating and analysing how they are normalized in particular ways through different social policies. This involves the subordination of migrant labour, voluntary work and domestic work as well as 'alternative' or 'informal' forms of work. Drawing on Marxist, feminist and post-structuralist (including social constructionist) approaches, we highlight work as part of a complex set of social relations. No single chapter utilizes all these theoretical frameworks. Different approaches are more explicitly used in some chapters than in others, but they share a concern to offer explanations of the multiple ways in which social policy, work and 'the personal' are mutually constitutive. Throughout the chapters a range of social science methodologies and different forms of research evidence are also highlighted, in the process illuminating diverse aspects of the connections between work, personal lives and social policy.

In this chapter we explore some of the ways in which work has been central to social policy in the UK, and we examine the contrasting meanings that can be attached to 'work'. We also consider some of the key trends in work and employment in post-1945 UK society that have helped to shape our understanding of work today. Drawing on Marxist perspectives in particular, we also analyse some of the ways through which the organization of work results in a loss of power and control for many workers.

Chapter 2 builds on the foundations of this chapter by analysing how welfare work involves managing personal lives in diverse and multiple ways. Welfare work, it is argued, relies on the production and regulation of different senses of 'the personal' – for both the welfare worker and the client/customer. Using Marxist, feminist and post-structuralist approaches, Chapter 2 draws on the concept of emotional labour to illuminate particular aspects of this relationship. By exploring contrasting forms of welfare work and voluntary work, it also highlights some of the ways in which developments in social policy help to shape 'the personal'.

Chapter 3 moves to consider the experience of a particular group of people defined in and against work – the 'retired'. Our first job is often a key milestone in our personal history. Likewise the transition out of paid employment can represent one of the most significant markers in our lives, one that is all too often surrounded by uncertainty and a fear for the future. Using feminist and post-structuralist accounts, this chapter explores the ways in which the social construction of 'the elderly' and 'the retired' is shaped by changes in social policy and considers the consequences of these for our personal lives.

Chapter 4 explores other aspects of work, notably the increasing emphasis on paid work in key areas of modern social policy. It uses the example of the Labour Government's welfare-to-work programme in the UK to show that specific policy frameworks inscribe particular individuals, groups and social activities as 'normal' or pathological, and in the process shape our personal lives in ways that are moralizing and prescriptive. Welfare to work, therefore, is among the most recent in a long line of social policies that have carried particular assumptions about the individual and how personal lives should be organized, in this instance around a particular understanding of work.

Chapter 5 pulls the main threads of the book together by considering some of the key shifts in work in recent decades, and the development of 'family friendly' policies and a concern with work–life balance (WLB) in the late 1990s/early 2000s, highlighting in particular the impact of neo-liberal economic and social policies on 'the personal'–work–social policy interface.

Aims The main aims, then, of this book are to:

- Examine some of the ways in which work as paid labour has become normalized through social policy, and the consequences of this for our understanding of the dynamic relationship between work and personal lives.
- Explore the ways in which 'the personal' and work overlap and are mutually constitutive.
- Disrupt the construction of a binary divide between paid/unpaid work, formal/informal work and home/workplace.

2 Conceptualizing work

Thus far we have side-stepped the highly contested issue of what we mean by 'work', though, as we have seen in section 1, we need to avoid equating work with paid employment. To explore the different ways in which work and our personal lives interrelate, we must understand work as a much broader set of activities and social relations. In this section we problematize work and examine why certain kinds of work are valorized and given privileged meaning, and how social policy helps to reinforce and consolidate this. To aid us in this task we initially turn to cultural theorist Raymond Williams who has traced the historical development of the concept of work.

ACTIVITY 1.1

Read Extract 1.1 from Raymond Williams's *Keywords*. How does his unpacking of the notion of work help us to understand the way in which work has come to be dominantly constructed and understood in contemporary society?

Extract 1.1 The shifting meaning of 'work'

As our most general word for doing something, and for something done, its range of applications has of course been enormous. What is now most interesting is its predominant specialization to paid employment. This is not exclusive; we speak naturally of **working** in the garden. But, to take one significant example, an active woman, running a house and bringing-up children, is distinguished from a woman who **works**: that it to say, takes paid employment. The basic sense of the word, to indicate activity and effort or achievement, has thus been modified, though unevenly and incompletely, by a definition of its imposed conditions, such as working for a wage or salary: being hired ... The specialization of **work** to paid employment ... is the result of the development of capitalist productive relations. To be **in work** or **out of work** was to be in a definite relationship with some other who had control of the means of productive effort. **Work** then partly shifted from the productive effort itself to the predominant social relationship. It is only in this sense that a woman running a house and bringing up children can be said to be not **working**. At the same time, because the general word is necessary, a person may be said to do his real work on his own, sometimes quite separately from his job. Time other than that spent in paid employment is significantly described as 'your 'own time', 'free time', or as 'holiday ... or as 'leisure time'.

(Williams, 1976, pp.281–3)

Figure 1.1 Work

COMMENT

As Williams highlights in Extract 1.1, work has largely come to be equated with formal paid labour. He illuminates the distinction between productive effort and the social relations of wage labour that underpin paid employment in capitalist societies. Work comes to be understood as an activity that is clearly demarcated from all others, for example, leisure pursuits, holidays and, ultimately, personal life. In this extract, work is constructed as a

rational, impersonal domain of activity, taking place in particular public settings for financial remuneration, ignoring that we go to work as gendered, racialized and often sexualized beings, reflecting also our class and other social positions.

The way we view work is further shaped by history and by our social position in relation to class, gender, 'race' and age, and we might also add geographical location. Following Williams, Ray Pahl (1984, p.18) suggests that it was towards the end of the eighteenth century when the contemporary meanings of 'worker' emerged, while it was not until the development of political science in the nineteenth century that idea of 'work' itself became a central concept. The hegemonic meaning attached to work (as public, formal paid employment) in the late twentieth and early twenty-first centuries is overwhelmingly a product of the rise of industrial capitalist society.

While Williams helps us to unpack some of the differing senses of 'work', it is apparent that the meaning attached to work has not been a problem for policy-makers, and all too often neither has its analysis by many academics. Gøsta Esping-Andersen, for example, has produced one of the most widely discussed explanations of the relationship between work and welfare systems. He argues that welfare systems – or regimes – can be differentiated by the extent to which they are premised on redistributive social policies and by the degree of **decommodification** of labour. Decommodification refers to 'the degree to which individuals or families can uphold a socially acceptable standard of living independently of market participation' (Esping-Andersen, 1990, p.37). Decommodified social benefits would include pensions based not on individual contributions but on citizenship rights, and a universal and non means-tested system of income maintenance. Work thus occupies a central position in this argument. Again though, work is equated with paid employment and other forms of work are neglected. The ideas of commodification and decommodification imply different entitlements and very different connections between work and 'the personal'. But, in Esping-Andersen's thesis, the separation of 'the personal' from work is assumed and unchallenged. Here, as in much of UK social policy, as well as in its academic analysis, 'the personal' is an absent presence.

decommodification

There has long been a common sense around work: 'work' was something that men and – particularly since the 1960s – increasing numbers of women, went to (even though paid work also took place in the home). Consider the everyday language that is often mobilized in relation to 'work': we refer to going to work, out working or away working. Thus, the 'public' and the 'private' are inscribed with particular spatial and temporal referents ('from nine to five' or 'five days a week'). However, this notion of 'work' is being challenged by the growing number of 'home workers': not only does this category often involve extremely low-paid (and often almost 'invisible') jobs, but it also includes the increasing number of freelance consultants operating from home. There are also those who run businesses from their home (and the mail order agents, party 'reps', dog walkers, cat sitters, house watchers, bin-washers and childminders). Such examples demonstrate that the boundaries between formal and informal categories of work, and 'public' and 'private' spheres are both fluid and increasingly porous, and that the meanings and definitions of work cannot be understood in a common-sense way. Further, over time the shifting meanings of 'public' and 'private' impact on how work is defined and understood. Care and mothering are two obvious cases in point. With care, Janet Fink suggests that there is an increasing overlap between formal and informal caring arrangements, though policy-makers continue to see them as occupying distinctive spheres (**Fink, 2004**).

In presenting these arguments we are concerned to avoid essentialist, universalistic and ahistorical definitions of work – though these still tend to be prevalent in explorations of work in contemporary societies – and to recognize the diversity of work instead. This allows us to challenge those normalizing constructions of paid work, which in constructing the boundaries of 'the personal' define as a result areas for legitimate state intervention. If the equation of work with public paid employment has been, and is now, increasingly subject to question and criticism, it is in part the result of contributions by feminist theorists such as Ann Oakley (1974), who have argued that the home is also a workplace, predominantly for women. Other feminists have also reminded us that much of wage labour for women takes place in other women's homes. Leonore Davidoff (1995), for example, estimates that over one million women were engaged in domestic service of some form or another in the 1920s and 1930s. In particular, socialist feminists have been instrumental in drawing our attention to the links between gender inequalities in the labour market and in unpaid domestic labour, in the process helping to reformulate the notion of 'work'.

Central to this reformulation of work has been the concerted effort to reject the 'public/private' spheres dichotomy and to understand the increasingly blurred nature of formal/informal categories of work. It is now generally accepted that the position of both men and women in the labour market is interconnected with their situation in the domestic or household economy. But, does this help us to understand all forms of work? In a study of 'community work' in the town of Kitchener-Waterloo in Ontario, Canada, Beth Moore Milroy and Susan Wismer (1994) explored women's involvement in volunteering. In their study, community work does not refer to formal, paid community work performed by welfare professionals, but rather to the unpaid volunteering that takes place both outside paid employment and the economy (see Chapter 2). They argue that the exploration of community work in this sense raises important questions about the relationship between the 'public' and 'private' spheres. To locate this kind of community volunteering in either the public or private sphere is problematic as it is both non-familial and non-economic (at least in the sense of paid work or commercial activity). They argue that this form of work 'explicitly connects the concerns of both spheres – the worrying over the failures, excesses and gaps and absences of both, as well as the desire for better things' (Moore Milroy and Wismer, 1994, p.83). By extending this analysis of community work we can see that 'the personal' pervades work in all its different forms, and it helps us to understand some of the ways in which the boundaries between work and 'other' areas of life are rarely, if ever, clear-cut. However, we need to take our understanding a step further as the kinds of volunteering and community work that women have often participated in have in the past been heavily prescribed. The case of middle-class women philanthropists in the late nineteenth century is an obvious example of this (see Mooney, 1998), while more enduringly particular forms of 'church' and some 'charity' work have often been constructed as the preserve of women volunteers. In the process this has helped to gender particular forms of 'welfare work' as well as shape social policy agendas.

Other researchers have drawn attention to 'alternative work relations' that also 'fall' between informal and formal categories of work. In their study of Local Exchange Trading Schemes (LETS) in Stroud and Brixton, Theresa Aldridge and her colleagues interpret these LETS as 'community orientated trading organizations' that attempt to develop the exchange of goods and services within a particular community (Aldridge et al., 2001, p.566). In 2002 there were around 450 LETS schemes in the UK, with 40,000 participants (Letslink UK, 2003), and LETS have been seen as a vehicle through which 'alternative work relations' can be constructed.

ACTIVITY 1.2

Read the following quotations from LETS Interviewees. How might these schemes shape 'the personal' in ways that are different to more conventional undertakings of work? What different meanings of work are traceable here?

> I'm out of work at the moment, and I thought that LETS sounded like a good idea so I joined. It's a way to get goods and services without having to pay out the little cash I've got, and I can offer my services to other people, and when I'm ready I might be able to get back into work, paid work. At the moment I'm still in recovery but I can do things, I can offer my crafts though LETS and word processing. And it's good to be able to make a contribution.
>
> (Female Stroud LETS Interviewee)

> I joined LETS because I have a lot of things to offer and I want to offer them, I'm eager to work, I am not a person who is lazy and I want to work. What I like about LETS is the fact that ... everybody has a place in the world, everybody has something to offer and that by joining, you create your own place, you create your own employment in a way.
>
> (Female Stroud LETS Interviewee)

> There was a whole angle which was about the whole inflexibility of the five-day week, nine to five job syndrome where you were defined by your job ... and everything else that you did was your hobby or relaxation and actually people have got five or six things that they like doing ... So it was a way of building space outside the system where things could go on.
>
> (Male Brixton LETS member)

(Aldridge et al., 2001, pp.570–2)

COMMENT

This LETS study deployed a combination of quantitative and qualitative research methods. The use of in-depth interviews allowed the researchers to uncover some of the different meanings that the participants accorded to their involvement in LETS. People join these

LETS for different reasons, but many of those who are involved feel it provides some way of exerting control over work. Through their involvement there is a greater sense of personal 'worth', of being 'useful'. However, despite the obvious attractiveness to many people, there are many limitations to what LETS can achieve. While LETS do challenge some of the traditional constructions of paid employment, it is also clear from the Stroud and Brixton study that they do not undermine class and gender relations in any significant way. In negotiations of the price to be exchanged for the services provided, the study also found that women from higher level occupational groups were able to demand more 'units' – the exchange 'currency' – compared with less skilled or unemployed women. Aldridge and her colleagues concluded that confidence in negotiating a 'price' for the job or service rendered was both class and gender related (Aldridge, et al., 2001, pp.576–7).

While the examples of community work/activism and LETS allow us to begin to challenge both the notion of separate spheres and the related construction of work as paid employment, they cannot account for the diversity of activities and labour that contribute to 'work' in a general sense. In section 2.1 we consider other research which has furthered our understanding of work.

2.1 The total social organization of labour

Miriam Glucksmann is one of several writers who, in the process of deconstructing the notion of work, has reminded us of the dangers of collapsing everything under the umbrella of 'work', which leads to a situation where we find it impossible to distinguish between 'work' and 'activity':

> As deconstructionist ideas filter through to the study of work their effect is to interrogate the term, asking what is meant by 'work', and whether indeed it denotes anything distinctive at all. Once paid employment has been recognized as constituting only one mode of work, rather than being its defining characteristic, obviously the question arises of where to draw the line between work and non-work. Should we understand taking the dog for a walk as work or single people doing their own cleaning as work? Are wives 'working' when they remember to buy birthday cards for their husbands' relatives? While it is necessary to ask such questions, certain types of answer may not prove so helpful.
>
> (Glucksmann, 1995, p.64)

Total Social Organization of Labour (TSOL)

Glucksmann's response is to reconceptualize work in ways that avoid essentialist, universalistic and ahistorical definitions. She develops the notion of the **Total Social Organization of Labour (TSOL)** through her research on the lives of working-class women in Lancashire in the 1930s. Glucksmann focuses on the relationship between the labour market and households in Manchester, Salford and Bolton in her study of 'cottons and casuals'. Her research captures the diversity of working lives among different groups of women weavers in the textile industry, the 'cottons' of the title, and the 'casuals', married women whose work was more irregular in 'all sorts' of 'little jobs' (Glucksmann, 2000). Not only does this research remind us that women's paid labour was central to the reproduction of many working-class households and communities prior to the Beveridgean welfare state, it further highlights the connections between paid and domestic labour, and to the unequal interdependencies between formal and informal economies. Cottons and casuals differed in their material circumstances. Many of the cottons were employed in an industry that tended to be relatively unsegregated in gender terms, and in which there was a degree of convergence between female and male rates of pay. The cottons purchased child care from neighbours and friends, while their regular income contributed to a clear demarcation between leisure and domestic labour time. The casuals, on the other hand, were dependent on irregular paid work both within and outside the home, often selling their caring labour to women working full-time. In other words, the casuals enabled the cottons to undertake formal paid work. As Glucksmann demonstrates, this contributed to their self-identity as principally wife and mother – and as neighbour – not as 'worker' in the publicly sanctioned sense. Any 'free' or 'leisure' time was severely limited by comparison with the cottons as a result of their reliance on a mix of different forms of work, both within and outside the home. What is evident though is that the differing – and unequal – relational networks, activities and connections to the labour market that both cottons and casuals depended on, and generated, contributed to the TSOL in the respective localities. According to Glucksmann, the notion of the TSOL refers to:

> the manner by which all the labour in a particular society is divided up between and allocated to different structures, institutions and activities. The total social organization of labour is a kind of higher level division of labour, referring not to the technical division of tasks within one institution or work process, but rather to the social division of all the labour undertaken in a given society between institutional spheres. It is the organization of activities from the standpoint of their economic constraints and relations.
>
> (Glucksmann, 1995, p.67)

It was Marx who first drew a distinction between the technical and social division of labour – that is, how labour is divided in the work (or *labour*) process and the wider social relations around which work is organized within capitalist society (see section 5). In this quotation Glucksmann helps capture the complex means through which domestic and formal economic activities are bound together in a 'wider system of labour'. We can identify different types of activity – production, services, welfare, education, domestic labour and so on – that comprise a particular TSOL, as well as analyse the ways in which the 'public' and the 'private' come at particular times, and in particular places, to be regarded as separate spheres of activity and personal life. However, we can also understand that 'the personal' runs through and across this range of different types of activity.

Glucksmann's approach helps us to understand the organization of 'work' and the wider division of labour in a society. She writes:

> 'Work' would refer to activity necessary for the production and reproduction of economic relations and structures in a particular TSOL, irrespective of how and

Figure 1.2 Women textile workers in a mill in Lancashire in the 1930s

> where it is carried out ... Rather than starting out from the idea of an economic system and then defining activities as economic or non-economic, work or non-work, the relational approach involves instead looking from the inside out, starting from how activities connect to each other and would not 'work' without each other.
>
> (Glucksmann, 1995, p.69–70)

Glucksmann's work is important for the discussion in this chapter in a number of respects. She draws our attention to the importance of linking place and history – that is the *spatial* and *temporal* – in terms of how labour/work is organized and understood. The employment histories, cultures and traditions of different parts of the UK remind us that we need to avoid overgeneralizing from the story of one locality and one type of industry when we are exploring work and highlighting its different effects and impacts on personal lives. Over the past century and a half the traditions of female employment in textile towns, and in towns such as Dundee where the jute industry had a long history, were very different from the largely male-dominated labour markets that characterized coal mining communities and industrial centres such as Glasgow, Cardiff or Newcastle, with their dependency on shipbuilding, iron and steel, and heavy engineering. Glucksmann also highlights that the relations and structures of 'work' – conceptualized though the TSOL – also involve economic, political, cultural and gendered elements. Research such as this enables us to question the extent to which our personal lives are something remote from the formal arrangements that surround work. It has also opened up the idea of separate spheres to increasing scrutiny, and in the process has highlighted how the 'public' and 'private' are interwoven.

A wider concept of work, reformulated in some of the ways suggested above, can account for any activity that involves the expulsion of human energies, as feminists and community activists among others have claimed. However, in the process of undertaking this reformulation it is important that we do not lose sight of the unique character of paid work under capitalism. Paid employment is different from unpaid work for obvious reasons. While some kind of **labour process** exists in all human societies, only in capitalist society is it premised on, and systematically organized for, the purposes of extracting surplus, that is profit. Such arguments derive from Marxist social theory, and there is an important difference here between the arguments of Glucksmann and Marx. For Glucksmann what is central is the aggregate amount of work conducted in a society, irrespective of where it takes place and in what form – the TSOL. For Marx, by contrast, the social division of labour has an entirely different meaning as it focuses on the centrality and specificity of commodified labour power under capitalism – processes that involve the exploitation of wage labour. Thus, for Marxists one limitation of the TSOL argument is that it can obscure the source of profit (wealth) in capitalist society: the systematic extraction of surplus from workers. But, for Glucksmann the advantage of the TSOL notion is that it highlights the centrality of other forms of work to the maintenance and reproduction of capitalist society.

labour process

Glucksmann's research and analysis opens up the notion of work and helps us to grasp the different ways in which work and personal lives are interrelated. Different groups of female textile workers had very contrasting personal lives, with the lives of 'casuals' being much more centred on the family and home and as a result, seemingly more limited. But, in what ways does social policy help to define and construct these personal lives?

3 Work, welfare and social policy

Work is, or will be, central to the lives of most people, albeit in very different ways. Our eligibility for welfare is also shaped by our relationship with work. Work and welfare are historically deeply interconnected – if often imagined as separate domains. Taxation policies, employment and labour market policies, pensions and benefits policies, are all easily understood as linked in some ways to work. We can also add Health and Safety laws to this list, along with Trade Union legislation and Industrial Relations policies – all of which have enormous impacts on 'the personal' of many workers. It is in relation to the provision of welfare benefits, however, that some of the most significant constructions of 'the personal' take place.

Social policy is full of assumptions about 'the personal' and how it should be organized. We have observed that governments tend to make a number of links between work and welfare (couched in terms of 'dependency'). While the notion of national insurance, which was such a cornerstone of the post-1945 welfare state, implied a contribution from current earnings for future welfare support, in general work and welfare tend to be constructed as opposites. There has, however, always been a link between work and welfare – albeit one that is historically specific and conditioned. Under the Labour Government in the late 1990s and early 2000s, however, it has undergone something of a revival. A key element of its social policy has been the welfare-to-work programme, while in the USA under the Democrat administration of Clinton during the mid 1990s there was some attempt to combine work and welfare under the label of 'workfare' (see Chapter 4). As Brown and Lauder (2001, pp.204–5) have noted: 'The extent of our obsession with waged work is evident when single mothers are forced to leave their children with a childminder, while they look after someone else's children for a wage, in order to demonstrate their contribution to society'.

The idea of a work ethic or a strong moral compulsion to work has a long history (Beder, 2000). As Cochrane (1998, p.294) highlights, the central principle of the New Poor Law of 1834 (for England and Wales) and 1845 (in Scotland) was to discourage what is now often referred to as 'welfare dependency'. Employment, no matter how poorly paid or horrendous the working conditions, was to always pay more than state welfare. This regime was backed by a discourse that preached duty and individual responsibility – particularly of a married man for his wife and/or 'dependants'. The threat of the 'workhouse' was the alternative for those considered to be lacking in the necessary moral fibre and requiring character 'reform' (see Chapter 3). Thus, a distinction was drawn between those who could be reformed through the work ethic – the **deserving poor** – and those considered resistant to the work ethic – the **undeserving poor** or the **underclass** (Mooney, 1998). From the early days of welfare policy then, particular assumptions about work and independence as opposed to welfare and dependency came to be constructed and sedimented in the social policy developments that followed over the next 150 years. To be defined as eligible for welfare often meant that certain freedoms had to be surrendered and it also entailed undergoing what were frequently the most degrading and intrusive of state interventions. Since the New Poor Law, notions of deserving, responsibility and personal morality have come to be inscribed as the key threads that weave together the work–welfare–personal lives relationship in policy-making.

deserving poor
undeserving poor
underclass

The assumption of a male breadwinner that lay behind the Poor Law legislation was also central to the Beveridgean Welfare State in post-1945 Britain. The ideal citizen was constructed as a male breadwinner with dependent wife and children (**Lewis and Fink, 2004**). In his report on *Social Insurance and Allied Services* in 1942, Beveridge was tasked to develop:

> a plan for Social Security to ensure that every citizen of the country, on condition of working and contributing while he can, has an income to keep him above want when for any other reason – of sickness, accident, unemployment or old age – he cannot work and earn an income sufficient for the honourable subsistence of himself and all who earn an income sufficient for the honourable subsistence of himself and all who depend on him, an income sufficient though he has nothing else of his own and not cut down by any means test if he has anything of his own.
>
> ...

> During marriage most women will not be gainfully occupied. The small minority of women who undertake paid employment or other gainful occupation after marriage ... require special treatment differing from that of a single woman. Such paid work in many cases will be intermittent; it should be open to any married woman to undertake it as an exempt person, paying no contributions of her own and acquiring no claim to benefit in unemployment or sickness. If she prefers to contribute ... she may do so, but will receive benefits at a reduced rate.
>
> (Beveridge, 1942, p.50)

What is notable here is the subordination and marginalization of women workers – at the very time when nearly eight million women were engaged in formal paid work (Thane, 1994, p.394). The post-1945 welfare system assumed a *natural* division of gendered labour: regular full-time (though in reality often *poorly paid*) male employment with women constructed in the process as dependent (and *unpaid*) domestic workers. However, a 'pure' male breadwinner model rarely existed given that some women were always engaged in paid labour, and that male earnings were often insufficient on their own to sustain a family. At the level of prescription, however, of what *ought* to be the case, this division occupied a strategic position in the post-1945 welfare state. Beveridge's proposals also constructed and shaped the personal lives of both men and women. Male workers were to be moral citizens: responsible for both themselves and their family through participation in paid work. By contrast women were denied an independent status – their personal lives were defined by and limited to the realm of family and child care.

ACTIVITY 1.3

To develop an understanding of the ways particular forms of work are privileged and become sedimented in policies, read closely the following quotation from Harriet Harman, the Minister for Social Security in the Labour Government of 1997. How is 'work' being understood and represented by Harriet Harman?

> Work is central to the Government's attack on social exclusion. Work is the only route to sustained financial independence. But, it is also much more. Work is not just about earning a living. It is a way of life ... Work helps to fulfil our aspirations – it is the key to independence, self-respect and opportunities for advancement ... Work brings a sense of order that is missing from the lives of many unemployed young men ... [The socially excluded] and their families are trapped in dependency. They inhabit a parallel world where: income is derived from benefits, not work; where school is an option not a key to opportunity; and where the dominant influence on young people is the culture of the street, not the values that bind families and communities together. There are some estates in my constituency where the common currency is the giro; where the black economy involves much more than moonlighting – it involves the twilight world of drugs; and where relentless anti-social behaviour grinds people down ...
>
> (Harman quoted in Fairclough, 2000, p.57)

COMMENT

There are a number of highly contentious assumptions here. It is clear from this quotation that what is being privileged is a sense of 'work' as paid employment, as the norm. In the final sentence there is both a pathological construction of the 'black economy' and of working-class housing estates, thereby ignoring, or at best marginalizing, the importance of irregular or hidden work for many poor communities. Informal work of different kinds is an important means of survival for those classified as 'undeserving' in an increasingly authoritarian and means-tested welfare system. There is reference also to the 'lives of many unemployed young men' – though not women – as being accorded 'order' through work. This links work and 'the personal' in a very specific way: for Harman (and the Labour Government in general) the discipline of paid labour is presented as the key route to salvation – to social inclusion. The boundaries of 'the personal' are thus inscribed through particular social policies, delineating legitimized state regulation. Where personal lives do not meet the standards defined as 'normal', they are as a result constructed as pathological and deviant. Thus, links are made through social policy between work, 'the personal' and welfare – even while they are seen as remaining separate. It is this connection that underpins much UK social policy. However, in the quote from Harman, the claim that work '*is a way of life*', that it creates '*a sense of order*' and that it is '*the key to independence, self-respect and opportunities for advancement*' can be subject to widespread criticism. There are many workers in Britain who do not regard work as the route to any of these goals but as little more than a daily drudge, for poor pay and with little hope of advancement. Little wonder then that the idea of paid 'work' as the source of salvation – of *social inclusion* – has been so heavily criticized (see Levitas, 1998).

Work as formal paid employment was clearly not *a way of life* for the million or so who were officially registered as unemployed at the time of writing this chapter. Then there are the estimated 1.5 million 'others' who are officially classified as out of work, but have either been disqualified from unemployment/job seekers allowance, or have been pushed off the unemployment register onto sickness and incapacity benefit (Beatty et al., 2002). There are also growing numbers of workers who are subject to what is often referred to as labour market *churning* – periods of irregular employment interspersed by unemployment – and the increasing numbers of workers in both the public and private sectors who have multiple jobs through economic necessity. Saying that 'work is a way of life' means something very different for these groups of workers and for workers in the home. This highlights the multiple ways through which our personal lives and paid employment are interconnected. It raises issues of personal value, of self-esteem, of hardship and survival, and the vast range of individual experiences and histories that are shaped by work in its different forms.

All of our lives are affected by the dominant view of work as paid employment – whether we are formally employed or not. In this sense, then, Harman's notion of parallel worlds – of separate spheres of activity and life – bears little or no resemblance to the day-to-day lives of the vast majority of people. Some state benefits (such as unemployment benefit) are dependent on work-related financial contributions, others on how much we earn. Increasingly, as Chapter 3 illustrates, pension provision is also work-dependent. There is, however,

Figure 1.3 Public sector workers striking against the impact of New Labour's public service 'reforms' on their working conditions in the early 2000s

another dimension to the social significance of work – the suggestion that our lives *should* revolve – or be ordered – around work as employment. Here the idea, again evident in Harman's speech, of work as a source of *advancement*, of *independence* and *self-respect*, is important. Of course some forms and types of work do provide these, but certainly not for everyone. Work is both a source of inequality and a reflection of wider social divisions within society. The intersecting social relations of class, gender, 'race', age and sexuality, then, underpin work and it is to this issue that we now turn our attention.

4 Trends in paid work and employment since the 1950s

Developments in UK social policy since the Second World War have taken place against a backdrop of significant social, economic, political and cultural change. For some sociologists such far-reaching change necessitates the development of:

> a framework of thinking and policy-making that seeks to adapt social democracy to a world that has changed fundamentally over the past two or three decades ... to help citizens pilot their way through the major revolutions of our time: globalization, transformations in personal life and our relationship to nature.
>
> (Giddens, 1998, p.26 and p.64)

Discourses of change are central to discussions of work and employment in the UK today. Change arises at different, though interconnected, levels. At the macro level there are the major changes in paid employment, in the occupational structure and in the social composition of the labour force. At the micro level is what Giddens terms the 'transformation in personal life', which he argues is one of the major 'revolutions of our time'. This section will explore some of the links between macro level labour market changes and the ways in which this impacts on and involves changes in personal lives. However, it is important to acknowledge from the outset that general shifts in employment can hide micro level changes, such as experiences of change that occur in different places and at different times.

Social scientists agree that we live in a world that has undergone profound change in recent decades. There are few areas of society where this is more marked than in relation to the organization of paid work and employment. But, what is open to question and debate are the nature, extent and durability of those changes. These are matters of theoretical dispute that cannot simply be 'read off' from an examination of empirical trends. For example, while there is complete agreement that manufacturing employment has been in long-term decline in Britain (since the late 1950s or mid 1960s depending on the measure used), this gives rise to a range of competing interpretations. Further, we need also to recognize that the official classification of employment categories often changes. The classification of work is premised not on the content of labour, but on the form that jobs take. Workers performing the same job in different sectors of the economy can be classified in different ways. One obvious difficulty is that the traditional separation between manufacturing and 'services' is now arguably less helpful given recent technological developments and changes in the organization of production. Further, *quantitative* changes in employment (for example a growth in white-collar work) are taken to imply *qualitative* shifts in work relations, in matters of power arrangements, inequalities and social stratification. Post-industrial theorists, for example, interpret employment change as marking the arrival of a post-industrial society, seen in the collapse of manual and blue-collar work and the rise of service-based work. This is perceived as the development of more fulfilling and rewarding employment as well as the restratification of society with the emergence of new middle or service classes (see Bell, 1973). Against this we have more Marxist-inspired arguments that white-collar service work will be subjected to the same processes of job degradation and deskilling that have taken place in relation to blue-collar work (see section 5) contributing to a growing **proletarianization** of the lower middle classes. Further, change is often presented not only as inevitable or at least the consequence of forces out of our apparent control – such as 'globalization' – but as a positive development. In this respect many explanations of change not only tend to conflate the *description* of change with their *prescription* of how the world, the economy or society, *should* be organized, they also mobilize a particular sense of the past in the process. Analysis of change is then the focus of much theoretical debate and argument. While different theorists and approaches will prioritize and seek to use different kinds of evidence, even where the same evidence is being used it is

proletarianization

interpreted in very different ways. As ever in the social sciences the relationship between theory and evidence is far from straightforward.

Figure 1.4 From manufacturing to services: towards more satisfying work?

4.1 From the 'golden age' to the 'silver age': a story of rising risk and insecurity in work?

The 'world of work' is plagued by myths – particularly when we are exploring changes in work and employment. Taylor (2002a, p.7) comments that 'no other subject arouses so much unsubstantiated generalization, dogmatic assertion and sweeping prescriptions for change as does the world of work'. One of the recurring and most potent myths that surrounds the discussion of economic and social change in post-1945 British society is that the period from the mid to late 1950s to the early 1970s was a 'golden age' for British society (see Howlett, 1996). This was the period in which, according to Conservative Prime Minister Harold MacMillan, the people of Britain 'never had it so good'. It was an era characterized by historically unprecedented economic growth, low unemployment and low inflation. It is commonplace to refer to the 1950s and 1960s as a time of relative prosperity, full employment, and as a period when the welfare state was steadily extending its scope of activity as reflected in the growth in state housing, education and the NHS.

There was a material basis to claims that this was a period of affluence and prosperity. This was due to the historically unprecedented conditions created by what has been widely referred to as the 'long boom' – the global economic growth following the end of the Second World War. The dominant image of this era remains one of economic security and certainty about the world and how it was organized, a key component of which was the assumption of a gendered division of labour between 'home' and 'workplace'. The post-war welfare regime, then, played a crucial role in structuring and ordering the life-course for men and women, in the process institutionalizing the gendered division of labour.

Table 1.1 Numbers of males and females in employment in Britain, 1959–1999 (thousands)

	1959	1971	1979	1992	1996	1999
Females	7174	8207	9435	10,395	10,693	11,477
Males	13,817	13,433	13,176	10,911	10,916	11,967
Total	20,991	21,640	22,611	21,307	21,609	23,444
Proportion of workforce that is female (%)	34.2	37.9	41.7	48.8	49.5	49.0

Source: based on Noon and Blyton, 2002, p.35, Table 2.2

This 'golden age' is marked by low unemployment and, in relation to paid work, five days a week, nine to five jobs with relative job security (for many, but not all, white men if for few others). During the late 1950s the male employment rate was 96 per cent compared with 46 per cent for women (Philpott, 2002). Since then, however, there have been significant changes in the proportion of men and women in employment: while the overall labour force has increased substantially, by 1992 the male employment rate had fallen while the proportion of women in employment had risen. But, this disguises marked geographical differences between different towns and regions across Britain. By the late 1990s women workers comprised almost 50 per cent of the entire paid labour force – a marked change when compared with the 1950s. In 1981 men filled 3.2 million jobs more than women, but by 2001 men accounted for 12.8 million jobs and women for 12.7 million, 50 per cent of which were part-time (Office of National Statistics, 2003). Between 1979 and the end of the 1990s, he number of men in employment fell by over 3.5 million, a trend that was particularly marked among men aged 50 years and over, a group referred to by Chancellor Gordon Brown in April 1999 as 'a lost generation' (quoted in McDowell, 2001 p. 451).

One of the most significant changes that helps us to explain the contrasting trends in the proportion of men and women in the labour force since the 1950s is the large-scale decline – and in some localities the total *collapse* – of the coal, iron, steel, engineering, manufacturing, and shipbuilding industries.

deindustrialization

The umbrella term for this trend is **deindustrialization**. However, deindustrialization has been uneven, varying geographically *between* different parts of the country, and *within* different localities. The impact has also varied within the manufacturing sector itself – some sectors (for instance car production) have been in long-term decline, while others such as computer components have seen a steady growth since the 1950s. Between 1971 and 2000, manufacturing employment declined by 49.8 per cent while over the same period service employment increased by 63.6 per cent (Noon and Blyton, 2002, p.34). The manufacturing and heavy engineering sectors were always more important for white male employment than for women, though many minority ethnic men were also made redundant as a result of the contraction of manufacturing in the North of England and West Midlands

segmentation

during the 1980s and 1990s. The **segmentation** – or segregation – of the labour force meant that women were overwhelmingly employed in service industries. Many of these jobs reflected assumptions about women's place in the home, their caring and child-rearing role and how their personal lives were (or *should be*) organized. Women workers were largely concentrated in personal services: in teaching, nursing, catering and related jobs. One of the most significant trends in the growth of 'services' is the expansion in finance and banking, retail, tourism and leisure – all sectors with a substantial number of women workers. The welfare state is also a major employer of women. While some 2 million public sector jobs were lost between 1981 and 1999, mainly as a consequence of various privatization measures (Beynon et al., 2002, p.120), in 1998 some 5.8 million workers remained in employment in government, medical and welfare sectors, a number that was greater than in the whole of manufacturing and construction (Webb, 1999, p.748).

Reflecting on your experience, knowledge or awareness of your own family history, what would you see as the key changes – and continuities – in relation to work as paid labour? How have these impacted on your personal life?

Kevin Doogan argues that the changes in the structure of the labour market in Britain are also accompanied by an ageing workforce and by the increasing use of those workers in the 'silver age' of their life course. Between 1992 and 1999, the relative size of the 30-plus age group increased from 69 per cent to 74 per cent of the total workforce (Doogan, 2001, p.429). A significant consequence of the ageing of the workforce is that there are contrasting shifts in work histories for men and women. There has been an expansion of employment among older women, in particular during the 1990s. For women aged between 50 and 74 years, the rate of employment increased from 30 per cent in 1992 to 40 per cent in 1999, primarily in the 50 to 54-year-old age group (Bardasi and Jenkins, 2002). Many male workers aged over 50 find themselves able to obtain only part-time and episodic work – and often poor quality and low-paid work. Younger male workers also find themselves at the lower end of the job market and they often find it the most difficult to obtain regular employment. As Linda McDowell (2001, p.455) notes, 'These young men are probably the first generation of male workers – at least in the post Second World War period – who will experience downward mobility compared to their fathers'. Here we can see age, gender and class intersecting in diverse and unequal ways in the labour market.

ACTIVITY 1.4

In what ways have rising risk and insecurity in work impacted upon the subjects in Extracts 1.2 and 1.3? The extracts provide two different personal narratives of work and employment change. Extract 1.2 is from an interview with a male factory worker in the West Midlands in the early 1980s. Extract 1.3 is from a biographical account about Tony, a former London Transport worker.

Extract 1.2 A 'world' that is lost

There's a sense of continuity if you like, a sense of dedication. You find this on most of the steel works except for the newer ones, you've got fathers and grandfathers and sons, it gives a sense of pride. I can't imagine such a sense of pride being born out of the Post Office or Woolworth's. At the last works we used to regularly have the pensioners back for a night or a dance and this is the tragedy of what's happening now, people who work here tend to associate it with something that's permanent, it will be there for their sons and their sons' sons, and so it's worth putting something into it, making it that bit better or at least keeping it as good as it is. But when there is talk of closures you find the sons take apprenticeships with other works or GKN and you lose that sense of craftsmanship and continuity and it is a fight to keep it going, it is a fight. There is still a large reliance placed on individual capability.

(Hedges and Beynon, 1982, p.68)

Extract 1.3 Tony's story

'It's almost like leaving home, isn't it?'

This morning Tony is packing up work. 'The guv'nor' allowed him out at 12 o'clock, and Tony is walking down to the pub in order to check out the details of the ceremony. It is a bright day, happily; it would be too sad to leave under a sky pouring with rain. With the collection given by the colleagues, Tony and his wife Margaret have bought a clock. They have wanted it for a long time. It will be a long time before Tony forgets this day. Every time he looks at the clock, he recalls this day vividly. He recalls the tear in his eye when he was given a kiss on the cheek by a young and pretty female colleague who had arrived in the job a few weeks before, and who had been very supportive during this time. Maybe, thinks Tony, this was because she had remembered her own father taking early retirement and how at the time she had wondered whether or not he would cope. In the end, however, he got on all right.

First comes the tear: 'It's almost like leaving home, isn't it', and then Tony laughs. Life is made of contradictions. 'That was a memorable day, a sad one but in a way it was enjoyable.' Thanks to the weather, positive feelings take precedence over negative ones.

It was a fine day, actually, it was a lovely day, it was a nice, bright day. I'd hate to have left in the winter when it was pouring down with rain. It would have been a drab day, a miserable day. But no, it was a good day.

How flimsy is Tony's final assessment of the event! Shall I, from a scientific point of view, give you the final toll of Tony's life? Certainly not, because it is not finished, and also because the joy and pain of a single individual are only subjective indicators. What I will tell you, though, is how these balance out in Tony's subjective experience, in his reflexive and his unreflexive consciousness. It is not by chance, in my opinion, that Tony uses the metaphor of 'leaving home' a few minutes into the interview, having referred to the situation of people living in the streets, unable to get a job because they do not have a home, and who are unable to get a home because they do not have a job. This is not to say that Tony is experiencing his journey out of work as an experience of being slung out of home. Certainly not, because Tony points out that the people on the streets have the privilege of being liberated from the burden of responsibility:

Is life worth living? Is it worth the trouble, is it worth the problem? I am sure there's a lot people out on the streets because, if you have nothing, you haven't got to worry, that's the end.

Tony is not on the streets and he does have to worry. He has been enormously worried at work, worried to the point of being sick, and he is still worrying a great deal after his retirement, to the point of being sick. Leaving work more or less as freely as one leaves home, he could not leave his burden at work; he packed up the burden and took it home, it is hidden in the clock: 'It is still in my system' ...

Let us go back to Tony's wedding day, 28 years ago. Everybody is there, family and mates from East London. Margaret's family too, farmers, although they are not overjoyed by her marrying a 'townie'. Eventually, they will accept Tony as a reliable person, which he certainly is. Before he got married, he was making a living in the City, doing odd jobs that might eventually have led into white-collar work. After the wedding, however, he will quickly leave these jobs and will do as his father did, as his brother does: he will work locally for London Transport. It is time to get a stable position in order to become a reliable male breadwinner for Margaret, who quits work when the children are born and will not return to work. And he has to pay for the house, bought with a mortgage. Tony starts as a cleaner and does not hesitate to work overtime. He goes from day work to night work, amounting to up to 26 days or nights every four weeks, leaving not more than two days for leisure. Look at the clock, every minute is money. However, his recollection is rosy. Tony's enthusiasm for work is endless; it is still evident today. London Transport means 'a job for life' – stability, and solidarity between colleagues, including colleagues in positions of command. A post-war spirit, a spirit of openness and camaraderie, very British in a sense, because of the war experience, but distinctive of the public services too, in France as well as in other countries.

...

Tony should be happy: he earns £20,000 a year. Money, however, does not buy happiness. 'Worry, don't be happy', the song *should* say. From the beginning of the 1990s up until now, Tony's life has been a burden. First, he loses his work security. London Transport workers are obliged to sign a new three-year contract. The old contract 'was not worth the piece of paper it was written on. I still don't understand how they were allowed to do that'. Nor do I. In my eyes such a murder of the word given, of the promise made, is not only a fact of London Transport; it is akin to a society lying to its members like a breakdown of the social contract ...

The fear of being blamed, fired, or privatized settled into London Transport. People felt 'their backs to the wall'. At first, the unions said 'don't sign' the contact, then said 'sign it'. Tony cannot recall the day he signed this new contract: 'Everybody was do disgusted, they just didn't want to remember'. Tony has never been politically active, even if his bitterness feeds a more critical view on society as a whole: 'I never used to think that the world was so bad'. The new contract forces him back to shift work, including night work, which is associated with sleeping problems for Tony, who is now aged 50 and has worked on day shifts for 14 years. Intensive training sessions are delivered in order to implement the extra workload that includes a large number of new tasks. Tony is snowed under: 'It was a struggle ... More often than not you couldn't remember back that far (how to do a task for which you might have been trained 18 months before)'.

How can the problem be solved? Tony's world is falling apart: 'A whole spectrum of life just seemed to collapse'. London Transport does not reward him any more: 'I am doing my best and I give my best at my job ... I was always reliable, conscientious and I felt they were not reciprocating'. A wall has been built between the executives and the staff: 'The consultants encouraged the company not to get emotionally involved with the staff'. Tony is conscious that it is a collective problem: 'It was a very sad time, not just for myself but for the majority'.

(Murard, 2002, pp.99–101)

COMMENT

There are a number of different ways in which 'the personal' and work are inseparable. What comes across strongly, in both the extracts, is that a sense of work often underpins our identity and life story. Reflecting the experience of factory workers, in Extract 1.2 there is a lifelong commitment to, and relationship with, a particular form of work, employer or factory. This is valued since it brings a sense of continuity, not just for individual workers but also for their families. There is also a strong sense of a 'working community': life is shaped around the factory and the 'working day', and this both structures and enables wider social events. This, in turn, encourages a sense of personal worth and value that leads to greater input to the job. For Tony, by contrast, the implementation of a new contract by London Transport management is portrayed as a betrayal of everything that he has worked for. In taking early retirement 'his world' threatens to 'fall apart'. But, he can never completely leave it behind – it is, as Tony expresses it, 'hidden in his system'. This point is worth noting: transitions in and out of work – that can represent some of the key turning points in our lives – are rarely as smooth and problem-free as employers and politicians would have us believe. Young workers in regular, paid work often find themselves in a world of intense day-to-day control. For Tony and the growing number of workers who take early retirement – whether through choice or coercion – there are very different kinds of work–life transitions. These are not transitions between different worlds, but rather a process of negotiating new paths and struggling with the reconfiguration of daily life while maintaining some sense of personal worth (see Chapters 3 and 4). Our past work continues to shape this to varying degrees given that we often remain influenced and identified with it. But, for many younger workers the experiences portrayed here are ones that are likely to remain alien to them as they move from job to job and find themselves vulnerable to periods of unemployment.

These two personal narratives relate to a world characterized by a job for life, in one or possibly two firms with opportunities to move up a career ladder. That clearly defined world of work, it is often suggested, used to be characterized by some sense of commitment between workers and employers, and work and personal lives were deeply intertwined. Social and leisure time were often work-related – work provided friends, jobs for family members and, often, opportunities for marriage. Work and personal life reinforced and reconstituted each other in many different ways. However this continues, 'the personal' and work remain deeply intertwined, but in different and arguably more uncertain and diverse ways. But, we should also recognize that personal histories of working life can vary widely for different people. For example, few women or migrant workers have been in the same job for their entire working life, or had the opportunity to move up career ladders. The ways in which work and 'the personal' might influence and shape each other continues to differ in relation to the social divisions of class, gender, ethnicity, and the other social positions we occupy.

4.2 Goodbye to the 'old certainties'?

It is widely assumed that the 'old certainties' that governed life in post-war Britain have been, if not completely eroded as a consequence of recent social and economic change, at least undermined. The consequences of changing patterns of work and employment are viewed as having far-reaching consequences for the social structure of contemporary society. The idea of 'work' as a way of life has come to be seriously disrupted in concepts such as

end of career

'**end of career**' (see for example Flores and Gray, 1999), with 'lifelong identities' giving way to more floating and shifting identities, in which work plays less of a role. As Diane Perrons (2003, p.67) has suggested in relation to the careers of new media workers, 'the lives of wired people are more like collections of short stories than the narrative of a bourgeois novel'. However, the life story implied by the idea of the 'end of career' represents only one kind of personal work history – and that, as we suggested, was 'real' only for a particular group of male workers in the golden age of the 1950s and 1960s. This golden age stands in contrast to the mass unemployment and insecure employment of the 1920s and 1930s – and also against the labour market as it has been restructured since the 1970s. In many respects the golden age represents an aberration when compared with what went before and what has occurred since.

Other continuities should be highlighted at this point. There is little that is new in employers pursuing greater flexibility. Anna Pollert has forcefully argued that the pursuit of 'flexibility' in the 1980s and 1990s was driven by the Conservative Government in an effort to legitimize their social and economic attacks on workers and their living standards through greater labour market deregulation (see Pollert, 1988; Taylor, 2002a). The story of employment change and changes in the organization of 'work' since the 1950s and 1960s is thus more complex and multi-layered than a simple story of a linear shift from a golden age to a silver age. A relatively new language of 'rationalization', 'downsizing', 'modernization', 'outsourcing' and 'restructuring' has emerged, but the processes to which they relate are not new. As we stressed earlier, the post-1945 era was never a golden age for many groups of workers. The idea that we are now in an era of rising insecurity and uncertain employment is certainly more relevant to some than it is for others. Further, the idea that we can construct work around our lives raises questions of opportunity and, importantly, of power. Relatively few workers are able to organize their work

work–life balance

or lives in the way that the notion of a **work–life balance** implies (we return to this in Chapter 5). For growing numbers of workers, however, the end of career will mean more *living to work* and less *working to live*. Our sense of self has been affected in different and highly unequal and uneven ways by these far-reaching changes in the structure of work and employment. But, what might this mean for the working experience of particular groups of workers?

ACTIVITY 1.6

Extract 1.4 is taken from two studies of ancillary and portering work in the NHS. The journalist, Polly Toynbee, conducted both studies. She gained employment in the two hospitals concerned at two different periods. What do these two studies in Extract 1.4 tell you about some of the continuities and changes in NHS work?

Extract 1.4 Continuity and change in nursing work

The nurses were a mixed group. They came and went week by week, and in this ward, only half of them actually belonged to the hospital. The rest were freelance agency nurses, who, like temporary secretaries, could make more money by being hired out to hospitals by the week, than by being attached to any one place. In between hospital work, they would try and get more lucrative jobs as private nurses. This only happens in the poor hospitals where no one wants to go. In the big teaching hospitals all the nurses actually belong. You could tell the agency nurses apart as they all wore different uniforms, the uniforms of the hospitals they had originally trained at. They held themselves apart from the others, thinking themselves a superior breed. Almost all the resident nurses were Irish or black. Apart from Sister, only one nurse in the ward was white and English.

The permanent nurses were the most miserable and down-trodden. And the more down-trodden they were, the worse they treated the patients. There was always a shortage of them in the ward, and they worked extremely hard. There wasn't time for them to think much about the patients as people, even if they had the energy and encouragement to do so. They shouted and quarrelled and bustled around, and sat down whenever the Sister's eye wasn't on them. The uniforms of the resident nurses were old and frayed although clean, and it was hard to see why they went on with the job at all. They worked very hard for no visible reward. The status outside the hospital of being a qualified nurse may have kept them going a bit, but they weren't out of the hospital very much. The romantic vision of 'Dr Kildare' or 'Emergency Ward 10' had nothing to do with life at St Mathilda's.

(Toynbee, 1971, pp.55–6)

... some things had not changed, or had changed for the worse. Then as now the pay was bad and in those full employment times there was the same hectic turnover of staff, the same wasteful stream of low-paid labour, stop-gap workers on the look-out for something better, treated badly. Then many ancillaries were Maltese, Italian or Spanish; now many were West Indian, Asian or East European. I can't claim that being directly employed by that hospital in those days engendered great emotional loyalty to the NHS because, then as now, the low-paid were treated as cheap and expendable labour. There was no miraculous St Stephen's Hospital ethos among the exploited ancillary workers. But at least back then all employees were interviewed and employed by the hospital, by the supervisor who would be responsible for them and their work. I knew who had employed me, what I was supposed to do and whom I was answerable to. Now, arriving as an agency worker, I belonged to no one, no one was responsible for me nor me to them. The supervisors I would work to in the new hospital had not hired me and did not pay me. I was casual, temporary and entirely detached from the greater life of the institution. I did not even work for the contractor.

What really startled me was this: my wages as a ward orderly ... [then] were £12.50 a week. Now, as a porter in the new hospital, they were £4.35 an hour or £174 a week. How does that compare? The Institute for Fiscal Studies made this calculation: if my pay had kept pace with general earnings, that £12.50 a week should now be £210. So I had actually fallen behind in the last thirty years, a story repeated all too frequently across the public sector ... For these people there has been no progress, only a falling-behind. True, there was now a fine new hospital and a far better working environment but the pay and conditions were worse. My work was not only relatively lower paid than thirty years ago, it was entirely insecure, day-to-day agency employment. Back then at least I had the security of joining the staff of the NHS from day one: it was a safe job for life if I wanted it, but now everything is shifting sands for the low-paid. It is called 'flexibility', and in the name of 'flexibility' the hospital had shed or 'outsourced' all its ancillary workers. I was about to learn the full meaning of contracting out.

(Toynbee, 2003, pp.56–7)

COMMENT

These participant observation studies by Polly Toynbee were conducted between 1970 and 1971, and then again between 2002 and 2003. The picture she presents of work in St Mathilda's in the early 1970s reminds us that even at this high point in the post-1945 welfare state, the nature and conditions of employment in the public sector were difficult and divisive. We can see that class, gender and 'race' intertwine in constructing the experience of work, and particularly in ensuring a sense of security. Insecurity of employment – with the possible exception of the 1950s and early 1960s – has always been the lived experience of the working class. This is not to deny that there have been real changes, but as Toynbee notes these have tended to be for the worse. Qualitative studies such as these help us to reflect on the examples of work in a more critically informed way. They also show that working life is often a story of daily struggle and 'making do' in circumstances over which workers have little immediate control. Work, particularly in nursing and in other areas of the welfare sector, also involves what has been termed **emotion work** or **emotional labour**. These are explored more fully in Chapter 2, but in both of Toynbee's studies in Extract 1.4 what also comes across is the dynamic relation between work and personal life, and how the different socio-historical contexts shape that relation.

emotion work
emotional labour

Many social scientists have argued that the changes in work and employment explored above have led to fundamental changes in the class structure of modern capitalist societies. The deindustrialization of the British economy and the long-term decline in blue-collar manual work have both been interpreted as signalling either the 'end of work' or the erosion of class – or at least the demise of the working class (Beck, 2000; Giddens, 1998; Gorz, 1999). Similarly, Offe (1985) has argued that 'work is no longer the key sociological category'. There are two elements to this: that sociology has moved beyond a concern with work-centred divisions and inequalities, focusing instead on issues such as the role of consumption and lifestyle in the shaping of identity, and that the moral compulsion to work has been eroded by the provision of state welfare. Beck (1999) has surpassed this, claiming that we are facing the imminent collapse of 'wage slavery', and the emergence of a 'new' world where work is more fulfilling.

There have been wide-ranging critiques of these arguments, particularly from theorists working in the Marxist and feminist traditions (Beder, 2000; Ferguson et al., 2002; McDowell, 2001; Mooney, 2000; Skeggs, 1997). Marxists draw attention to the fact that globally, the working class is larger than ever before. Here, the argument made against Beck and Gorz among others is that while the class structure may have been reshaped, exploitative class relations remain its foundation. They also point to the continuing class-based and material inequalities that both structure and reflect work and employment in the UK and beyond (Callinicos, 2003). McDowell (2001, p.454) further claims that 'a number of the recent analyses of the future of work are based on the oddly paradoxical claim that waged work at the end of the millennium is becoming less and not more important in the construction of personal identity' at a time when women's employment has been increasing steadily. For McDowell the weakness of such claims is that they generalize from the experience of male employment at particular times, in particular places, and from particular kinds of work. As we have seen, the experience of regular full-time industrial work has been far from the norm. In addition, the re-emphasis by successive governments in the 1990s and early 2000s on work as a source of self-worth and of social inclusion means that work has been re-centred in the lives of many people against the claims by Offe (1995) – and not only for those in paid employment. People who are counterposed to work through being constructed as the unemployed or 'workless' or 'retired', may often define themselves in rather negative terms. As we saw in Extracts 1.2 and 1.3, work can remain central to a sense of self, while policy-makers have often sought to refocus work as central to policy interventions in personal lives.

The 'revolutions' in work and working lives have many direct and indirect consequences for how people attempt to construct their lives. The norm of a male breadwinner continues to have a powerful resonance in society today, and so for many men, and in particular for those who are middle-aged and perhaps can remember 'better times', the restructuring of work has profound consequences for their sense of self and their ability to construct a personal identity that is not work-related. Such issues were played out in popular British films of the 1990s. *Brassed Off* (1996) and *The Full Monty* (1997), for example, explore questions of masculinity, identity and gender politics in the context of long-term male unemployment in areas of the north of England that have been subject to widespread deindustrialization.

How is the relationship between work and personal life constructed in social policy at the time of writing in 2004? The New Labour Government has placed considerable emphasis on self-help and responsibility. This includes individual responsibility for seizing opportunities and for constructing a working life. Against the 'end of career' argument it is suggested that changes in work and employment have created new routes through which workers can manage their own career and employability, re-skilling, training and engaging in life-long learning. But, 'the capacity of people to organize their own working lives and work biographies and plan their lifetime finances continues to vary now, as in the past' and these capacities remain highly structured by the inequalities of class, 'race', gender, age and stage in life (Perrons, 2003, p.72).

The future of work for some commentators promises hope and, as Beck puts it, an end to wage slavery. Work can potentially offer more than daily drudgery, though for many theorists this would necessitate far-reaching social and economic transformations. For Richard Reeves, among others, paid work offers more opportunity for personal fulfilment than 'other' areas of life. He argues that:

> while the workplace is growing in attractiveness, for many people home or 'life' is looking a bit gloomy. For dual-earner couples with children, life outside work is one of fixed timetables (child care), conflict (whose turn is it to pick up the kids?), low-skill work (cooking, cleaning, nappy disposal) and thankless masters and mistresses (the kids). As work enters the post-industrial era, home life has become industrial.
>
> (Reeves, 2001, p.128)

There is an obvious neglect of the pay and working conditions of those who increasingly service the dual-income households referred to by Reeves. But, this is not the only weakness of his argument. He also draws a distinction between 'work' and 'life' – constructing them as opposites instead of seeing them as interrelated, that the 'gloominess' of home may reflect the pressures of paid work, and also the thankless drudgery and long hours. What are we to make of Reeves's arguments here? It is clear that he mobilizes and constructs 'the personal' in a particular way: he appears nostalgic for a time when it might be thought that family and domestic life were 'problem-free' – at least for some men. For the vast majority of women, however, was it ever different from the picture he presents above?

We can see that there is a complex story of both continuity and change in relation to work and employment in recent UK history. A number of theorists have drawn our attention to the intersections of class, gender and 'race' in relation to how work is shaped, organized and experienced (see Bondi and Christie, 2000; McDowell, 2001; Skeggs, 1997; Vail et al., 1999). Class inequalities and the exploitative nature of work relations continue to be key forces shaping work in contemporary society. For Taylor (2000a, p.8), 'it is hard not to reach the conclusion that class and occupational differences remain of fundamental importance to any understanding of our world of work'. In section 5 we consider some aspects of this more fully.

5 Class divisions and alienation at work

labour process

The class struggle between capital and labour – between employer and worker – is for Marxism the central dynamic of capitalist societies. It is this pivotal relation that structures and shapes working lives – and our experiences of it. One of the key concepts used to analyse work regimes and to interrogate the relationship between capital and labour in the workplace is **labour process**. This concept was first developed by Marx (1867/1976) in *Capital* (Volume 1), as part of his wider theory of the organization of work relations under capitalism. For Marx there are two key components in the labour process: the means of production (the raw materials, tools, technology and so on that are used in the production process) and the purposeful activity of human beings – labour. As we noted earlier, some form of labour process is a condition of all human societies, but only in capitalism is it systematically structured and organized for the purpose of making profit, through the exploitation of those workers actually producing the products or services. For Marx this exemplifies the distinctiveness of paid labour under capitalism: a process in which the worker or direct producer has no control over the product of his or her labour. Instead, this belongs to and is disposed of by the employer and for which, in turn, workers are paid a wage, but a wage that does not equate with the value of what they have produced. In pre-capitalist societies people used their creative abilities to produce goods that they themselves would either directly consume, exchange or sell. Under capitalism many workers will often be unable to purchase the item they have just produced, whether it be a new computer, a car, designer jeans or items of sportswear. Referring to the horrendous working conditions and low-wage economy that are a central feature of the 'export process zones' of the Philippines in the late 1990s, Naomi Klein comments that 'zone wages are so low that workers spend most of their pay on shared dorm rooms and transportation; the rest goes to noodles and fried rice from vendors lined up outside the gate. Zone workers certainly cannot dream of affording the consumer goods they produce' (Klein, 2000, p.210).

For Marx such conditions and work relations are alienating. The product of a worker's labour confronts them as an 'alien object' – produced by them, but beyond their control. Writing in 1844 he argued that:

> labour is external to the worker, that is it does not belong to his essential being; that he therefore does not confirm himself in his work, but denies himself, feels miserable and not happy, does not develop free mental and physical energy, but mortifies his flesh and ruins his mind. Hence the worker feels himself only when he is not working; when he is working he does not feel himself. He is at home when he is not working, and not at home when he is working. His labour is therefore not voluntary but forced, it is forced labour. It is therefore not the satisfaction of a need but a mere means to satisfy needs outside itself. Its alien character is clearly demonstrated by the fact that as soon as no physical or other compulsion exists it is shunned like the plague.
>
> (Marx, 1844/1975, p.326)

alienation

While the idea of **alienation** is increasingly used and referenced freely in the media and even in everyday conversation, for Marx it had a particular meaning and significance. He argued that alienation is not about feeling 'out of sorts'. It is an objective, not psychological state, in which all workers find themselves, whether they are conscious of it or not. In selling their ability to work to an employer, workers transfer control over their work and when it should take place. Thus, the control of work and the worker becomes the prerogative of the employer or their delegates, managers and supervisors. For Marx (1867/1976, p.713) the result of this is that under capitalism work is necessarily a dehumanizing and degrading activity: 'all the means for developing production are transformed into means of domination over and exploitation of the producer; that they mutilate the worker into a fragment of a human being, degrade him to become a mere appurtenance, make his work such a torment that its essential meaning is destroyed'.

Workers are not only alienated from what they produce but also from their fellow workers and those around them – and from themselves. Instead of allowing them to realize their creativity, work instead becomes *forced labour*, in the process the worker becomes estranged from him or herself.

living labour
dead labour

The capitalist labour process involves, then, the domination of **living labour** (workers) by **dead labour** (capital, tools, technology and so on) – the products of the labour of the previous generation of workers. This involves management strategies of different kinds operating to 'deaden' labour. Harry Braverman, in one of the most important studies of management strategies at work, explored the ways in which the production-line management techniques employed by the Ford Car Company have, during the second half of the twentieth century, increasingly spread to the office and to white-collar service work. Ford's system of worker control relied upon the principles of '**scientific management**' as devised by Frederick Taylor in 1911. Taylor's system was driven by the pursuit of efficiency: it was the role of management to allocate tasks to employees, and in the process to control each and every aspect of the job itself. According to Taylor, this process would be made easier if each job was broken-down into different parts. This would allow each part of the job to be controlled more effectively, thus reducing the costs of production (Thompson, 1989, pp.72–3). Braverman emphasizes that the growing separation of the conception and execution of a task, that is, an increasing divorce of mental and manual labour, is leading to the widespread **deskilling** of work. As Braverman notes in relation to the scientific management or **Taylorist** system:

scientific management

deskilling
taylorist

> Thus, if the first principle is the gathering and development of knowledge of the labour process, and the second is the concentration of this knowledge as the exclusive province of management – together with its essential converse, the absence of such knowledge among workers – then the third [step] is the use of this monopoly over knowledge to control each step of the labour process and its mode of execution.
>
> (Braverman, 1974, p.119)

This would seem to fit well with the experience that many workers have of their day-to-day work: though they may struggle individually and collectively against this, many workers find their autonomy and 'freedom' at work, their sense of value and worth, increasingly undermined, restricted and controlled. This does not only involve the control of physical labour, but also increasingly the control of emotional labour. Changing work practices and the meanings given to work are thus central to the constitution of our personal lives.

6 Conclusion

There has always been a relationship between work, personal lives and social policy. It is dynamic and ever changing, affecting people in different ways. Policy assumptions that our lives are organized around separate spheres of activity neglect the interconnections between work as paid employment and the pivotal role that unpaid domestic, community and caring work play in its reproduction and organization. In the chapters that follow we will explore some of the different ways in which work provides a crucial lens through which we can think about and analyse the relationship between personal lives and social policy.

In Chapter 2 we consider the increasing use of emotional labour/emotion work and the experience of different groups of 'welfare workers'. We stress the role that class, gender, 'race' and other forms of social differentiation play in the experiences of people in the workplace and the structuring of employment. Different spheres of work carry, and are characterized by, their own social relations. Our personal lives are shaped by our working experiences of multiple and different kinds – by the intensity of work (in both the domestic and formal economies), by its uncertainty (often as a result of low wages), and by forms of work that are subject to strict management control and regulation. The devaluing of particular forms of work such as caring – in both formal and informal settings – can also affect our feelings of personal worth. Retirement can potentially be a period of personal fulfilment as we seek out the opportunities of what is now referred to as the 'third age'. But, being 'retired' can also undermine one's sense of self (see Chapter 3) as can being a 'client' of the New Deal for Young People programme (see Chapter 4).

'The personal' helps to shape our understanding and experience of work. Increasingly different companies and organizations – from call centres to welfare providers – seek to utilize and exploit our 'personalities', and other 'personal qualities' such as our friendliness, humour and sensitivity. In this process increasing efforts are made to structure and shape these qualities in particular ways. Again while this use of what is increasingly referred to as emotional labour may take on new and more pervasive forms, we should not forget that employers have long sought to shape our personal lives in other ways. The moral regulation of the family and household life (through, for example, regular house inspections and the policing of alcohol consumption) was part and parcel of the 'model villages' of the eighteenth and nineteenth centuries as developed by Robert Owen at New Lanark, the Levers at Port Sunlight and the Cadbury's in Birmingham among others. In the inter-war period, the Ford Car Company in the USA employed social workers to manage the personal lives of its workforce, especially those considered as 'heavy drinkers'. As Huw Beynon noted in his classic study *Working for Ford*:

> [Ford's] ... Sociological Department did help many immigrant workers to learn English and to protect themselves from the worst manifestations of the racketeering frontier city. But, the paternalism which the whole [welfare] programme expressed often degenerated into petty and heavy-handed interference in the private lives of vulnerable people. In Nevin's words: 'Doubtless the spectacle of an earnest inquirer writing down an array of facts on his blue form aroused conflicting emotions in many breasts. The investigators...were asked to throw 'a deep personal interest' into every visit. Sometimes it was tinged with suspicion; the mere word of an employee that he was married was not taken as sufficient, and agents were instructed to use some ingenuity in getting this information positively. Branch managers were instructed, for example, to be vigilant and to make sure 'beyond a shadow of a doubt that the money is paid to those deserving, and to no others' ... Those families who did not meet the specification of the Sociological Department were put on probation.
>
> (Beynon, 1975, pp.22–3)

From Ford through to the Labour Government of the late 1990s and early 2000s, 'the personal' and work are both brought together yet constructed as separate spheres. Here, we have argued that we take our 'personal' to work with us – wherever that work is conducted and in whatever form. But, we have also seen that work helps to shape and construct 'the personal' in particular ways. Social policy has tended to construct work as paid work and in the process it has normalized paid labour. In turn other forms of work, including domestic labour, voluntary and caring labour, are subordinated and devalued. This has, as we shall see, far-reaching consequences for the ways in which our lives are shaped and structured for our rights and responsibilities as citizens.

Further resources

There are numerous books and other sources on the general theme of the sociology or work. Paul Thompson's *The Nature of Work* (1989) provides an excellent all-round account of many of the key areas of work discussed here, and it has extensive discussion of what has come to be termed the 'labour process debate'. This can be supplemented by the much more recent Noon and Blyton volume entitled *The Realities of Work* (2002).

For statistical data on trends in work and employment, together with other information on the economy in general, along with social and welfare policies, and national/regional economic profiles the government's National Statistics office has a very accessible website at http://www.statistics.gov.uk.

The Economic and Social Research Council (ESRC) has funded a far-reaching investigation of changes in different aspects of work in Britain in recent times. We have used some of this research in this chapter (Taylor, 2002a; 2002b). You may want to refer to more reports from the ESRCs Future of Work

Programme at http://www.esrc.ac.uk. (These websites were last accessed on 13 January 2004.)

Finally, Alex Callinicos's *Social Theory: A Historical Introduction* (1999) provides a well-grounded exploration of the key ideas of Marx and a wide-range of other social theories.

References

Aldridge, T., Tooke, J., Lee, R., Leyshon, A., Thrift, N. and Williams, C. (2001) 'Recasting work: the example of local exchange trading schemes', *Work, Employment and Society*, vol.15, no.3, pp.565–79.

Bardasi, E. and Jenkins, S.P. (2002) *Income in Later Life: Work History Matters*, Bristol, Policy Press.

Beatty, C., Fothergill, S., Gore, T. and Green, A. (2002) *The Real Level of Unemployment 2002*, Sheffield, Sheffield Hallam University Centre for Regional Economic and Social Research.

Beck, U. (1999) 'Goodbye to all that wage slavery', *New Statesman*, March 5, pp.25–7.

Beck, U. (2000) *The Brave New World of Work*, Cambridge, Polity Press.

Beder, S. (2000) *Selling the Work Ethic: From Puritan Pulpit to Corporate PR*, London, Zed Books.

Bell, D. (1973) *The Coming of the Post-Industrial Society*, New York, Basic Books.

Beveridge, W. (1942) *Social Insurance and Allied Services* (The Beveridge Report), Cmnd 6404, London, HMSO.

Beynon, H. (1975) *Working for Ford*, Wakefield, EP Publishing.

Beynon, H., Grimshaw, D., Rubery, J. and Ward, K. (2002) *Managing Employment Change: The New Realities of Work*, Oxford, Oxford University Press.

Bondi, L. and Christie, H. (2000) 'The best of times for some and the worst of times for others? Gender and class divisions in urban Britain today', *Geoforum*, vol.31, no.3, pp.329–43.

Braverman, H. (1974) *Labour and Monopoly Capital: The Degradation of Work in the Twentieth Century*, New York, Monthly Review Press.

Brown, P. and Lauder, H. (2001) *Capitalism and Social Progress: The Future of Society in a Global Economy*, London, Palgrave.

Callinicos, A. (1999) *Social Theory: A Historical Introduction*, Cambridge, Polity Press.

Callinicos, A. (2003) *An Anti-Capitalist Manifesto*, Cambridge, Polity Press.

Cochrane, A. (1998) 'What sort of safety-net? Social security, income maintenance and the benefits system' in Hughes, G. and Lewis, G. (eds) *Unsettling Welfare: The Reconstruction of Social Policy*, London, Routledge,

Davidoff, L. (1995) *Worlds Between: Historical Perspectives on Gender and Class*, Cambridge, Polity Press.

Doogan, K. (2001) 'Insecurity and long-term employment', *Work, Employment and Society*, vol.15, no.3, pp.419–41.

Esping-Andersen, G. (1990) *The Three Worlds of Welfare Capitalism*, Cambridge, Polity Press.

Fairclough, N. (2000) *New Labour, New Language?*, London, Routledge.

Ferguson, I., Lavalette, M. and Mooney, G. (2002) *Rethinking Welfare*, London, Sage.

J, Fink (2004) 'Questions of care' in Fink, J. (ed.) *Care: Personal Lives and Social Policy,* Bristol, The Policy Press in association with The Open University.

Flores, F. and Gray, J. (1999) *Entrepreneurship and the Wired Life: Work in the Wake of Careers*, London, Demos.

Giddens, A. (1998) *The Third Way: The Renewal of Social Democracy*, Cambridge, Polity Press.

Glucksmann, M. (1995) 'Why "work"? Gender and the "total social organization of labour"', *Gender, Work and Organization*, vol.2, no.2, pp.63–75.

Glucksmann, M. (2000) *Cottons and Casuals: The Gendered Organization of Labour in Time and Space*, Durham, Sociology Press.

Gorz, A. (1999) *Reclaiming Work*, Cambridge, Polity Press.

Hedges, N. and Beynon, H. (1982) *Born to Work*, London, Pluto Press.

Howlett, P. (1996) 'The 'Golden Age', 1955–1973' in Johnson, P. (ed.) *Twentieth Century Britain: Economic, Social and Cultural Change*, London, Longman.

Klein, N. (2000) *No Logo*, London, Flamingo.

Letslink UK (2003) *UK LETS and Complementary Currencies Development Agency,* http://www.letslinkuk.org (accessed 25 March 2003).

Levitas, R. (1998) *The Inclusive Society?*, London, Macmillan.

Lewis, G. and Fink, J. (2004) '"All that heaven allows": the worker citizen in the post-war welfare state' in Lewis, G. (ed.) *Citizenship: Personal Lives and Social Policy,* Bristol, The Policy Press in association with The Open University.

Lindsay, C. (2003) 'A century of labour market change: 1900–2000', *Labour Market Trends*, vol.111, no.3, pp.113–44.

McDowell, L. (2001) 'Father and Ford revisited: gender, class and employment change in the new millennium', *Transactions of the Institute of British Geographers*, vol.26, issue 4, pp.448–64.

Marx, K. (1844/1975) 'Economic and philosophical manuscripts' in Marx, K. *Early Writings,* Harmondsworth, Penguin.

Marx, K. (1867/1976) *Capital,* Volume 1, Harmondsworth, Penguin.

Mooney, G. (1998) '"Remoralizing" the poor? gender, class and philanthropy in Victorian Britain' in Lewis, G. (ed.) *Forming Nation, Framing Welfare*, London, Routledge in association with The Open University.

Mooney, G. (2000) 'Class and social policy' in Lewis, G., Gewirtz, S. and Clarke, J. (eds) *Rethinking Social Policy*, London, Sage.

Moore Milroy, B. and Wismer, S. (1994) 'Communities, work and public/private sphere models', *Gender, Place and Culture*, vol.1, no.1, pp.71–90.

Murard, N. (2002) 'The shortest way out of work' in Chamberlayne, P., Rustin, M. and Wengraf, T. (eds) *Biography and Social Exclusion in Europe*, Bristol, Policy Press.

Noon, M. and Blyton, P. (2002) *The Realities of Work* (2nd edn), London, Palgrave.

Oakley, A. (1974) *Housewife*, Harmondsworth, Penguin.

Offe, C. (1985) *Disorganized Capitalism*, Cambridge, Polity Press.

Office of National Statistics (2003) *National Statistics Online*, http://www.statistics.gov.uk (accessed 26 March 2003).

Pahl, R. (1984) *Divisions of Labour*, Oxford, Blackwell.

Perrons, D. (2003) 'The new economy and the work–life balance: conceptual explorations and a case study of new media', *Gender, Work and Organization*, vol.10, no.1, pp.65–93.

Philpott, J. (2002) *Work Audit 1952–1992*, London, The Chartered Institute of Personal Development.

Pollert, A. (1988) 'Dismantling flexibility', *Capital and Class*, no.34, pp.42–75.

Reeves, R. (2001) *Happy Mondays: Putting the Pleasure Back into Work*, London, Momentum.

Skeggs, B. (1997) *Formations of Class and Gender*, London, Sage.

Taylor, R. (2002a) *Britain's World of Work – Myths and Realities*, Swindon, ESRC.

Taylor, R. (2002b) *Diversity in Britain's Labour Market*, Swindon, ESRC.

Thane, P. (1994) 'Women since 1945' in Johnson, P. (ed.) *Twentieth Century Britain: Economic, Social and Cultural Change*, London, Longman.

Thompson, P. (1989) *The Nature of Work* (2nd edn), London, Macmillan.

Toynbee, P. (1971) *A Working Life*, London, Hodder and Stoughton.

Toynbee, P. (2003) *Hard Work: Life in Low-Pay Britain*, London, Bloomsbury.

Vail, J., Wheelock, J. and Hill, M. (eds) (1999) *Insecure Times*, London, Routledge.

Webb, J. (1999) 'Work and the new public service class?', *Sociology*, vol.33, no.4, pp.747–66.

Williams, R. (1976) *Keywords: A Vocabulary of Culture and Society,* London, Fontana.

CHAPTER 2

Managing Personal Lives: Doing 'Welfare Work'

by Janet Newman and Gerry Mooney

Contents

1 Introduction

There are many things that contribute to our well-being as citizens of welfare states. Some are the product of direct encounters or relationships, such as receiving a service from a member of staff in a government office or being looked after when ill by a family member or friend. Others result from more impersonal relationships (for example, receiving a pension), or from struggles to be free from extreme poverty, to have access to clean water, or to be able to live without fear of racial or sexual harassment. And people may take some responsibility for their own well-being, for example by eating in a healthy way. Each has a different impact on the personal lives of both welfare users and providers.

Producing welfare involves welfare as work, in different forms, in different settings. It can be formalized – and commodified – as paid work (teachers, social workers or managers of voluntary organizations). But, much of it remains low level and invisible, taking place informally in households and communities and through volunteer labour. Welfare work entails providing services, but also includes the labour involved in co-ordinating the fragmented patchwork of social policy provision in order to meet the needs of individuals and groups.

However, the term 'welfare work' might seem an unusual focus for this chapter since 'work', as highlighted in Chapter 1, tends to be thought of as something apart from 'welfare'. Work is associated with paid employment – and independence – while welfare is more closely associated with our mutual dependence on each other and reliance on state services. Paid work is viewed as something that takes place in the impersonal realm of economic exchange, while welfare touches us more deeply in our 'private' lives.

This opposition between work and welfare is based on a number of implicit dualities. While there are many different forms of welfare, most are based on relations of care that are strongly gendered (**Fink, 2004a**). The close association between 'welfare' and 'care' contributes to the low status (and low pay) of much welfare work and its historical construction as predominantly 'women's work'. The provision of welfare within households and through voluntary work – both often dependent on women's labour – is viewed as somehow less tainted by the cash nexus and closer to the human spirit of care. Welfare is also viewed as something that we are most likely to receive when young (such as, education and child health services) or past retirement age (for example, pensions and social care for the elderly). The age dynamics of work and social policy are explored in Chapters 3 and 4. Welfare work is frequently associated with private or intimate relationships and forms of support, areas that are seen as necessitating a close personal involvement for workers with their clients. We return to consider some aspects of this later in the discussion; here we highlight a central thread running through the chapters that comprise this book: the idea that work and 'the personal' cannot be easily separated.

The dualities and oppositions between welfare and work are constituted in, and reproduced by, social policy discourse – getting people into paid work is viewed as a means of reducing their dependence on state benefits/welfare, for example. Following Chapter 1, we challenge the discursive separation between 'work' and 'welfare' by considering welfare as a product of work. We do so by examining the dynamic interrelationships between welfare and work, and how these interrelationships are constituted in and through social policy.

Aims This chapter aims to:

- Explore the labour processes that characterize welfare work, considering if they are qualitatively different from other forms of labour.
- Examine some of the ways in which the providers and recipients of welfare work experience this form of labour.
- Uncover how social policy constitutes the relationship between informal, voluntary and paid welfare work, and the ways in which this balance shapes the personal lives of specific groups of welfare workers and welfare users.
- Consider how welfare work is changing as a result of shifts in social policy and how such changes influence our personal lives as both the providers and recipients of welfare work.

Before we proceed any further, however, we need to highlight the type of evidence that is used in this chapter. We have used a number of quotations from paid workers and others who are engaged in welfare work. These accounts have been deliberately selected because they illustrate particular dimensions of welfare work: the affiliations and identifications of the individual concerned, the skills they use and the resources they draw on, and the way in which each defines the meaning of the work they undertake and the impact of change on that work. These are 'grounded' accounts. The extracts and quotations tend to derive from unstructured or semi-structured interviews rather than questionnaires and structured interviews. Such qualitative data allow us a more in-depth understanding of people's experiences and attitudes and the meanings attached to them. However, we should also remember that there are a multiplicity of meanings relating to welfare work and that an individual's understanding of them will be shaped not least by the particular intersections of class, 'race', age, gender, sexuality and (dis)ability in their personal lives, as well as their location in the life course. The accounts we draw on in this chapter can, therefore, provide only a snapshot of the meanings of welfare work for they have been captured within specific research conditions at a particular moment in time.

1.1 The relational context of welfare work

In this chapter we are concerned primarily with two forms of difference: between sectors and over time. These are interconnected in important ways. But, we want to start by thinking about differences between sectors by considering some everyday forms that welfare work might take. For example, helping a child cross the road on her/his way to school might be done by a lollipop lady/man, a parent, or by someone taking children to school as part of a reciprocal arrangement. Supporting someone on a low income might mean a family member lending money to a young person setting up home; or it could be done through the government's social fund, or through a charity. So, there are diverse forms of welfare work: informal work provided by relatives, neighbours or friends; paid work in statutory or voluntary organizations; and voluntary unpaid work. The boundaries between these forms of welfare work are not always clear, but the categories signal the importance of understanding the social dynamics of welfare work as well as the economic conditions under which it is carried out. For example, cooking a meal for a person who is unable to care for her/himself may be paid or unpaid work. The financial and social relationships surrounding the production and consumption of the meal are likely to be very different depending on whether this is done by a relative or neighbour, a social care organization such as 'meals on wheels', school pupils as part of their community activities, or a café providing a takeaway meal delivered to, and paid for by, the person consuming it.

Welfare, then, is something that is produced as well as consumed. It is a form of work, and it is performed in the context of a set of social relationships. This is what is meant by the 'relational context of welfare'. In discussing welfare in terms of 'production' and 'work' it might seem that we are suggesting it is just another commodity that gets produced, distributed and consumed by customers. But, welfare is different from other commodities in a number of ways:

- First, as we have seen, it does not necessarily involve paid labour, but it is often produced informally in homes and neighbourhoods and through voluntary work. This means that welfare work involves relationships of reciprocity – based on our ties, commitments and obligations to each other – as well as economic exchange.
- Second, the 'customers' of welfare may not choose to receive it, or have little choice about the way in which it is provided. Caring for someone with mental health problems, for example, may involve coercive forms of care such as 'sectioning' in the UK (placing someone in care, possibly against their will, under the Mental Health Acts 1983 and 2001). Patients may have little choice about where and when their health needs are met, and people receiving community care may have little say over the worker who visits them at home.
- Third, welfare work tends to be characterized by inequalities of power between those who produce it (whether paid or unpaid) and those who consume it.
- Fourth, welfare work often involves intimate relationships that bring an emotional element to the work itself.

1.2 Managing personal lives

managing personal lives

Welfare work also involves **managing personal lives**. We have chosen this phrase as the chapter title because it signifies the ways in which welfare work mediates aspects of social policy and personal lives. You might think that 'managing' is a strange term to use because of its usual associations with 'management' as a particular group in an organizational hierarchy. But, in everyday language the word 'managing' has many uses that are relevant to our analysis, as shown in the following phrases:

> 'I can't really manage on (x) pounds a week.'
>
> 'I have to manage getting my elderly mother up and dressed before going to work.'
>
> 'I managed not to seem upset when my child was diagnosed with (x).'
>
> 'I finally managed to get the increase in my benefits I had been struggling for.'

These examples suggest that welfare work involves managing other people, managing the coordination of services to meet one's own needs or those of other people, and managing the self and one's own emotions. These popular uses of the term 'managing' to mean coping, organizing, smoothing and coordinating, are all part of the everyday experience of managing personal lives. We begin to unpack these meanings in the next section by considering welfare work as *emotional labour*.

2 Managing the self: welfare work and emotional labour

Welfare work has long been constructed as sites that deal with highly intimate and private arenas (Gunaratnam and Lewis, 2001, p.135). Welfare workers, including those involved in community and voluntary services, tend to come into contact with service users exactly when an individual's personal life, or that of their family, is defined in some way as requiring intervention or 'support' of different kinds. There are numerous examples of this: a volunteer working in a welfare advice centre, absorbing the distress of a stream of people sitting across the counter whose problems she feels unable to solve; a neighbour visiting an elderly person's home to see if they need any help and having to cope with their emotional as well as physical needs; a teacher attempting to pacify a parent who has come to the school to complain about the treatment of their child. In each example, the welfare worker is engaged in **emotional labour** and has to 'manage' the emotional dimensions of work. Personal lives, then, are at the core of each of these encounters and relationships.

emotional labour

The boundaries between emotional labour and other forms of work are not clear-cut. One study cites the case of a worker in a care home who had previously had caring responsibilities but whose job had been redefined:

> my job is boring and monotonous and there is not a great deal of satisfaction ... Previously, I knew more about the clients, but I'm not allowed to have the input that I had before ... the emotional side of caring, for example, comforting residents if someone's wife or husband is in hospital ... I put my mop or broom

> away to sit down with a client if they are crying. I'm not supposed to take them to the toilet, but I do if they are wet. I'm not supposed to, but they get verbal and resentful if you don't.
>
> (Rainbird et al., 1999, p.37)

commodified

The person in the quotation is paid as a cleaner. Cleaning, then, forms the **commodified** element of her job. The caring work that she chooses to do, in addition to the cleaning work, is unpaid. But, not all emotional labour is uncommodified – sometimes it forms the core of the job of a paid employee. Such commodification is common in service industries where emotional labour is used to add value to the customer experience, and thereby profits to the enterprise. Hochschild (1983) described the management of 'feelings' or 'emotions' as an integral element of the work of female flight attendants in their interaction with passengers. Emotional labour is part of the effort made by airlines to cultivate the long-term loyalty of customers. This work was defined by airline companies, management and in-flight crews themselves as 'women's work' as it was deemed to involve skills – *essentialized* skills – which 'women are seen to posses simply by virtue of being women' (Taylor and Tyler, 2000, p.86). Caring, emotional and 'personal servicing' skills were said to be particular female skills, while female cabin crew were also expected to present themselves and their bodies as feminine. For Hochschild, the commodification and control of femininity and female sexuality was integral to the emotional labour process in the airline industry. However, the increasing employment of men as flight attendants suggests that emotional labour can be undertaken by either sex and is not a specifically gendered skill. This example shows that men often do work that is constructed as feminized – as flight attendants, and as care workers in hospitals and nursing homes (see **Fink, 2004a**).

While emotional labour has long been identified as a key component of retail and personal service work, a number of researchers have pointed to its importance in rapidly expanding sectors of the economy such as call centres and telesales work (Callaghan and Thompson, 2002; Taylor and Bain, 1998). However, we need to distinguish between the types of emotional labour that are used for commercial gain – commodified emotional labour – and those that have tended to characterize professional welfare work. It is argued that the notion of emotional labour does not transfer well from private sectors such as the airline industry to nursing or other welfare work where profit is not necessarily the main organizing force:

> Caring professionals are basically different to the majority of workers who produce a service in that they are not closely supervised in their emotion work; their skilled status allows them to retain autonomy, within the confines of professional norms and client expectations, over how they carry out the emotional part of their job.
>
> (Hochschild quoted in Bolton, 2000, p.582)

Let us look more closely at what we mean by emotional labour in welfare work. It draws on particular resources that welfare workers bring to the labour process, such as empathy and care. However, in addition, emotional labour

Figure 2.1 Advertising images of female flight attendants from the 1960s and 1990s

involves managing the emotions of others, for example when workers have to manage the frustrations and distress of clients. This is evident in the quotation from the cleaner at the start of this section who talks of 'comforting' clients when they are upset, but also of coping with their resentment and verbal abuse. And it means managing the self. The following is an account based on the experiences of staff caring for a patient called Joan (pseudonym) and it provides an insight into the experience of nursing cancer patients:

> Once upon a time there was a patient – Joan – who was dying slowly of cancer. Her quality of life was not great. She couldn't walk, she was incontinent. And she felt sick so much of the time that she couldn't enjoy her food. No medicine seemed to help her very much.
>
> The staff were good and kind. But the more they cared for Joan, the more she demanded of them. Nothing was ever right and she was never grateful. She cried a lot about her situation and she shouted out for the nurses even when she didn't want anything. She craved attention and control.
>
> At first her carers were pained by Joan's pain and did what they could to alleviate it. But because of her behaviour, feelings changed, and working with Joan became an act which had a personal cost – they had to put aside their own feelings of anger and frustration at her demands, and her lack of feeling for them. They had to smile and be nice to her.

> Everyone had to do this but they did it in different ways. Acting patiently and obligingly came easily to some and made them feel better towards Joan. Others had to really work on their feelings of resentment in order to nurse her well. For some it was all in an irksome day's work but they just got on and made light of it. Some got very upset and took their feelings home with them. There were very few carers who were free of feelings of conflict about her – a woman dying without much dignity, and with some of her problems self-inflicted.
>
> (Lee, 2002, pp.144–5)

The emotional work described above in this account involves comforting patients and giving them attention. But, the nurses also had to manage themselves – controlling their own feelings of hurt and irritation at Joan's behaviour. Managing the self in these types of welfare work situations might mean 'performing' emotions that you may not actually feel: acting patiently and obligingly, smiling and being nice. Or it might mean finding strategies to deal with the feelings that arise.

ACTIVITY 2.1

Drawing on the example of nursing described above, think about what the work of managing one's own emotions and the emotions of others might entail in other welfare contexts. See if you can think of examples to put in the grid below.

	Managing one's own emotions	Managing the emotions of others
Policing		
Being a mental health worker		
Getting children ready for school		
Chairing a meeting of a community or voluntary group		

Of course not all welfare work is purely emotional labour: nursing involves physical work (handling patients), mental work (assessing the best treatment) and emotional labour (reducing anxieties, giving the patient confidence in their care). You might like to think about areas of your own work – paid or unpaid – and how far the labour might comprise physical, mental and emotional features.

The account above illustrates two different levels of emotional labour: 'surface' (working on your facial expressions, putting on an act) and 'deep' (managing your feelings in order to change them) (see Fineman, 2003). Some strategies of managing the self might involve reducing the emotional dynamics of the interactions between the people involved so that personal boundaries are not crossed by either the worker or the welfare recipient. This may have negative consequences (think, for example, of going to a doctor and receiving a diagnosis in medical terminology that you do not understand and not having the implications of diagnosis explained to you). But, sometimes it may have positive results in that the boundaries could afford the welfare recipient a sense of respect despite the deep inequalities that might be involved in the welfare relationship. For example, the US sociologist Richard Sennett draws on his own experiences of growing up in Chicago's Cabrini Green, an area that had a very negative image in Chicago, to argue that respect has to be part and parcel of a progressive welfare system (Sennett, 2003). To respect the autonomy and rights of the welfare recipient, he believes that a degree of reserve and distance has to be maintained. According to Sennett, this in turn will lead to mutual respect that can reduce the inequality in relationships between recipient and welfare worker.

Creating the distance that Sennett talks about involves managing one's own feelings so as not to disclose them to the recipients of welfare. The idea of 'managing the self' does not simply suggest that we have to suppress our feelings, as for example the feelings that nurses might have to suppress when dealing with 'difficult' people. Rather than containing or suppressing our sense of self, emotional labour can also demand the performance of a self that is acceptable in the work place or welfare relationship and that can be deployed to achieve a particular effect. This could include for example:

- presenting a 'caring' self despite being tired or needing emotional support oneself;
- performing a neutral, dispassionate self although one is deeply affected by the circumstances of others we relate to in welfare work, as in the Sennett example;
- performing a 'responsible' self when visiting a doctor or other professional with the power to intervene in our personal life;
- producing an 'enterprising' self fitted to the culture of the organization we work in, one in which we appear to be committed to its values and mission.

interpellated

All these 'selves' are **interpellated** in and through different welfare practices and discourses that are themselves associated with different sources of power, knowledge and authority. However, it is the emotional dynamics of welfare work that also produce powerful identifications and allegiances which are the basis for advocacy or social movements through which social policy is contested. These allegiances also mean that individuals and groups are often inspired to work 'for love' – to give their labour with no economic reward. We consider this further in section 3.

alienation

Marxist, feminist and post-structuralist theoretical perspectives can help us to understand welfare work as labour process in general, and managing the self and emotional labour in particular. For Marxists, the key concept mobilized here is **alienation**: the process through which we become separated from ourselves, other human beings and what we produce. It is, for Marx, the loss of control over key areas of our lives which is central to our increasingly alienated existence under capitalism. The focus of feminist analysis is the gendered nature of much welfare and care work (**Fink, 2004a**). Feminist analysis highlights how emotional labour is associated with 'women's work' and how such work is often viewed as a 'labour of love', which is freely given and somehow separate from the impersonal domain of economic exchange and paid employment. Feminist theory also explores how women's bodies and capacities become commodified as part of an exchange relationship in some types of emotional labour, for example, as in the case of the flight attendants discussed by Hochschild (1983). Post-structuralist theory highlights the multiple identities and attachments of being a worker (**Carabine, 2004**). Managing the self means producing the self and performing the self within a range of different discourses. A post-structuralist view would also note how welfare work is constituted as caring, committed and dedicated. This helps explain both why welfare work tends to be low paid and the difficulties that can arise in subjecting it to **Taylorist** working practices (see Chapter 1, section 5).

Taylorist

However, these theoretical perspectives can interact with each other in important ways. An account of welfare work might begin by using a Marxist analysis to highlight how personal dimensions of welfare work are influenced by the broader social structures and processes that shape, and are mediated through, social policy. As welfare services become more fragmented with a number of agencies across the public, private and voluntary sectors producing different elements, they have to be brought together and coordinated. A feminist analysis would note how this is typically done by women on behalf of their families, doing welfare work as mothers and daughters, and also coordinating other sources of support from the fragments of services available from different groups and agencies. And as some elements of welfare are transferred from the state to the private sphere of individual responsibility, the way in which we live our personal lives becomes subject to greater scrutiny and intervention. As some forms of welfare work are transferred to the user-as-producer, this requires new forms of self-management that can be analysed through a post-structuralist perspective.

The concept of emotional labour, then, reminds us that you do not leave your personal life behind when you undertake welfare work. 'The personal' is something that you bring with you, which may be a commodified resource in the labour process itself. Emotional labour involves elements of managing the self. We may come to 'perform' particular selves in order to deal with the requirements of welfare work. Such selves are partly produced in and through discourses and ideologies, but may also form sites of new identifications and allegiances through which dominant social policy ideas and assumptions may be challenged. One such site is voluntary welfare work, which is the focus of the next section.

3 Working for love or loving to work? Voluntary work and social policy

This section explores voluntary and informal welfare work because of their centrality both in the discourses of social policy and to the way in which individuals experience the delivery of welfare services. The 'voluntary sector' is a term that many writers have discarded because of the difficulty of collapsing a huge variety of different kinds of organizations, from large professional bureaucracies to small neighbourhood-based groups. But, wherever it is located, voluntary and informal welfare work tends to be a source of allegiances and identifications that are deeply embedded in our personal lives.

ACTIVITY 2.2

Read the three quotations in Extract 2.1 and think about how the work described in each one is shaped by specific sets of allegiances and identifications. What concepts of 'community' does each quotation invoke?

Extract 2.1 Allegiances and identifications

In my local church I've been what we call a society steward, that is one of the leading lay people who organize things, along with the property and finance stewards. And circuit wide, that's a group of Methodist churches, I've been a circuit-wide steward. I'm on the committees related to the circuit and also district wide I got involved and also what used to be [name of meeting hall] and it involved a fair few opportunities there ... I suppose one of the other things is we had a friend who was a member of the church although, because of her illness, she's got MS, she couldn't attend. Well, my wife in particular, she was on my wife's visiting list, that's when anyone really wanted help we used to get involved. Finally she had to go into a nursing home, and we got her transferred in there and then when finally she died we looked after all her affairs all the way through and we cleared the house etc and the selling of it. So there was some involvement all the way through.

(Barnes et al., 2001/2002)

I was involved in the Nigerian Union. My duty as a Welfare Officer, is that, if someone, say, there is a problem with any of us, I visit them, see if they are OK, something like that, and then the children of the members, I send them birthday cards ... And if they stay we get involved with the family. And I would do things like going to funerals ... [and] we get together for things like the children's Christmas parties. And we celebrate our Independence Day the 1st of October – Nigerian Independence Day.

(Barnes et al., 2001/2002)

The reason why I got into this job was because I had a keen interest in seeing HIV prevention done amongst gay men ... and because politically I wanted to be involved in a job that had something to say to me personally, something that gave me some kind of personal fulfilment, and about which I knew a lot, because I've been involved in like, gay politics and gay organisations for a long time.

(Outreach worker doing HIV prevention work with gay men, quoted in Deverell and Sharma, 2000, p.29)

COMMENT

'community'

postcolonial

The examples in Extract 2.1 suggest various kinds of affiliations and different possible definitions of **'community'** (see Hughes and Mooney, 1998). The first example alludes to religious affiliations and a church community, though note how the respondent talks about the work of *his wife* whose motivations and attachments we know little about. The second example reveals a **postcolonial** attachment to a diasporic community in part identified with an allegiance to a nation state. And the third suggests a paid worker, but one whose allegiances are drawn from political attachments and identification with a 'gay community', and whose search for fulfilment has strong affinities with work in the voluntary sector.

Voluntary (uncommodified) work tends to be distinguished from paid (commodified) work in that it is assumed to be freely chosen, motivated by altruism and driven by ethical values. Working for the well-being of others, without expectation that they then become obligated to you, may bring emotional satisfaction. However, as the third example in Extract 2.1 suggests, the distinction between commodified and uncommodified welfare work is difficult to sustain. Paid welfare work may be motivated by similar sets of values and may include an element of 'volunteering', for example, a teacher running an after-school club or providing extra support for a child facing difficulties because of domestic or economic circumstances. At the same time, informal and voluntary welfare work is becoming subject to pressures that blur the demarcation with paid work. Many carers are increasingly subject to training and accreditation that opens their personal lives to new processes of surveillance and control, while there is greater emphasis now on the audit and inspection of these sectors as they come to play a larger role in the delivery of different kinds of welfare service. Some voluntary workers may receive payment for their work, while much of the voluntary sector is becoming subject to an array of standards, targets and regulations that blur the boundary between the experiences of paid and unpaid workers.

communitarian

People undertake voluntary and informal labour for different reasons. However, we need to challenge the representation of voluntary work in popular culture, where it is portrayed as altruistically 'doing good', and in social policy discourse, where it is viewed as integral to good citizenship and as an expression of civic or **communitarian** values. Its diversity encompasses a number of different motivations including:

- gaining access to powerful networks – for example, volunteering to do unpaid research for a member of parliament or serving on the management board of public sector bodies;

- improving one's chances of gaining paid employment or access to training – for example, undertaking voluntary work in order to expand or strengthen a résumé;
- finding new forms of sociability to enhance one's circle of friends and acquaintances;
- aiding the transition out of paid work and into retirement through, for example, working for a charity;
- forging links with others who share one's cultural or ethnic identity, for example, when part of a minoritized group;
- finding expression for one's beliefs, for example, by working for a political or religious organization;
- working on a local project as part of community service following a court conviction;
- doing voluntary work as part of a welfare-to-work programme.

These last two examples challenge the idea that all voluntary work is freely chosen – both are elements of more coercive social policies. The examples also suggest something of the ways in which class, gender and ethnicity inflect voluntary welfare work. These inflections are, however, not stable. Who does welfare work, where it is done and under what conditions, all change as a result of shifts in social policy.

3.1 Social policy and voluntary welfare work

The state has always relied on voluntary and informal labour as well as paid work:

> the family, in its multiple forms, and, in particular, women's caring work (and) ... voluntary organisations ... filled in the gaps and articulated and connected the needs of individuals, often under conditions of severe duress, with the services which existed [in the welfare state]. They patched together needs, resources, and institutions in highly complex and creative ways, which the Italian sociologist, Laura Balbo, has compared to the making of a patchwork quilt. Indeed, without these concrete intermediaries to connect individual and social provision, the state sector or large organizations in general could not function.
>
> (Showstack Sassoon, 1996, pp.185–6)

This intermediary work, Showstack Sassoon suggests, provides the conditions for state policies to be effective and ultimately for the economy to function. But, as the welfare state has undergone change, the state sector no longer consists of the same 'large organizations' that Showstack Sassoon had in mind. Services have been contracted out to a range of organizations in the private and voluntary sectors, and social welfare provision is increasingly fragmented. For example, community care services may initially be accessed through a GP. But then those receiving services – or their relatives, partners or friends – must negotiate with and coordinate a range of diverse service providers including: social services departments in order to have their needs formally assessed; a hospital-based occupational therapy service to get equipment for the home; the workers at the equipment store itself; individual care workers and their supervisor; a social security office; local firms providing home hairdressing, paediatric and other services; churches or voluntary sector groups providing outings, clubs or events for older people; a community transport organization; and a network of neighbours, family or friends to cover the gaps that paid care workers do not fill, or to stand in for emergencies.

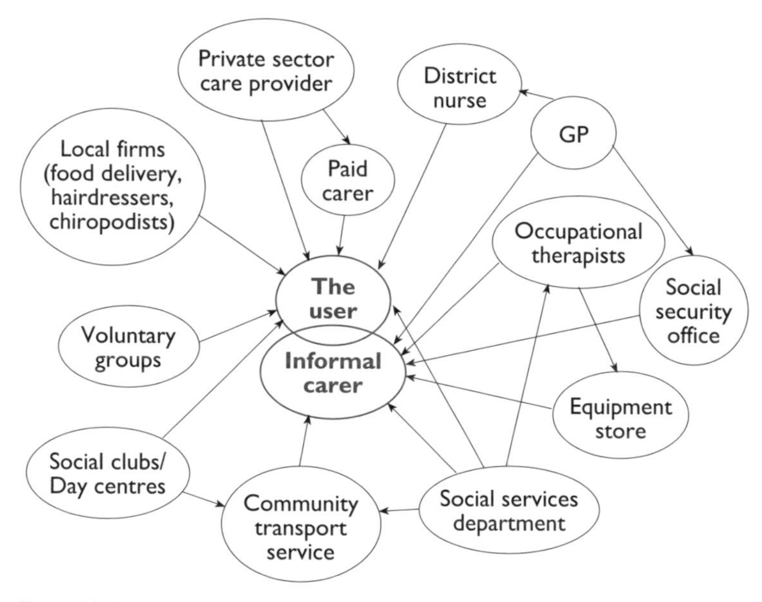

Figure 2.2 Emotional labour: coordinating welfare services

The work of intermediaries must be viewed as labour, and labour with a high emotional cost for both the service recipient and those who negotiate on his or her behalf. The relationships of mutuality, dependence and independence, of trust and mistrust, of power and powerlessness that inflect these networks have profound implications for the personal lives of the service user, of the workers providing the services, and of the families, neighbours and friends who often do much of the work of coordination.

active citizenship
social capital

The debates on the role of voluntary work have been transformed by the development of ideas of **active citizenship** (see Social Exclusion Unit, 2004; Cabinet Office, 2004) and **social capital** (Fine, 2001). Here, the key claim being advanced is that involvement in a diverse range of networks and activities not only creates and cements relationships, but enhances the greater social good. New Labour emphasizes the crucial importance of fostering an active civil society (Giddens, 1998), and the election of the Labour Government in 1997 led to greater mainstreaming of the voluntary sector into social policy. That is, social policy promoted a professionalized voluntary sector, working in partnership with government and business. This led to a bifurcation, with large voluntary organizations growing increasingly distinct from grassroots organizations. The professionalization of voluntary work produced a greater emphasis on standardized working practices that, it is argued, squeezed the capacity of the sector to be innovative and to challenge mainstream social policy. These increasingly semi-formalized aspects of voluntary work change the experience of doing it, and many organizations have struggled to recruit volunteers because 'there is a particular and very significant tension between a professionalized managerial approach and a more traditional volunteering ethos' (Morrison, 2000, p.109).

However, this narrative of change tends to mask the complexity and diversity of voluntary organizations and their capacity to reconcile conflicting goals. The boundaries of the voluntary sector are extremely blurred: at one extreme (for example the commercialized and entrepreneurial housing associations) it shares many characteristics with the private sector and at the other end of the spectrum (for example, faith-based groups that provide services and welfare activities) it is closer to informal, unorganized welfare work. Some groups have a strong advocacy, or political, role, while others are more concerned with providing services. There are also differences between groups with rural roots and those based in urban settings. The class, gendered, racialized and age composition of the voluntary labour force will vary significantly depending on a group's history, location and purpose.

Accounts of voluntary sector transformation also underestimate the ways in which voluntary sector organizations manage to reconcile seemingly conflicting goals and values. Voluntary organizations are located in what can be termed a 'field of tensions' between the rationales and discourses of the state, business and community (Evers, 1995). To illustrate this, let us look at the field of tensions experienced by one organization – a women's advice centre in a major city of the UK. The advice centre supplements state welfare by offering a service and is part funded by the local authority. It therefore has to work within a 'professional' discourse of quality, accountability and standardized practices that shapes the work of its volunteers and makes it closer to the experience of paid work in the public sector. However, the centre also works with an 'advocacy' discourse, seeking to influence policy and promote social change. It also draws on a 'business' discourse in order to win resources from potential funders, which requires entrepreneurial and political skills. Finally, it works with a strong, feminist-inflected set of discourses that emphasize the empowerment of women volunteers and the need for an ethos of equality and anti-discriminatory practice. Each of these discourses positions workers in a different way and calls on them to manage not only the tensions between different working practices and their own individual capacities and skills, but also the boundaries between different ethical commitments.

As we have seen, then, voluntary work is hugely diverse and evokes many different forms of commitment, identification and allegiance. The boundaries between informal work, voluntary work and paid work within the statutory sector are blurred and change as a result of shifts in social policy that have deep impacts on the personal lives of both those providing, and those receiving, welfare work. However, the narrative of a voluntary sector becoming increasingly incorporated into social policy as the partner or agent of the state is too simple; voluntary organizations are cross-cut by multiple discourses and operate in a context of contradictory pressures and tensions, and managing these tensions is part of welfare work. Such tensions are not confined to the voluntary sector but are experienced by public sector workers, whose experience we consider in the next two sections.

4 Managing welfare work: welfare professionals and state restructuring

Whether paid or unpaid, the labour involved in providing welfare work has undergone profound transformations as a result of the restructuring of the welfare state in the UK over the last two decades. While there are many continuities in the actual working process – giving care to an individual, managing housing repairs, running a youth group or day centre for older people, planning a community event – the context in which these activities take place has changed radically as core assumptions about the professions and the public sector have become unravelled. These shifts have had profound consequences on social policy and therefore on the personal lives of both workers in, and users of, state services.

Think about changes in policies relating to the care of older people and consider how these might shape welfare work and personal lives.

We thought of at least four ways in which policy change might have an impact on welfare work and personal lives:

- The provision of care in residential homes for the elderly has often been 'contracted out' to the private sector. This has significant impacts on pay and conditions of work, and on the ways in which the work itself is organized. Such changes have consequences for the personal lives of care workers and also for the personal lives of the residents of care homes.
- The squeeze on social services budgets means that resources are being increasingly targeted on older people who are deemed to be most in 'need' or at risk. This has consequences for those who perform care work and where it is done. Those who do not qualify for state provision are increasingly being looked after at home, while the nature of the care work in residential settings is intensifying because of the higher levels of dependence of residents.
- The emphasis on 'care in the community' has affected different kinds of welfare work. This also creates new forms of work for family members or friends as they strive to coordinate the work of multiple providers to ensure that someone living on their own receives a reasonably consistent quality of care.
- There is a greater expectation that we each have to take more responsibility to look after ourselves to ensure that we can have a relatively healthy old age and remain independent for as long as possible.

What effects do these processes of policy change and restructuring have on those engaged in paid work? Welfare services are traditionally associated with certain professions and para-professions: teachers, social workers, probation officers, doctors, nurses and others. The key features that characterize professional work and differentiate it from other forms of occupation include:

- claims that social problems require expert judgement and the application of expert knowledge;
- claims for autonomy based on the self-regulation of both entry into the profession and the maintenance of standards through a professional body;
- an emphasis on the special and privileged quality of professional/client interactions;
- defence of this space in which professional judgement can be exercised and must be trusted.

Professionalism is, thus, both a form of work and an occupational strategy that enables workers to negotiate the power and rewards due to them in return for their expertise (often based on long periods of training), and to control entry to the profession. Their power has, however, been significantly challenged over the last two decades through successive cycles of state restructuring and **managerialization**, which has introduced a business ethos into the public sector, and prioritized decision-making based on economic rationality (efficiency or value for money) over affective or personal judgement (Clarke and Newman, 1997; Newman, 1998). Managerialism has also led to the standardization of many working practices, reducing the discretion enjoyed by professional workers. So, for example, social work has become a more technical process of assessing needs and then purchasing services from a range of providers, rather than serving the needs of clients directly on a one-to-one basis (Jones, 2001). Managerialism involves the introduction of Taylorist forms of labour process. This means professional knowledge and judgement (such as, assessing needs) is captured by an organization and incorporated into standardized procedures that can be operated by lower-grade staff (such as, completing an assessment form). This has fragmented the professional–client relationship into a number of encounters between welfare users and different grades and types of staff. As a consequence, the professional–client relationship has become more impersonal, codified and transient, with profound implications for service users as well as professionals themselves.

managerialization

These processes have been underpinned by a less tangible but equally significant challenge to professional power in the form of the discourses through which restructuring is legitimated. Much professional work continues to enjoy high levels of autonomy because of the complexity of the tasks (for example, diagnosing a disease) and the nature of the professional–client relationship. However, professionals have, like other staff, become subject to a range of discourses through which the professional self is reconstituted. One such discourse is that of **empowerment**. The authority and knowledge base of the professions has been challenged from below, for example, by user activity such as the women's movement, disability movement and anti-racist struggles, each of which has introduced new knowledges and practices into professional work. That is, they have become part of professional discourse

empowerment

Figure 2.3 Client/professional interactions

itself. Some professions have also been influenced by calls for more recognition of the importance of the self – the experiences, values and feelings of the workers – in professional–client interactions (Williams, 1993).

consumerism
accountability

Alongside empowerment, the linked discourses of **consumerism** and **accountability** have informed a range of policy reforms under both the Conservative and Labour Governments of the late twentieth century. Welfare services have been opened up to much greater scrutiny, giving users and the government information on the comparative performance of different service providers. Charters and league tables have exposed state organizations by providing users with information about access and rights. Consumerism has also led to a proliferation of consultation exercises, with for example mental health service users being invited to comment on mental health legislation.

Consumerism intersects with pressure from user movements: many of the reforms have been put in place as a result of the changing awareness of the diverse needs and claims of different groups of users. Thus, the managerial imperative towards consumerism has been – rather uncomfortably – articulated with issues of power, rights and accountability arising from social movements and struggles.

These social policy discourses – empowerment, consumerism and accountability – are now so prevalent in social policy that they have had a significant impact on personal lives by reconstituting the relationship between professionals and service users.

ACTIVITY 2.3

Imagine yourself in three common instances of welfare interaction:

- visiting your GP;
- contacting your local social services department to ask for help for a frail or older relative;
- choosing a school for your child.

What do you think might be the consequences of the discourses of empowerment, consumerism and accountability for the way in which you experience the encounter? And for the professional concerned?

COMMENT

Empowerment might mean that you, as a user, feel you have more right to be heard and to get the service you feel you are entitled to. You might have used the Internet or other sources to get information (say about the best treatment for your illness). Accountability might mean that you have more information about the performance of the service provider, for example the GP surgery, school or social services department. You might also be able to complain if you do not get a satisfactory service, and to have your complaint treated seriously. Consumerism may imply that you have been consulted about the service and asked for feedback on it, and that you are treated with politeness and efficiency, as customers of other service industries might expect. But, it will not necessarily give you any more choice or power in the delivery of the service itself. What of the consequences for the professional? The key sources of their power – information, knowledge and expertise – are no longer under their own control. They might welcome more empowered and informed (and thus responsible) users, but they may also become fearful of a public more inclined to make claims against public authorities when things go wrong. This so-called '**litigation culture**' is producing more defensive practice and changing the service users', as well as the professionals', experiences of their encounters.

litigation culture

However, as in the case of the voluntary sector, this narrative of change is rather too simple. Professional identities are constituted within a number of different discourses; some are traditional (linked to the origins and development of specific professions) and others are emergent (linked to new policy agendas or arising from challenges to tradition from within the profession). Some professional workers may appropriate emergent policy discourses such as partnership work or evidence-based policy, in order to create new forms of power and identity (Newman and Nutley, 2003, for example, describe how the 'what works' agenda has been a source of renewal for the probation service). Others may engage positively with a managerialist agenda and so create new, hierarchically-organized distinctions between 'managerial' and 'service-oriented' professional roles. Hopfl describes the effects of this in nursing:

> Nurses have sought to reinforce the technical exactitude of their work, to give emphasis to the managerial demands that are placed on them and to underscore their commitment to service and dedication. However, such values carry fundamental contradictions and this leaves nurses open to the exploitation of their ambivalence. Their career orientations are radically different from those of potential managers and, by their attachment to service values, their political position is radically weakened. Virtue it seems is not rewarded but 'managed'.
>
> (Hopfl, 2003, p.181)

In addition, professional workers may also rely more heavily on a recasting of the technical basis of professional knowledge and expertise (as in some branches of medicine). The power of the welfare professions, then, rather than being eroded, is being reshaped in multiple ways. This has consequences for the hierarchical ordering – including the gender hierarchy – that occurs both within and between welfare professions.

This provides us with a different perspective on emotional labour – it is labour that is strongly linked to the service values that Hopfl contrasts with managerial or entrepreneurial values. It reminds us that different forms of welfare work are not only associated with different identities, attachments and allegiances, but also with different sources of power, knowledge and authority. The power bases of the welfare professions have always been highly gendered. The professions associated with caring and service were the basis for the expansion of female employment and professional education in the mid twentieth century. As the professions undergo change, with increasing numbers of men employed in traditionally female domains, we should not assume that questions of gender and power disappear from the analysis.

As we have seen, social welfare has traditionally been associated with professional work within the welfare state. The process of state restructuring has profoundly reshaped this work, and the professions have become subject to processes of managerialism that have challenged the quality of the professional–client relationship. Professional power has also been challenged by the discourses of empowerment, consumerism and accountability. These too have changed the nature of the professional–client relationship. Professionals, then, operate in a field of tensions between different discourses, each of which constitutes welfare work in a different way and which produces different patterns of subjectivity and identification in both the producers and users of welfare services. They are also the source of different forms of professional knowledge and power.

5 Working on the margins: modernization and its discontents

In this section we explore the consequences of the 'modernization' of public services for low-paid welfare workers – care assistants, nursing auxiliaries, classroom assistants, cleaners, low-grade administrative staff, school dinner supervisors, hospital porters, street cleaners and so on. These workers tend to be younger women and men, women returning to the labour market and older workers who are either close to, or above, retirement age. As a result, such work tends to be linked to particularly sharp patterns of disadvantage around age, gender, class and 'race' (see Chapters 1, 3 and 4).

work intensification

The process of 'modernizing' the labour force involves a number of different dynamics of change. Some involve **work intensification**: reorganizing the work in order to extract the maximum value from each worker. In a study of workplace-based inequalities in public sector employment, an interviewer describes how a kitchen assistant in a school meals service experienced this:

> when she had started work ten years previously, the job had been hard, the people were nice and 'the girls [other staff] treated each other as friends'. She felt that the attitude of the employer was now 'we will get as much out of you in the shortest possible time for the same pay' ... She felt they were [now] skimping because there was no time and they were short staffed. Whereas she had felt pride in her job, she now felt unable to do it properly.
>
> (Rainbird et al., 1999, p.35)

deskilling
multi-skilling

The findings of the same study by Rainbird et al. (1999) also highlight substantial elements of **deskilling** as a result of the routinization of many tasks, and a shift towards generic work organization (**multi-skilling**) with the removal of traditional lines of demarcation between jobs. The authors of the study suggest a number of possible reasons for these shifts:

- the introduction of 'single status' agreements in local government and local bargaining in the health service, leading to a move away from national pay and grading structures;
- legislation on community care and child protection, producing a different 'skills mix' among workers, for example, 'home helps' becoming care assistants;
- the introduction of '**best value**' producing a reconfiguration of services in the drive for efficiency and customer satisfaction.

best value

These reasons suggest that theories of the labour process that can account for 'deskilling' and the shift towards Taylorist forms of work organization that were discussed in Chapter 1 may be too general: the state is an important actor in shaping employment relations in the public sector, and the changes in specific welfare sites will be influenced by a range of social and political, as well as economic, processes.

flexibility

Calls for increased flexibility are a central imperative of the modernization of the workforce. **Flexibility** is a normative term, but in contrast to its potential opposites (inflexibility, entrenchment) it has positive connotations. As such it has been deployed in a range of discourses, reflecting different interests and different kinds of argument. However, the dominant meaning denotes workforce flexibility in the interests of the employer. One shift has been towards greater *numerical* flexibility based on a growing distinction between the 'core' workforce (on full-time, permanent contracts) and the 'peripheral' workforce of part-time workers, workers on short-term contracts, term-time only contracts and consultants. The trend towards numerical flexibility can be viewed as a **casualization** of the workforce as people move from full-time to part-time contracts and more irregular work. This, of course, brings with it increased financial insecurity and risk. It may also bring benefits: many workers are choosing to opt for the better paid, albeit less secure, work available through agencies supplying nurses and teachers. Whatever the reason, numerical flexibility also has implications for the quality and continuity of the services provided as Figure 2.4 illustrates.

casualization

Standards warning on supply staff

Ofsted says temporary teachers cost schools £150,000 and 'damage learning'

Figure 2.4 Headline from *The Guardian*, 16 December 2002

Functional flexibility occurs where workers are required to undertake different duties as the needs of the enterprise change, as in the examples of multi-tasking and multi-skilling mentioned above. Both forms of flexibility potentially enable employers to adapt to the shifting demands of the enterprise. To these conventional views of flexibility we want to add a further dimension: **flexible citizenship**. This is a term used by Aihwa Ong (1999) to explore the impact of globalization on citizenship regimes. Flexible citizenship is about spatial flexibility based on transnational mobility. Britain's colonial past has meant that it has had a wide and deep pool from which to draw labour to support the expansion of the welfare state and to fill gaps in the labour market (Figure 2.5). In the UK, the flexible labour market in welfare services is, then, profoundly racialized.

flexible citizenship

This racialization cannot be simply attributed to the economic processes that underpin the supply and demand of labour. It is mediated in important ways by Britain's colonial legacy and the state's policies on immigration, and by cultural

Figure 2.5 Image from *The Guardian,* 19 February 2003

practices that inform attitudes about the value and status of different forms of work. Immigration policy underwent significant shifts at the end of the twentieth century, becoming increasingly focused on people seeking asylum, with attempts to construct clear distinctions between 'genuine' and 'bogus' asylum seekers, the latter, often termed 'economic migrants', being excluded from entry to the UK (**Saraga, 2004**). The continued reliance on migrant labour to meet skills shortages in nursing, social work and other occupations has profound implications for the nations from which the labour is drawn.

ACTIVITY 2.4

Read the following newspaper extracts, both of which were taken from *The Guardian* in early 2003. What do you think these tell us about the relationship between personal lives and social policy? Think about the ways in which the terms 'personal lives' and 'social policy' apply across, as well as within, national boundaries.

Draining the south

Britain's public services are increasingly reliant on foreign workers, but the knock-on effect has been staff shortages in poorer countries

David Batty

New Labour has staked its political future on modernizing Britain's public services. It pledged more than £101 billion in last year's Budget and the comprehensive spending review to improve the state of our hospitals, schools and local government services.

But the main obstacle to achieving the government's ambitious goals – such as cutting waiting lists and class sizes – is no longer money; it is staff shortages.

Ministers have launched a series of recruitment drives to tackle a growing workforce crisis. ...

To fill the gaps, employers are increasingly looking abroad. The Department of Health (DoH) has launched a huge overseas recruitment drive, attracting nurses from countries as diverse as Spain and the Philippines. The bulk of the global recruitment market is controlled by independent recruitment agencies, which have reported a sharp upturn in demand in recent years. There are now 42,000 foreign nurses working in the health service, more than double the number three years ago. The number of overseas social workers in Britain has quadrupled in the past 11 years, from 227 in 1990–1991 to 1,175 in 2001–2002. Thousands of foreign teachers have been recruited since 1997. While 5,056 overseas doctors were registered to practice in the UK in 2001, compared to 4,281 new home-grown recruits. ...

Britain is now reliant on this international workforce. It is cheaper and easier to hire overseas staff. ...

There are clear advantages to working in the UK. One million Filipinos work abroad, including tens of thousands of nurses, contributing $6 billion (£3.75 billion) to the country's economy annually. In South Africa a social worker is commonly responsible for 500 cases, yet the average salary is only 36,000 rand (£2,850). British social workers usually deal with 12 cases and earn on average £24,000.

The ethics of overseas recruitment are increasingly under scrutiny, however. Following a plea by the former president of South Africa, Nelson Mandela, the DoH banned NHS trusts from recruiting nurses from developing countries because many face staff shortages. But less than a third of private recruitment agencies have signed up to the guidelines. The number of South African nurses in the UK has risen five-fold in four years.

Even those countries long considered to have a surplus of care staff are now feeling the strain. Turnover at Philippine hospitals is so high that many operating theatres are staffed with trainee nurses.

The crisis facing schools and social services in the developing world is just as acute. Zimbabwe's Department of Social Welfare has only an eighth of the staff required to function effectively because more than half of the country's 3,000 social workers now work in Britain. And Jamaica lost 600 teachers, mainly to England and the US.

The Philippine board of nursing is pressing their government to make foreign hospitals cover the costs of training new recruits every time a nurse is lost from the country. The UK's Commonwealth Secretariat is drawing up a code of conduct on the recruitment of health and social care staff following pressure from poorer member states.

(*The Guardian*, 11 March 2003, p.5)

Crippled by ambition

Exodus from Zimbabwe highlights winners and losers

David Batty

Up to half of Zimbabwe's social workers are now employed in Britain following a dramatic rise in overseas recruitment over the past decade that threatens to cripple the African country's welfare system.

About 1,500 social workers have come to Britain from Zimbabwe as a result of the country's economic slump and poor working conditions.

Christopher Chitereka, president of the National Association of Social Workers (NASW) in Harare, says the majority of Zimbabwe's social workers are now employed overseas, and nearly half of the total workforce of 3,000 are in Britain.

Another NASW official, who wishes to remain anonymous, says Zimbabwe's department of social welfare now has barely a quarter of the social workers required to function effectively. He says: "The situation is desperate. At most, there are 100 social workers left at the department out of a staff of 400." The official estimated that between 20 and 40 people are leaving the department to work in Britain every year.

...

Overseas recruits accounted for nearly a quarter of new social workers in Britain last year, according to the General Social Care Council (GSCC), the regulatory body for social care professionals. The GSCC's annual report on overseas recruitment shows that, over the last 11 years, the number of overseas social workers verified as eligible to practise in Britain has quadrupled, from 227 in 1990–1991 to 1,175 in 2001–2002. There has been a particularly sharp rise over the past two years – by 66% in 2000–2001 and 47% in 2001–2002.

(*The Guardian*, 19 February 2003, p.6)

COMMENT

The personal lives affected by these flows of labour are multiple. We might consider, for example:

- the lives of the Philippine nurse or the Zimbabwean social worker moving across continents and cultures and living apart from family and friends;
- the consequences for their own families – for example, children or elderly parents may have to be cared for by other people; such are some of the more pervasive consequences of the spreading of global care chains (see **Fink, 2004a**);
- the personal lives of those in the source countries as they seek to use public services drained of their key resource;
- the shaping of UK welfare workers' personal lives through their engagement and interaction with workers recruited from Africa and/or the Philippines.

5.1 Contesting modernization

The continued efforts to 'modernize' the labour force are a site of potential conflict between welfare workers and employers. Examples include the calls in November/December 2002 for greater workforce flexibility as part of the negotiation of new pay deals for two groups of key workers – fire-fighters and health workers. For fire-fighters, extra pay beyond inflation was offered in exchange for 'modernization'. This included a number of different forms of flexibility: fire-fighters being required to act as paramedics, the move to shared call centres with ambulance services and having fewer fire-fighters on duty at night. These conditions were fiercely resisted by fire-fighters, and the dispute led to a number of strikes and the deployment of the armed forces to provide basic cover during the periods of industrial action. Fire-fighters also offered their own definitions of 'modernization' that emphasized improving knowledge and skills, and developing a more diverse workforce. Management and employer-led 'modernization' strategies undermined the identity of fire-fighters (of who they are and what they do) and, in turn, their sense of self and self-worth.

At the same time nurses were offered long-term pay rises in exchange for modernization. The provisions included support workers taking on tasks traditionally done by nurses, such as giving injections, and nurses taking on tasks traditionally done by doctors, for example prescribing drugs. There was also a new system for rewarding 'unsocial' working hours in order to give better cover for weekend and evening services. This did not receive the same kind of resistance from employee organizations, though this does not imply that labour relations in nursing are 'conflict-free'. Resistance and contestation are central to work place experience in both nursing and the fire service.

Why do you think there was more resistance to modernization, and the flexibilities it required, on the part of fire-fighters?

There are complex issues here including problems of recruitment and retention in some of the health professions, leading to the increasing use of agency staff to cover basic services. Then, there is the question of the relative power of the trades unions in the two sectors and the longer tradition of trade unionism in the fire service. Some nurses were offered higher status in the creation of a new grade of 'super-nurses'. Then, there are differences in the gendered and racialized composition of the two labour forces concerned. This is important in understanding the flexibility strategies of employers. As we have seen, flexibility strategies tilt employment towards cheaper labour, and in the process worsen conditions of employment by outsourcing labour to the private sector. This increases the proportion of the workforce in part-time, low-paid and insecure work, precisely those categories of work most likely to be done by working-class women and by members of minority ethnic groups.

This section has focused on the experience of low-paid welfare workers in order to highlight:

- the way in which low-paid work intersects with gender and 'race' – there is less focus on class in the research we cited, but it is also of central

Figure 2.6 The 2003 fire services dispute

importance in attempting to understand the way in which the labour process is organized;

- changes in the patterns of work for the low paid that result from the process of restructuring the welfare state – we noted the importance of de-skilling and casualization, but also highlighted the ways in which some jobs were being redefined around generic skills in order to introduce more functional flexibility;
- the ways in which 'flexibility' can be a site of resistance and struggle, and how this takes different forms in different occupations;
- the multiple links between personal lives, and low-paid work – for example, that processes of 'modernization' can undermine a sense of identity and worth.

6 Managing the changing relationships of welfare work

The changes in social policy that we have been considering in this chapter mean that much of the task of co-ordinating and managing welfare provision for individual users has been 'privatized' to the informal sphere of welfare work done by friends, families and communities. This has profound implications for personal lives. Let us consider the hypothetical example of Mr X, the user of a community care service. Mr X is the spouse of an older woman who has recently been discharged from hospital. Mrs X needs help to get dressed and undressed, with toileting and washing, and in preparing food. Mr X has only recently retired and is not familiar with running a household. He has his own health problems. He has to manage the care of himself and Mrs X, but in doing so has to manage a number of different relationships including those with: the hospital occupational therapy service (which provides 'aids' that supposedly enable someone discharged from hospital to be cared for in their own home); social services staff who purchase services; care staff from whom services are purchased; neighbours and friends to cover for him when he is away; and, of course, Mrs X. Each of these, too, involves a considerable amount of emotional labour. Many of you reading this will be all too familiar with the emotional management that is involved here – or in other similar situations.

In what ways do you think that the feelings and experiences of Mrs X are being marginalized by the focus on Mr X?

Being a carer or providing care for others in the community is much discussed in the literature on welfare provision and is a high profile form of informal welfare work receiving considerable attention in social policy (see **Fink, 2004b**). But, other forms of activity contribute informally to the welfare of others, some of which are illustrated in Extracts 2.2 and 2.3. These are taken from interviews with citizens participating in forums set up by public bodies to consult with users, citizens and voluntary sector organizations. The first speaker is a past member of a user forum on disability issues, the second is the coordinator of the women's advice centre described in section 3.

Extract 2.2 Making a difference

I only went to a few meetings (of a group on disability issues). It sounds awful but I can't think of another way to put it, but I was past that. I didn't want to sit in meetings for 2 hours. We're all at different stages. Some people were at the stage where they wanted to come together and talk about how crap their lives are and talk about the problems they have had with THEIR home help and THEIR carer, and I was like: this is good, we need to do this, but I want to go and I want to speak to the Director of Social Services and tell him the whole service is ... do you know what I mean? My time was really limited and I didn't want to spend it in a, like, a support group because I didn't need that. I wanted to be making a difference.

(Barnes et al., 2001/2002)

Extract 2.3 Working for change

I am not an expert on anything at all. What I am is someone who is prepared to lead basically. But, I like to take the lead from other people ... it's not for me to say 'this is where we ought to go'. However, you do get drawn in, because once you start to move into those decision-making arenas, it is you that actually initiates the movement a lot of the time, and you have to recognize that. I see myself as the person ... you know when you are at school and everybody's going 'do you think we should?' 'Do you think we should do it?' I'd say 'I will. I'll go and have a look and I'll come back and tell you if it's alright'. That's the way I work, I'll go and dip my toe in, and I might come back and say 'too much for us at the moment' ... or I might go out and come back and say 'Yes. We can do that'.

(Barnes et al., 2001/2002)

These extracts suggest how the concept of welfare work needs to encompass those working for changes in social policy. Extract 2.2 challenges the usual constructions of welfare users as needing support: this interviewee clearly wanted the opportunity to influence the policies and practices of the service provider. Extract 2.3 highlights the difficulty of thinking of management/workforce relationships in simple terms. Here the manager's role is to help other women build the confidence and skills to change their own circumstances and to act in the wider policy arena.

The interaction between welfare work and social policy is, then, the site of social and political agency. There are many barriers to our capacity to influence policy from below. However, each of these respondents clearly wanted to 'make a difference'. 'Making a difference' is shaped by the attitudes, values and experiences of particular individuals, and by their involvement in welfare work. Within the world of welfare work there are challenges – or at least the potential for challenges – to dominant social policy norms and assumptions. Such challenges often involve the reshaping of the personal lives of those involved.

7 Work, personal lives and social policy

The world of 'work', formal and informal, paid and unpaid, is shaped by social policy in a number of important ways. First, the interaction between policies concerned with the provision of welfare benefits and the management of the economy to provide enhanced employment or training opportunities is fraught with difficulty. Successive governments have struggled with the task of balancing the need to provide support for those in poverty due to unemployment, sickness and disability, on the one hand, and the need to provide incentives to encourage claimants back to work, on the other. If welfare benefits are too generous, it is argued, there is likely to be little incentive to do paid work, especially the kinds of low-paid, 'flexible' job opportunities that exist on the margins of economic activity. On the other hand, people can get stuck in a 'benefits trap', as Extract 2.4 from a woman involved in the Disability Rights Movement shows.

Extract 2.4 Paid and unpaid work

At the moment I am not doing any paid work. I am really frustrated about that ... There is no reason why I couldn't do a part-time job. But I am stuck in the benefits trap ... I go to all these meetings locally and nationally and get really heavily involved and take on loads of tasks and I think what am I doing I should be getting paid for this. I could be doing something with all this experience. I go and see an independent living adviser and I know more than they do. That really frustrates me, but the system isn't there for me to work. If I was to work I would lose my disability benefits and I would lose my direct payment which I need. I need people to help me in the mornings, help with the running of the house and help me look after my child. That would all stop if I went to work. If I went to work I would still need that support, and would need a bit of support at work. Like that consultation thing I did. I could do it but I needed someone else to go round with a microphone. I could do it but I needed someone else to go around with a microphone and it really frustrated me.

(Barnes et al., 2001/2002)

Extract 2.4 questions the idea of a neat boundary between paid and unpaid work, but also suggests some of the ways in which individuals have to negotiate their way through and around it. Social policy oscillates between curbing welfare benefits to certain groups (for example, radically reducing the opportunities for early retirement on the grounds of ill health) and providing a standard minimum wage to make it worth the while of those on state benefits to re-enter the labour market. The tensions created by these oscillations produce dilemmas that people must manage in their personal lives, as illustrated in Extract 2.4. Shifts in social policy may also mean that more of people's personal lives come under the aegis of government help, intervention or scrutiny. Policies concerned with eradicating 'social exclusion' or combating child poverty produce interventions into what were previously seen as private decisions about, for example, whether to get a job or stay at home to care for children. But, Extract 2.4 also emphasizes the ways in which policy norms around work shape personal lives; workers are constructed as independent individuals who do not require welfare.

8 Conclusion

The recasting and restructuring of the welfare state (considered to be its *modernization* by successive governments), has major consequences for those involved in the managing of welfare and the personal lives of welfare users. The major shifts in welfare and public sector service provision that have been engineered since 1997 have led to widespread changes in the organization of welfare work, and in the day-to-day working experiences of diverse groups of welfare workers. These shifts have also, as we saw in section 5.1, contributed to increasing opposition by large numbers of welfare workers to what they view as the deskilling and increasingly alienating conditions of welfare work.

We have also highlighted the complex and diverse ways in which personal lives and social policy are mutually constituted. The messiness and complexity of this process serves to compromise and destabilize the orthodox dualities between paid and unpaid, formal and informal, work. Here, we have focused on some of the ways through which this mutual constitution underpins the relationships between welfare users and different groups of welfare workers: how 'the personal' of each is shaped through the welfare encounter, albeit in different and unequal ways. The next chapter explores the ways in which this mutual constitution comes into play in relation to one of the key life transitions – ageing and retirement.

Further resources

For discussions of the Labour Government's programme of welfare state 'modernization', *Modernising Governance* (2001) by Janet Newman provides an extensive discussion of the discourses deployed, while Martin Powell's edited volume of essays, *Evaluating New Labour's Welfare Reforms* (2002), considers the impact of the government's social policies on different sites of welfare between 1997 and 2001.

Another interpretation of the impact of modernization on welfare workers is provided by the independent *Labour Research* journal, which can be accessed at http://www.lrd.org.uk. This monthly publication provides an up-to-date account of changes in working practices and considers the impact of diverse aspects of government legislation (including local government, devolved government and European Community legislation) on working conditions across different industries. This can be usefully supplemented by the websites run by different public sector trades unions such as UNISON (http://www.unison.org.uk), the GMB, (http://www.gmb.org.uk), and the various teachers unions in different parts of the UK. There is (in the early

2000s) a growing emphasis on active citizenship, volunteering and the promotion of social capital from the government. Further information is available at the Cabinet Office site: http://www.cabinet-office.gov.uk and the Social Exclusion Unit site: http://www.socialexclusionunit.gov.uk/.(All these websites were accessed on 19 January 2004.)

The origins of the idea of social capital are explored by Ben Fine in *Social Capital Versus Social Theory* (2001), while for more on emotional labour we would refer you to Arlie Russell Hochschild's *The Managed Heart* (1983) and to Stephen Fineman's *Understanding Emotion at Work* (2003).

References

Barnes, M., Newman, J., Sullivan, H. and Knops, A. (2001/2002) 'Power, participation and political renewal', unpublished data drawn from ESRC research project under the *Democracy and Participation Programme*, Project L215252001.

Batty, D. (2003) 'Crippled by ambition', *The Guardian*, 19 February, p.6.

Batty, D. (2003) 'Draining the south', *The Guardian*, 11 March, p.5.

Bolton, S.C. (2000) 'Who cares? Offering emotion work as a "gift" in the nursing labour process', *Journal of Advanced Nursing*, vol.32, no.3, pp.580–6.

Cabinet Office (2004) Homepage, http://www.cabinet-office.gov.uk (accessed 19 January 2004).

Callaghan, G. and Thompson, P. (2002) '"We recruit attitude": the selection and shaping of routine call centre labour', *Journal of Management Studies*, vol.39, no.2, pp.233–54.

Carabine, J. (2004) 'Personal lives, public policies and normal sexualities?' in Carabine, J. (ed.) *Sexualities: Personal Lives and Social Policy,* Bristol, The Policy Press in association with The Open University.

Clarke, J. and Newman, J. (1997) *The Managerial State: Power, Politics and Ideology in the Remaking of Social Welfare*, London, Sage.

Deverell, K. and Sharma, U. (2000) 'Professionalism in everyday practice: issues of trust, experience and boundaries' in Malin, N. (ed.) *Professionalism, Boundaries and the Workplace,* London, Routledge.

Evers, A. (1995) 'Part of the welfare mix: the third sector as an intermediate area between market economy, state and community', *Voluntas*, vol.9, no.1, pp.11–38.

Fine, B. (2001) *Social Capital Versus Social Theory*, London, Routledge.

Fineman, S. (2003) *Understanding Emotion at Work*, London, Sage.

Fink, J. (2004a) 'Questions of care' in Fink (ed.) (2004).

Fink, J. (ed.) (2004b) *Care: Personal Lives and Social Policy*, Bristol, The Policy Press in association with The Open University.

Giddens, A. (1998) *The Third Way: The Renewal of Social Democracy*, Cambridge, Polity Press.

Gunaratnam, Y. and Lewis, G. (2001) 'Racialising emotional labour and emotionalising racialised labour: anger, fear and shame in social welfare', *Journal of Social Work Practice*, vol.15, no.2, pp.131–48.

Hochschild, A.R. (1983) *The Managed Heart: Commercialization of Human Feeling*, London, University of California Press.

Hopfl, H. (2003) 'Ministering angels and the virtuous profession' in Barry, J., Dent, M. and O'Neill, M. (eds) *Gender and the Public Sector*, London, Routledge.

Hughes, G. and Mooney, G. (1998) 'Community' in Hughes, G. (ed.) *Imagining Welfare Futures*, London, Sage.

Jones, C. (2001) 'Voices from the front line: state social workers and New Labour', *British Journal of Social Work*, vol.31, no.4, pp.547–62.

Lee, G. (2002) 'Emotional labour and cancer work', *Soundings*, vol.20, Summer, pp.144–5.

Morrison, J. (2000) 'The government–voluntary sector compacts: governance, governmentality and civil society', *Journal of Law and Society*, vol.27, no.1, pp.98–132.

Newman, J. (1998) 'Managerialism and social welfare' in Hughes, G. and Lewis, G. (eds) *Unsettling Welfare*, London, Routledge.

Newman, J. (2001) *Modernising Governance*, London, Sage.

Newman, J. and Nutley, S. (2003) 'Transforming the probation service: the 'what works' agenda, organizational change and professional identity', *Policy and Politics*, vol.3, no.4, pp.547–63.

Ong, A. (1999) *Flexible Citizenship: The Cultural Logics of Transnationality*, Durham and London, Duke University Press.

Powell, M. (ed.) (2002) *Evaluating New Labour's Welfare Reforms*, Bristol, Policy Press.

Rainbird, H., Munro, A., Holly, L. and Leisten, R. (1999) 'The future of work in the public sector: learning and workplace inequality', *ESRC Future of Work Programme Working Paper*, no.2, November.

Saraga, E. (2004) 'Who counts as a refugee? Personal lives and the shifting boundaries of citizenship' in Lewis, G. (ed.) *Citizenship: Personal Lives and Social Policy*, Bristol, The Policy Press in association with The Open University.

Sennett, R. (2003) *Respect: The Formation of Character in a World of Inequality*, London, Allen Lane/The Penguin Press.

Showstock Sassoon, A. (1996) 'Complexity, contradictions, creativity: transitions in the voluntary sector', *Soundings*, no.4, Autumn, pp.183–94.

Social Exclusion Unit (2004) Homepage, http://www.socialexclusionunit.gov.uk/ (accesssed 19 January 2004).

Taylor, P. and Bain, P. (1998) 'An assembly line in the head: the call centre labour process', *Industrial Relations Journal*, vol.30, no.2, pp.101–17.

Taylor, S. and Tyler, M. (2000) 'Emotional labour and sexual difference in the airline industry', *Work, Employment and Society*, vol.14, no.1, pp.79–95.

Williams, J. (1993) 'What is a profession?: Experience versus expertise' in Walmsley, J., Reynolds, J., Shakespeare, P. and Woolfe, R. (eds), *Health, Welfare and Practice: Reflecting on Roles and Relationships,* London, Sage/ Open University Press.

CHAPTER 3

Retiring Lives? Old Age, Work and Welfare

by Beth Widdowson

Contents

1 Introduction

Extract 3.1 Mrs Pullen

I don't think I mind being old, I try very hard to accept that I am old, but what makes it harder is that people think that old age is a write-off ... The reason it's brought home to you with such a jolt is because you give up work. You have to give up work – suddenly ... You see, I've spent many, many years in a job ... As I came up to retirement [at 60] I decided I really wanted to stay on for a couple more years and spend some time organizing my retirement. In fact it didn't work out ... so I decided I had to retire ... first I was anxious about whether I would be going the right way about acquiring a pension ... I am not managing on the [state] pension ... But I was also worried about the lack of companionship. No, not really that, more the daily social round. There were people there at work to talk to, to grumble to; they talk to you, you've had that for years and taken it for granted ... The thing about life at work is that it has to run along these rails, so you feel safe inside the rails. When you've given up work there's no timing, no guidelines, nothing. I was absolutely bewildered. As I came up to leaving work I was bitter, cynical and very cross that I couldn't stay at work at least one more year ... [W]hen I was at work free time often got taken up with getting ready for work. ... I did [look forward to having more time to myself when I retired], of course I did. I thought that was lovely and I liked the idea of not having to jump when somebody said ... I felt all these things at the same time. I really believe that it's the most difficult thing I have done in my life.

(Ford and Sinclair, 1987, pp.107–9)

Age and ageing are clearly part of our personal lives. Many experiences we hold to be private, intimate or unique in our own biographies are likely to be defined or anchored by age. Yet, 'aged' experience, such as being a young person, is powerfully shaped by the social policy context within which it is located (**Thomson, 2004**; **Goldson, 2004**). In this chapter we explore the way in which older age has been socially constructed, and focus particularly on how the identity of being an 'old age pensioner' (OAP) developed during the twentieth century. Examining the role that different social policies played in shaping this social construction, we look at the implications this had for the way older people experienced their personal lives during the period. Finally, we consider how the identity of being an OAP began to unravel at the turn of the twentieth century: a period in which the life course of older people became more fragmented and uncertain.

Extract 3.1 offers insights into one person's experience of being an OAP. Mrs Pullen had been retired for two years when interviewed in the mid 1980s, and her account gives insights into what this experience meant to her. It also allows us to see how aspects of the social are implicated in giving shape to the personal life she describes.

ACIVITY 3.1

Take a moment to think back over Extract 3.1. How, and in what ways, is the social implicated in shaping the experience Mrs Pullen describes?

COMMENT

Work – defined in terms of paid employment – or, more specifically, being excluded from work, perhaps represents the most prominent way the social is evoked within Extract 3.1. The experience Mrs Pullen describes seems predicated on the assumption that waged work is something that she, as an older person, is excluded from. This becomes evident if we reflect on the language she uses. While retirement is clearly something she looked forward to, her actual experience of this nonetheless reflects strong feelings of compulsion. So, for example, she says 'you *have* to give up work ... I *had* to retire'. As we move further through the extract, she reports feeling 'bitter' and 'cynical' about the compulsion she experienced. The second way the social is evoked involves her reference to the state pension. This firmly connects her personal life to the public domain of the welfare state. She reports feeling 'anxious' about obtaining the pension and indicates that she is not 'managing' on the income it furnishes. The overall impression generated by the extract is that this feature, combined with her exclusion from work, constituted her experience of retirement as one characterized by difficulty as she struggled to 'manage' both her immediate 'transition' out of paid work, and its aftermath. It further evidences how Mrs Pullen's experience of ageing, and becoming older, was constructed through the interplay of work and welfare, and that this constituted a key life transition.

The interplay between the different aspects of the social Mrs Pullen describes – between paid work and state welfare – are clearly implicated in shaping the personal life she outlines. Indeed it seems to represent a defining or critical moment in the context of her biography: marking a point where her identity as a 'worker', and the various contemporary meanings which attach to it (**Mooney, 2004**), becomes eclipsed by that of being 'retired'. The feelings she gives voice to are profoundly individual in the sense that they are grounded in her own biography. However, the association she describes between chronological age, retiring at 60 (or 65 if she had been a man in the same period), and being defined as 'old', can be seen as exemplifying the experience of many older people in the UK in the latter part of the twentieth and early part of the twenty-first century. As we will see below, by the 1960s and 1970s the accepted orthodoxy was that the 'normal' period of full-time employment ceased at 60 or 65 years: ages that also became conventionally defined as the point at which 'old age' started (Harper and Thane, 1989).

Yet, just as this orthodoxy was becoming cemented, fault-lines emerged. The 'right' or 'entitlement' of people to retire at 60 or 65 years, or to take early retirement in their fifties, was increasingly scrutinized towards the end of the twentieth century. So much so that during the early part of the twenty-first century it seems that we are bombarded on an almost daily basis with media reports forecasting some form of 'crisis' mapped around being or becoming older. For example, warnings of a 'pension gap' and 'pension shortfalls' are routinely wielded, along with prescriptions that we will need to work longer, save more, or do both if we are to realize anything more than a relatively impoverished, if longer-lived, older age. At the same time, companies like B & Q, Nationwide, and Marks and Spencer are highlighted and praised for their commitment to recruit and retain older workers. While at national government level, New Labour in response to European Union (EU) directives is, at the time of writing, drafting anti-age discrimination legislation. This is scheduled to be introduced by 2006. When enacted, this legislation is likely to make it illegal to discriminate against people on the basis of their age, in areas like paid employment, and health and social care services.

Nationwide plan for older workers

NATIONWIDE building society at the end of last year introduced a retirement age of 70 for its 15,000 employees.

Good on you, Nationwide. Other organisations are also keen on the idea of flexibility. Marks & Spencer, for instance, has no retirement age at all, letting people retire at any age after 50.

Old is a dangerous age

Still planning to retire at 65?

Bishops, judges and vets go on till 70. So might the rest of us

Figure 3.1 'Old' An uncertain age?

Anthony Giddens, a prominent sociologist, has added to these debates by calling for a fundamental re-think of the way the welfare state constitutes the identity and experience of older age in the post-war period. Thus, as the end of the 1990s he asserted:

> The concept of the pension that begins at retirement age, and the label 'pensioner', were inventions of the welfare state. But not only do these not conform to the new realities of ageing, they are as clear a case of welfare dependency as one can find ... We should move towards abolishing the fixed age of retirement, and we should regard old people as a resource rather than a problem.
>
> (quoted in Blackburn, 2002, p.24)

Irrespective of whether being older constitutes part of our present or future personal identity, two things are clear. First, the way it is constituted is changing. Second, shifting intersections of work and welfare are likely to play a crucial role in shaping this process of change in the future, just as they did in the past. In order to examine these processes of (re)constitution, this chapter aims to look at how:

Aims

- Experiences of being an older person are shaped through a historical and **mutually constitutive** process involving an interplay between the personal, work and welfare; and the points of continuity and difference this interplay illuminates.
- Personal experiences of being older are constituted not only through age divisions, but also through loci of social difference and inequality organized around class, (dis)ability, ethnicity, gender, 'race' and sexuality.
- Different social theories – Marxist, feminist, Marxist-feminist and post-structuralist – have attempted to account for, and give shape to, the personal lives of older people.

mutually constitutive

2 Making the 'house' into a 'home'? The enduring legacy of the 1834 New Poor Law

In this section, we explore how experiences of being an older person in the nineteenth century were constituted through the operation of the 1834 New Poor Law Act and the processes of industrial change that ran parallel to it. We examine the way this constructed the lives of older people as 'other' to the emergent 'normal' (adult, relatively youthful, male paid worker) and trace its legacy to reveal points of continuity and change.

2.1 Older lives and the shadows of the workhouse: mediating 'welfare' through the threat and control of the 'House'

For much of the nineteenth century, the experience of public welfare by older working-class people was mediated through the local administrations of the 1834 New Poor Law Act (a separate Act was introduced in Scotland in 1845) and the deterrent of the **workhouse** that provided its spine. The Act enshrined a particular set of social relations underpinned by the dominant liberal political ideology of laissez-faire. Predicated on a philosophy of non-state intervention, this ideology advocated minimal state intervention as the best guarantor of individual and social well-being. Work – defined as paid employment – occupied a privileged status within the social relations constructed by the ideology informing the Act. Elements of this remain in the present as the privileging of paid work continues to circumscribe social policies like welfare to work (**Fergusson, 2004**), and the over-arching two-tier principle that has informed public welfare policies in the post-war period. This principle – discussed further in section 3.2 – effectively privileges the

workhouse

benefit entitlements of social groups with relatively continuous records of full-time, paid employment. In public welfare terms, this privileging of paid work in the nineteenth century was mobilized through the principle of 'less eligibility'. Stipulating welfare recipients should have a harsher standard of living than paid workers, this principle lay at the heart of the 1834 Act: constructing public state welfare as the option of last resort in a mixed economy of welfare comprising private charities and family support.

The majority of older paupers experienced the Poor Law through the administration of outdoor relief. Involving small payments to support life outside the confines of workhouse walls, outdoor relief was used by older people to augment a patchwork of other income and support sources (paid work, charity, family). This meant older people often struggled to support a bare subsistence; as well-known and widely reported studies of poverty conducted by Charles Booth and Seebohm Rowntree at the end of the nineteenth century and early part of the 1900s indicated:

> the aged, when past work are dependent on someone; either on their children or on the [Poor Law] guardians or on the charitable or on all three. They very often live very hard lives and one of the most striking features throughout is the extreme smallness of their means.
>
> (Booth, 1894, quoted in Thane, 2000, pp.175–6)

total institutions

Around a quarter of older age paupers were subject to indoor relief. That is, they were workhouse 'inmates' and so inhabited regimes characterized by many of the features Goffman (1961) later described in his ground-breaking work on '**total institutions**'. Goffman coined this concept to capture the way large-scale institutions, like prisons and asylums, work to strip away the complex personal and social identities people carry with them when entering such institutions. Workhouses were literally that – places organized around reasserting and instilling the ethic and discipline of 'productive' work among their inhabitants. Their often imposing structures both symbolized and enforced the work ethic: the latter mediated through a regime in which all aspects of inmates' personal lives were scrutinized, managed and controlled. For instance, male and female inmates were segregated from each other. Such policies acted to strip away and regulate the space through which inmates could experience and express their individual autonomy – in terms of sexual and other forms of personal identity. Indeed, the control of workhouses could even extend into death, as Poor Law Authorities could supply the corpses of unclaimed paupers to surgical schools for dissection (Richardson, 1989, p.248).

Well-founded fears of the workhouse became an embedded feature of working-class mythology. Often dominating local landscapes, they represented a constant reminder to working-class people of the threat to liberty and autonomy which a failure to adhere to the capitalist work-ethic promised. The physical and symbolic shadows cast by workhouses, therefore, extended well beyond the personal lives of inmates, as the experiences of many living outside their walls involved a constant struggle to avoid entering their harsh regimes. Oral history testimonies offer powerful insights into the lengths people would go to in order to avoid entering the 'House', and how they would struggle to prevent family members from entering these draconian environments (Hussey, 2001). Indeed, the resonance of these fears continue to shape the consciousness of those living in the present, long after the real threat of the workhouse has passed (Richardson, 1989).

The number of older people in workhouses always remained small. However, figures show a marked and steady escalation over the second half of the nineteenth century. In 1851, 3 per cent of the population in England and Wales aged 65 and over were in workhouses. By the turn of the twentieth century this had risen to 5 per cent of the population (Thane, 2000, p.172). This feature can partially be explained in terms of the changing nature of employment over the period.

social model

Processes of capitalist industrialization and factory manufacture were expanding and becoming consolidated as employers increased their efforts to control the labour process and promote increased levels of productivity. The social and organizational context of paid work clearly has implications for the construction of worker identities, and what aspects of this become constituted as 'normal'. This point has been powerfully mobilized by the '**social model**' of disability, and the emphasis it gives to social as opposed to individual and/or biologically reductionist explanations of inequality mapped around differences of the body or the mind (**Shildrick, 2004**; Hughes, 1998). So, as the pace of work escalated during the nineteenth century, the boundaries between those constructed as 'fit' and 'unfit' to work were redrawn. Increasingly constituting workforce bodies as units of effort and labour, particular forms of physicality became emphasized. Bodies of social groups constructed as 'lacking' the productive effort required by new and intense rhythms of work – older people, people defined as disabled – were thereby constructed as 'other' through processes of labour market discrimination and marginalization (Hancock and Tyler, 2000; Laws, 1997). In the absence of widespread pension and retirement policies, workhouses therefore constituted the most obvious available 'welfare' solution to accommodating bodies constructed as being 'past' work, or 'worn out' by work.

In tandem with the increasing pace of work, other processes were changing the demography of workhouse populations in the early part of the twentieth century. This point is illustrated by Extract 3.2.

ACTIVITY 3.2

Read through Extract 3.2. As you do so, note how the workhouse population at Maldon in 1930 differs from that in 1870. Imagine yourself inhabiting the workhouse in both periods. What is the main difference between these two periods? How is this explained?

Extract 3.2 The changing demography of workhouse populations

At Maldon, relief lists show older people coming to dominate the workhouse in both absolute and percentage terms. In 1870, Maldon contained a highly diverse range of inmates: a six-month period ending in March of that year shows that the workhouse admitted 306 people, 81 (around 27 per cent) of whom were 60 and above. By the same six-month period in 1930 the sum of older people at Maldon represented 143 from a total of 257, a growth in percentage terms of 29 per cent ... [N]umbers of children admitted ... [fell] from 94 to 13 ... Popular and government distaste had slowly grown for mixed institutions, in which old and young, the sick and the healthy, the honourable and the feckless, the moral and the immoral could mingle. Answers to the varied social, physical and spiritual needs of this combined population were increasingly sought in separate institutions ... Single mothers were to reside in maternity homes and, after the Children's Act of 1908, orphaned or abandoned children were to be boarded out in children's homes or with foster parents.

(Hussey, 2001, p.200)

COMMENT

spatialization
specialization

Perhaps the first thing to note is that as an older person in the Maldon workhouse of 1930, you would be living in an environment where older people comprised the majority population. That is, you would inhabit a space that had become increasingly constituted through age relations – with the workhouse becoming constructed as the space and place of older people. Your experience of older age would, therefore, have been informed by processes of **spatialization**. In addition, and more by default then design, interrelated processes of **specialization** would have shaped your experience. Thus, sections of the workhouses' former population were no longer present as aspects of their personal identity– being a child, being defined as disabled – were emphasized; resulting in their relocation to specialist institutions like orphanages and asylums for people defined as having mental or physical impairments (Hughes, 1998). Involving a series of 'dividing up' practices, these processes of spatialization and specialization were articulated through a number of state-level reforms that would have both directly and indirectly shaped your experience as an older workhouse inhabitant in 1930 (Laws, 1997; Foucault, 1973, 1977, 1979).

2.2 Older lives and elder care homes: care and control

The de facto constitution of workhouses as 'older' spaces can be viewed as representing a precursor to public elder care homes as these developed later in the twentieth century. Indeed, the numbers of older people in such care homes today remains consistent with the 5 per cent of older people inhabiting workhouses at the end of the nineteenth century (Midwinter, 1997). Constituted as sites of care rather than control, these homes have nonetheless been subject to considerable critical scrutiny by social policy analysts. Their work chimes with investigations of the institutionalization of other social groups constructed as having 'special needs'. Emphasizing the complex relationship between care and control, such investigations demonstrate the tensions between the two; with care relations providing a medium through which various forms of control can be exercised (**Fink, 2004**; **Goldson, 2004**; **Shildrick, 2004**). Further demonstrating how institutional environments profoundly shape individual experiences in ways that deny and delimit social rights of representation, autonomy and privacy are the in widely reported accounts of elder and child abuse among 'cared for' groups in institutional settings. However, institutional care can also involve subtler, but nonetheless invasive, forms of control. This is illustrated by the interview extract below, in which Mrs Hatter describes a typical day in her life as an elder care home resident in the 1980s.

Extract 3.3 Mrs Hatter

Well, I get up by half past six, between six and half past, and of course it takes a bit longer to get dressed now ... Then we have a cup to tea about seven, and they come and give you a tablet ... I don't need it but you have to take it from them so then I put mine down the sink. Breakfast is at half past eight ... We get a cup of tea around quarter past ten but I've already told them I won't bother this morning because I don't want them coming in. After breakfast you just have to sit ... I do an awful lot of just sitting! They bring more tea and you can have a biscuit but then at half past five it's supper ... But I tell you what: least said, best said about lots of things here ... [There was a knock at the door and an attendant came in without waiting for a reply. He did not seem to have to come in for any particular reason and looked around and went out again.] You see, that's the trouble with this place [she whispered]. Often they don't even knock. I told them not to come in today.

(Ford and Sinclair, 1987, pp.34–5)

The presence of paid carers in shaping Mrs Hatter's experience of living in residential care is clearly important. As we saw in Chapter 2, paid carers intervene in some of the most intimate aspects of our personal lives: a feature that shapes the experiences of both carer and those for whom they care. In the account Mrs Hatter provides, it is apparent that the interventions of paid carers and her response to them give structure to the day. It is also clear that dimensions of 'control' are present: a feature that evokes subtle forms of resistance as Mrs Hatter attempts to define and maintain her personal boundaries and space. Therefore, although workhouses represented a harsher and more overtly controlling environment for older (and other) social groups, the controls mediated through practices of care in elder residential homes of the present are also apparent. This theme of control marks an important point of continuity between the two periods, in terms of constituting and delimiting how older people living within such environments experienced and experience their personal lives.

The growth of specialized elder care places such as sheltered housing, residential and nursing homes, provided the basis for an increasing commodification

commodification of care, and so created a growing and largely low-paid sector of care workers, as we saw in Chapters 1 and 2. Further, the composition of this workforce both mirrors and reproduces ingrained patterns of inequality mapped around differences of class, gender, and ethnicity. Further, these patterns of labour market inequality, as suggested below, often have a negative effect on the retirement incomes of such low-paid workers.

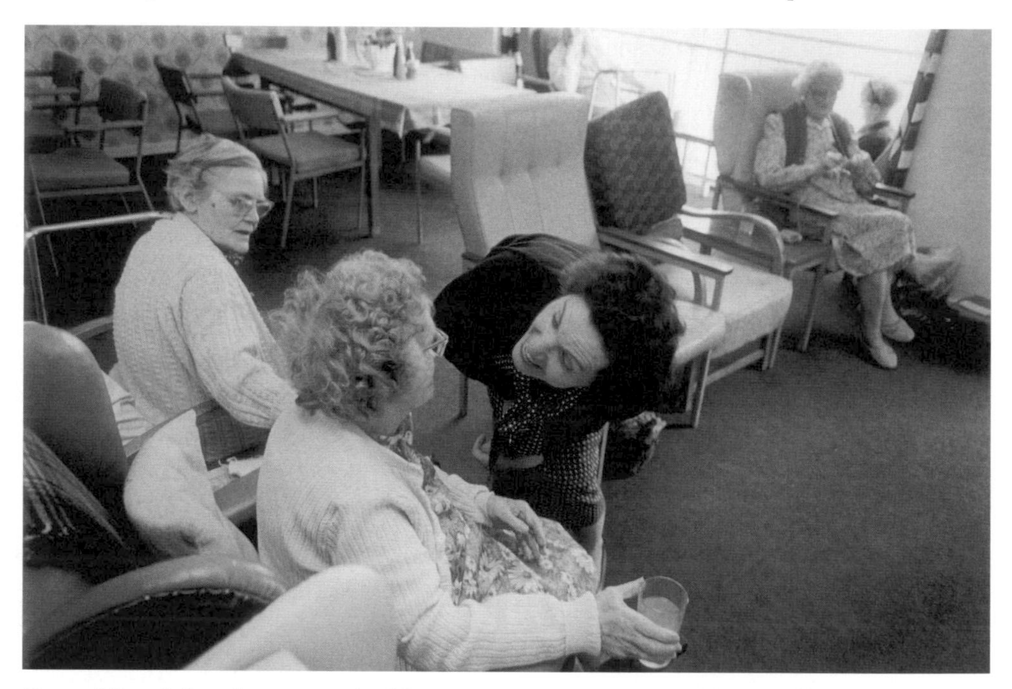

Figure 3.2 A female carer with older women residents in a public elder care home

ACTIVITY 3.3

Take a moment to study Figures 3.2, 3.3 and 3.4. As you do, think about the ways in which older people are constructed within them. Now read Extract 3.4, which describes the marketing of Sun Cities, a number of 'designer' retirement communities in the USA. What images of old age are suggested by this extract? How, and in what ways, do these differ from the constructions of older people represented in preceding images?

Extract 3.4 Sun Cities

Coloured brochures show golfing couples on a fairway in front of an artificial pond ... Other images include a team of women syncronized swimmers, lawn bowlers and a couple in formal wear enjoying 'fun-filled evenings out on the town in neighbouring Palm Springs' ... The level of activity in these images suggests that the reader could be perusing a brochure for a resort instead of a retirement community. The resort image is continued in an advertisement for a 'very affordable resort-style getaway' that invites potential residents to 'try it before you buy it'. Packages 'include deluxe accommodations, free 18 holes of golf, and access to our multi-million dollar recreational facilities, where you

> can play tennis, lounge by the pools and more'. Like cruise ships, Sun Cities are relatively self-contained. But, as with a cruise, residents can 'go ashore' to purchase goods and services not available on board.
>
> (Laws, 1997, p.97)

Tortoise goes into retirement

TORTOISES are famously retiring creatures, but few can be said to have officially retired, like the one belonging to Jean and Ernest Ray from Bicester, pictured above.

Tortoise – as he is known – is now a proud resident of a new retirement cottage, and he's probably the only pet truly old enough to qualify to live there!

His owners, Jean, 71, and Ernest, 93, have had Tortoise since 1947, when they found him in a pet shop in Battersea. The couple have bought one of McCarthy & Stone's St Birinus retirement cottages in Wessex Way, Bicester.

Jean said: "This is the first time any of the three of us have moved away from Battersea in our entire lives. Tortoise spent many years on a balcony in a block or flats, where he didn't have much space – now he can roam around freely."

Figure 3.3 New owners of a private retirement cottage

COMMENT

The images and extract are all focused on the experience of being older, and offer descriptions and representations of older spaces. Figure 3.2 showing older people with a carer in a public care home is perhaps one we are most familiar with. Here, it is clear that older people are being constructed as dependent, and so 'other' to the socially constituted 'norm' of an independent adult (paid) worker. Studies exploring the way in which older people are constructed within photographic representations indicate this to

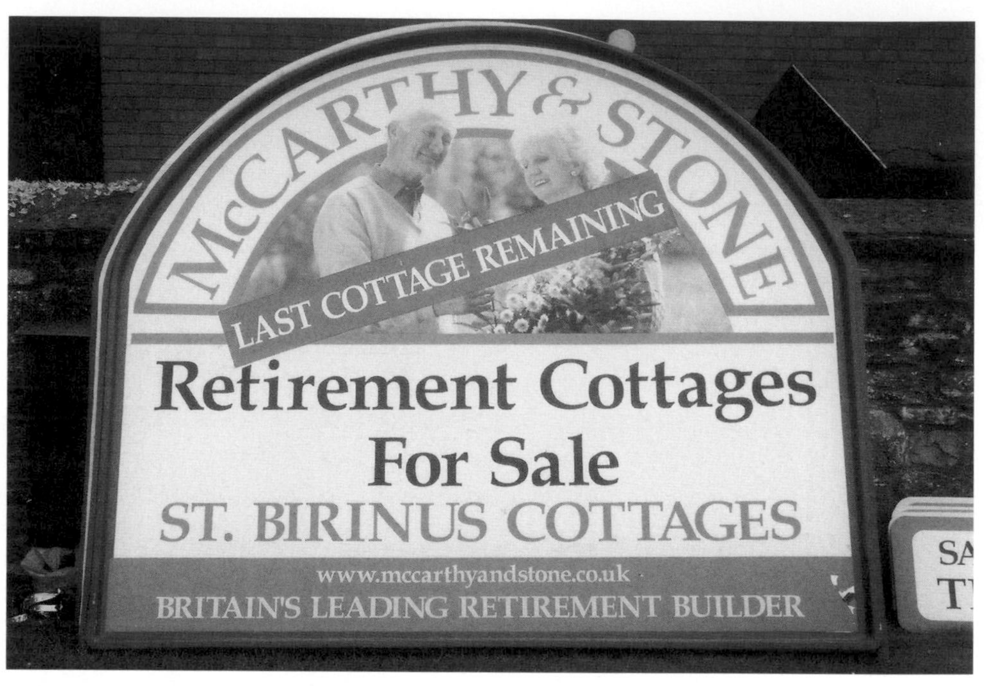

Figure 3.4 Marketing private retirement cottages

be the dominant form of representation (Johnson and Bytheway, 1997). Thinking about the inter-generational relationship suggested by the care home image, it is also apparent that older people are being shown as dependent on younger people; a feature concealing the ways older people themselves are often implicated in giving care – to spouses, adult off-spring, grandchildren, friends and others (**Fink, 2004**).

Figure 3.3 also sets the two older people apart, in the sense they have just bought a private residential development specifically built for older people. The humour of the image and the related newspaper feature suggests an implicit **ageism**, but nonetheless seems to invite us to share in the good fortune of the couple as they move into their new and relatively spacious accommodation. The marketing image for similar retirement 'cottages' in the same area, depicts a seemingly idealized image of an older, heterosexual white couple. The image of older age outlined in Extract 3.4 turns on active and conspicuous consumption. Living in Sun Cities is clearly only an option for relatively affluent older people who have accumulated significant amounts of wealth during their working lives. Further, it suggests an image of older age characterized by a lack of ethnic and sexual diversity, and exudes a sense of a youthful, mobile and independent older age.

ageism

All three contrasting representations are anchored in the material; in that the personal lives they represent evidence obvious and apparent economic differences and inequalities permeated by class inequality. This is most apparent in the case of Extract 3.4, which is predicated on wealth, and contrasts sharply with the relatively impoverished background of the elder care home. As we move through the following section, try to hold these different images of older age in your mind and think about how the different policies we explore might have been implicated in shaping the personal lives they suggest. For example, what kind of pension and employment biography might you imagine for the Sun Cities resident or the women living in the elder care home?

3 Pensions policies: the making and remaking of old age through the intersections of work and welfare

In this section we look at the way in which the personal lives of older people have been socially constructed through pensions policies over the last century. As we saw above, welfare policies and changes in employment in the latter part of the nineteenth century and early part of the twentieth century constructed the personal lives of older people as 'other' to the emergent normal of relatively younger, 'independent' paid workers. Here, we explore the way pensions policies during the twentieth century became implicated in this process, and the complex set of interests that informed this. Enabling older workers to be 'divided up' and divided out of the domain of paid work, we explore how pension policies provided a conduit through which the personal lives of older people could be constituted in and through the domain of private and public welfare. We also investigatge how shifting boundaries between work and welfare informed this process in a way that both reflected and reproduced social differences and inequalities of not only age, but also class, (dis)ability, gender, 'race' and sexuality.

3.1 The 1908 Pensions Act and the inter-war years: counting age and discounting older workers

state pension
non-contributory

The 1908 Pensions Act represented the first time welfare interventions in older age were based on chronological age. It set the pension age at 70 years. Prior to this, although chronological age was often noted in Poor Law records, it did not constitute the basis of eligibility. Rather, age, and older age specifically, was constructed in terms of particular forms of embodiment, with older people being defined as those whose bodies were 'past' work, 'worn out' by work or 'too frail' to work. The **state pension** was tax-funded and therefore **non-contributory** – meaning people did not have to make contributions to the scheme in order to receive the pension it offered. Trade unions and some women's organizations in the period leading up to the Pensions Act had stressed the importance of this feature, arguing that even small contributions would be prohibitive for low-paid workers and women. However, few other concessions were made to the demands of these organizations. In a period when the average trade union member died at the age of 50 years (Vincent, 1991, p.27) modest calls for a pension age of 60 or 65 were ignored. This feature effectively excluded many older, working-class people, as Extract 3.5 indicates. It is taken from a married women's work survey conducted by the Women's Industrial Council (1909–10), and refers to an interview with one woman, aged 69 and widowed, living in a Yorkshire woollen weaving district.

Extract 3.5 Not yet 70: a long and hard wait for the pension

She began work at the age of four selling tea-cakes from house to house; at eight began rag-picking and afterwards became a weaver ... [She] has worked regularly whenever she could get the work to do, until recently, when her health had broken down ... Her husband always sickly ceased work in 1886 and she had to work for both and meet the expense of a protracted illness. ... She went back recently to rag-picking at 10s. a week, in the hope of keeping off the Poor Law until she can claim her pension ... In spite of all her troubles and hard work [she] has brought up a large family. She has had fifteen children, of whom seven are living and 22 grandchildren. It is touching to learn that this old lady, having been ill, was fearful she would not live long enough to draw her old age pension.

(quoted in Thane, 2000, p.277)

The old age pension was set at a very low level. Consequently, it could only support subsistence in conjunction with a patchwork of other income sources older people had previously put together as recipients of Poor Law out-door relief. Only British citizens were eligible to claim the pension. Coinciding with a rise in anti-Semitism, this saw Jewish immigrants increasingly being denied citizenship, and so prohibited from any entitlement to the pension offered by the 1908 Act (Thane, 2000, p.223). Despite these and other limitations, take-up of the pension far exceeded government expectations. Just under half a million people claimed the first old age pension when it was paid in January 1909, around two-thirds of whom were women (Thane, 2000, p.226).

The 1908 Pensions Act represented the first time connections were drawn between chronological age and pensions, but it did not signify retirement in the sense of an end to paid work. However, such connections had become a sedimented part of state practice with respect to sections of its own workforce.

occupational pensions

Occupational pensions had long been a feature of the employment contract in the civil service. In the mid 1850s the system was reviewed and a retirement age of 60 years was recommended based on the argument that this represented 'an age at which bodily and mental vigour often declines' (Thane, 2000, p.240). Though not formally implemented, most civil servants did retire in their sixties; creating an apparent paradox. Thus, at the beginning of the twentieth century, relatively affluent (and overwhelmingly male) civil servants officially became 'old' earlier in life than did older poor women, who were not officially defined as 'old' until they reached 70 years of age and qualified for a pension under the 1908 Act.

Occupational schemes in the private sector were generally imposed from above by employers and usually only extended to male skilled workers (Thane, 2000). When making the case for the introduction of occupational schemes, the economic or business case was invariably emphasized, as the following quote from a speech made in 1906 by Seebohm Rowntree on the introduction of such a scheme in his family's firm indicates:

> Many firms may hesitate to adopt a Pension Scheme ... but it is probable that these very firms carry heavy costs in 'hidden pensions' without realizing the fact. If a firm establishes a liberal pension scheme it will doubtless at the same time fix a definite retiring age and will thus never find itself with a number of old workers ... not only does the firm lose on [these workers] individually but their presence tends to lower the pace and lessen the output of the whole shop.
>
> (quoted in Thane, 2000, p.243)

The emergence and ascendancy of Taylorist or scientific forms of management in the early part of the twentieth century further enhanced the control employers had exerted over labour through the expansion of the factory system in the nineteenth century. As we saw in Chapter 1, these developments have been cogently explored through a Marxist lens in the work of Braverman (1974). Driven by a strong deskilling dynamic, the introduction of assembly-line production marked the culmination of this process, as the ever increasing speed of the line provided the mechanism through which the skill and autonomy of labour became subordinated to the machinery of manufacture. Sections of the labour force constructed as being unable to keep up with this intensification of paid work were thereby constituted as surplus labour through processes of marginalization and exclusion, their participation in paid employment being represented as a threat or drain on levels of efficiency and productivity.

In 1925, the Conservative Government introduced the Old Age and Widows and Orphans Contributory Pensions Act. As the Act's title suggests, this involved a contributory insurance scheme as opposed to the non-contributory, tax-funded base of the 1908 Pensions Act. It reduced the retirement age from 70 to 65 years for those making contributions under the 1911 National Insurance Act. Predicated on the 'male breadwinner' model, the overwhelming majority of married women were only included in a subordinate and conditional sense as 'wives' or 'widows'. Effectively constituting their personal lives in terms of the domestic domain, this gendered hierarchy of entitlement also constituted the personal lives of men through the construct of full-time and continuous paid employment. Further, the inclusion of pensions provision under the umbrella of the 1911 National Insurance Act meant that the pension was effectively furnished through a tax on the working classes as the principle transfer of resources took place within the working classes (Vincent, 1991, p.37). Many of those in low-paid and insecure forms of employment struggled to pay this, while those not covered by the scheme continued to rely on the 1908 Act, and so were not eligible for a state pension until they were 70 years old.

collectivist
social reformist

In the period between the 1908 and 1925 Acts, Britain's political landscape changed significantly. Marked by intense class struggles and the mobilizations of the first wave of feminists, the period witnessed the extension of democratic voting rights by 1918 to all working-class men and some working-class women. Full female suffrage was achieved by 1928. **Collectivist** or **social reformist** political ideologies became increasingly influential. Arguing that proactive state intervention represented the best guarantor of individual and societal well-being, these challenged the laissez-faire, liberal ideologies which had dominated the British political arena during the nineteenth century.

The high levels of unemployment which characterized the Depression of the 1930s make it difficult to discern the impact of the 1925 Act on retirement rates, in that older people reporting themselves as 'retired' may actually have been expressing their difficulties in re-entering the labour market (Thane, 2000, p.281). Further, the link between unemployment and retirement became a significant feature of pension debates during the 1930s, with those on the Left and Right representing retirement as the solution to the problem of unemployment. This operated to construct the personal lives of older workers as outside the domain of paid employment, and within the arena of public and private welfare policies, and often coincided with calls for the exclusion of much younger workers. For instance, a draft of the 1929 Labour General Election Manifesto argued:

> Every year about 400,000 young children, inadequately educated and inadequately trained, are brought into the labour market; while at the other end there are hundreds of thousands of aged persons who are compelled by poverty to struggle for employment.
>
> (quoted in Macnicol, 1998, p.228)

patriarchal

The emergence of new industries and the expansion of clerical occupations, together with assembly-line production, witnessed a growth in female paid employment and off-set levels of unemployment amongst women. At the height of the Depression, women's employment fell by 3 per cent compared to 11 per cent for men (Walby, 1996, p.167). Nonetheless, **patriarchal** exclusions of women, and particularly married women, from paid employment provided one of the strategies through which the state, employers and trade unions representing the interests of male workers sought to address the problem of unemployment. Constructing the problem of unemployment as one that impacted on the lives of younger, married men, the personal lives of women, irrespective of their employment or marital status, were thereby defined in relation to unpaid labour in the domestic domain.

Connections between gender, class, age, unemployment and pensions were particularly emphasized by the National Spinsters Pension Association (NSPA). Founded in 1935, the NSPA was a broad-based organization representing the interests of lower middle-class and working-class unmarried women, which campaigned on the single issue of reducing unmarried women's retirement age to 55 years. Membership of the NSPA was particularly strong in and around textile towns in the north of England, which had traditionally employed large groups of women. Arguing that its members found it difficult to retain or enter paid employment once they reached middle age, the NSPA's calls for a reduction in the retirement age of unmarried women were linked to the role unmarried women often played as informal carers (**Holden, 2004**). Suggesting that 'dutiful' daughters often found it difficult to re-enter the labour market after they had left to care for elderly parents, the NSPA highlighted the way this could jeopardize any previous pension contribution record, as the following account from 1938 by one of its members indicates:

> I was in domestic service, and paid from the commencement of the Insurance Act ... My age is 56 in June next, just now I am looking after my aged mother who is 86 and have had to help to support her for the last 36 years. I found I could not keep on paying, I was in benefit till last year and now they write and tell me it has lapsed.
>
> (quoted in Macnicol, 1998, p.313)

Figure 3.5 On the march: single 'sisters' unite through the NSPA, London, 1939

In making this point, the NSPA not only illuminated the way in which the lives of its members often involved both unpaid care work and paid employment, it also underlined the tension that pension entitlements predicated only on the latter generated for older women. This tension, as we see below, shapes the lives of many married women too, given their frequent involvement in unpaid care work. However, the NSPA's demands were articulated in a highly sectional manner. Its calls for a reduction in the retirement age extended to unmarried women only and not to women per se. Further, in making this demand, it expressed considerable antagonism towards other groups of women, arguing that unmarried women's contributions represented an unfair subsidy to the pensions of widows, orphans and the wives of male pensioners.

The sectionalism informing the NSPA's platform alienated feminist organizations and other women within the labour movement. For example, feminist groups representing the interests of middle-class women expressed concerns that a reduction in single women's retirement age would make employers more likely to discriminate against them. Nonetheless, the NSPA did receive support from textile unions, though not from the Trade Union Council (TUC), which preferred to campaign for reducing the retirement age of all women. In 1940, the retirement age of all women was reduced to 60 years. However, despite claims made on its own behalf, it appears that the NSPA's campaign played little or no part in this policy shift. Though applied to all women, the reduction in retirement age reflected an apparent recognition that married women were on average five years younger than their husbands; a policy shift that effectively defined women's older age relative to that of men (Thane, 2000).

ACTIVITY 3.4

Take a few minutes to reflect on the divisions of class and gender illuminated by the NSPA's demands, and the rationale informing the eventual reduction of women's retirement age to 60 years. Think about how you might explain these from both a class and gender perspective. As you do, try to identify the intersections and tensions involved.

COMMENT

As we saw in Chapters 1 and 2, Marxist perspectives foreground inequalities mapped around class divisions, while feminist accounts emphasize differences and inequalities organized around gender. Analyses developed by Marxist-feminists attempt to explore the interplay between class and gender, and the processes of compromise and tension informing it (Walby, 1986; Skeggs, 1997). Processes of industrial restructuring in the textile industry had generated significant levels of unemployment during the period surrounding the NSPA's campaign. The support of textile unions for a reduction in the retirement age of single women involved an expression of class solidarity with sections of its female constituency. However, the unions' support can also be interpreted as articulating the patriarchal interests of their working-class male members, as a reduction in the retirement age of single women would have removed a section of female labour from the textile workforce and consolidated the position of male workers within the industry.

The TUC's position, echoed by the Chamberlain Government's ultimate decision to reduce the retirement age of all women to 60 years, can be interpreted as reflecting similar patriarchal interests. Further, from a feminist perspective, this gendered policy also reinforced the controls that men were able to exert over women's unpaid work in the domestic domain. Thus, the retirement of older women from paid employment did not signal their 'retirement' from unpaid work in the home, but rather reinforced women's role in this regard. Recent studies have demonstrated how the concept of retirement is profoundly gendered and thus highly problematic for women, as women's retirement from paid work rarely involves their retirement from unpaid work in the domestic domain. Constructed around men's experience of, and exit from, paid work, the concept does not therefore accurately reflect older women's experience of work – which often involves a continuity of unpaid labour long after their retirement from paid work (Arber and Ginn, 1995).

3.2 Beveridge and the move towards a 'species of universalism'

The 1942 Beveridge Report laid the foundations for the 1946 National Insurance Act and the creation of the welfare state. This represented a central plank of the post Second World War reconstruction. State pensions were viewed as offering a basic minimum income to old people, thereby constituting them as part of the nation's social citizenry. However, cultural and economic imperatives privileging the needs of the young over those of the old meant older people's citizenship rights were in reality limited even while they were rhetorically being extended. Beveridge, therefore, argued that 'it is dangerous to be in any way lavish in old age (until) adequate provision has been assured for all other vital needs, such as the prevention of disease and the adequate nutrition of the young' (quoted in Phillipson, 1998, p.68).

universalism

The **universalism** underpinning the social citizenship offered by the welfare state was always partial and contingent (**Lewis and Fink, 2004**). Bearing the imprint of nineteenth-century welfare policy distinctions between the 'deserving' and 'undeserving', this was mobilized in the post-war period through a two-tier principle. The first tier involved contributory benefits available to 'the deserving' with continuous employment records. The second turned on means-tested benefits paid to groups without such an employment record, who were thus constructed as 'less deserving'. However, this was compounded in the case of the universal pension in that the low level at which it was set – equivalent to 19 per cent of average male manual earnings in 1948 – meant that those without other income sources needed to apply for means-tested supplementary benefits. Further, the stigma attached to such means-tested benefits, and the nineteenth century Poor Law associations they evoked, meant that many of those who were eligible did not to apply. This is illustrated by the following quotations from interviews Peter Townsend conducted with older people in the early 1960s, while researching their family lives in the East End of London:

> I don't want to tell people all my affairs. They ask too many questions. I'm proud, I suppose.
>
> The pension is different. Everyone has a right to that. But the other, they have to come round every six months or so asking questions.
>
> (quoted in Elder, 1977, p.66)

old age pensioner

Further, those who did apply were frequently subject to invasive forms of official surveillance into their personal lives, as the following quotation from Gladys Elder's life history account of being an **old age pensioner** (1977) makes clear:

> Most pensioners recognize that when the social security officer calls he is more likely to be on the watch for any small improvements in their income, rather than those tell-tale signs that the allowance is too small. Indeed, pensioners admit that they actually appear guilty by the way they excuse themselves, feeling compelled to underline their gratitude and minimize their needs. This feeling of being suspected and being watched is a further indignity suffered by those on Supplementary Benefit.
>
> (Elder, 1977, p.39–41)

The extension of the contributory principle to the Basic State Pension (BSP) – in which entitlement is predicated on participation in full-time employment over a complete working lifetime – also meant that, as with the 1925 Act, women's personal lives continued to be defined through an assumption of their dependence upon men. Hence, although women's work was seen as playing an important part in the post-war reconstruction, it was conceptualized primarily in terms of unpaid work in the domestic domain. Women's personal lives thereby remained constituted in terms of unpaid labour; a gendered feature that the Beveridgean pension reforms both reflected and reinforced. This was mobilized through provisions allowing married women in employment to opt out of the BSP by making reduced National Insurance contributions, together with the half-test making void any contributions married women made to the BSP unless paid for more than half their married life. Effectively discouraging married women from contributing towards a pension in their own right when in employment, these features were further articulated through the principle of derived benefits. Linking pensions and other benefit entitlements to marriage, this principle operated to compensate women for their labour market exclusion and marginalization by reinforcing their dependency on men. In so doing, it also privileged the personal lives and experiences of some groups over others, by discriminating against lone mothers and gay and lesbian couples who lived their personal lives outside the heterosexual coupling dictated by marriage (**Carabine, 2004**).

pensioner movement

All of these factors gave the rhetoric of universalism a somewhat hollow sound for older people. So, for example, the National Federation of Old Age Pensions Associations (NFOAPA) – a radical, socialist, working-class **pensioner movement** which incorporated 400 branches in England, Scotland and Wales by 1940, and boasted a local membership in excess of 3,000 by 1942, concluded that the Beveridgean pension reforms meant that 'it was not a new world we are heading for, but merely a patched up old one' (quoted in Macnicol, 1998, p.388).

Britain was not unique in adopting a contributory approach to providing incomes in older age as the USA and most other European countries had introduced similar contributory state schemes by 1960 (Blackburn, 2002). In so doing, they had all moved towards what Blackburn characterizes as a:

> species of 'universality' still qualified by work record, gender and status. Thus the workings of the contributory principle ... meant that they did not in fact offer all citizens of a country, let alone all residents, a pension once they reached the age of retirement. ... There was a gendered assumption that men were the breadwinners and that women would be covered by wives and widows claiming entitlement via their husbands' work record. In practice, women were to be excluded from the full pension if they or their husbands did not have a consistent contribution record ... Many unmarried women had no proper entitlement and were obliged to apply for Assistance. ... Itinerant workers, or ethnic groups suffering social discrimination, or non-registered unemployed, or ex-prisoners, might all find it difficult to attain the minimum contribution record.
>
> (Blackburn, 2002, p.61)

Throughout the 1960s and 1970s a series of studies illuminating the extent, scale and experience of poverty among older people living in the UK were published (Townsend and Wedderburn, 1965; Coates and Silburn, 1970; Shaw, 1971). Informing a wider 'rediscovery of poverty', these studies offered compelling evidence of how the UK's 'species of universalism' translated into an impoverished experience of retirement for many older people. The persuasive power of such studies was further reinforced by the research methods deployed. Leaning heavily on in-depth interviews, these yielded a rich array of personal accounts that provided powerful insights into what if felt like to be older and poor in the UK during this period.

These accounts were further reinforced by biographical-based testimonies that older people offered of their own lives. A seminal text here involves Gladys Elder's (1977) *The Alienated: Growing Old Today*. In this, she blends her own life history with personal accounts offered by other older people, together with evidence from interviews and secondary sources. A staunch campaigner for older people's rights, Gladys Elder – a Scottish, working-class woman – was 75 years old when she completed the book, and died shortly before its publication in 1977. The autobiographical account she offers exemplifies the complex and mutually constitutive interplay between 'the personal' and the political. By offering a politicized reading of her own personal life, she shows how this was shaped by wider structures and processes of power, and the intersections of class and gender.

ACTIVITY 3.5

Read through the quotation below. Now read Extract 3.6, involving an interview with Miss Stewart. As you do, think back to 'Tony's story', Extract 3.1 in Chapter 1, in which Tony describes his experience of retirement and the factors that informed this. Try to answer the following questions:

- What do these accounts tell us about the interplay between age, class and gender?
- What kinds of research methods have been used to generate this data?

> One London Borough Council ran a sheltered workshop where pensioners packed thousands of contraceptives for a derisory hourly rate. I talked to a voluntary worker who had visited one such workshop, and she confirmed my fears of exploitation when she told me that she had seen a forewoman stop an old lady from talking. If she had allowed them to chat, she explained, others would follow suit instead of getting on with their work.
>
> (Elder, 1977, p.41)

Extract 3.6 Miss Stewart

... the headmaster ... said I was teacher material. Mum and dad wouldn't sanction it ... [s]o I sat the labour exam and left school at 13 ... I'd got a friend who was working in the dressmaking trade so I went in along with her and stopped in that all my life from being 14. I worked for one firm from when I was 26 until I finished work. ... When I was into my twenties I used to think if I'd gone to be a school teacher I should have been on a good pension. It's not only the money because I liked school, but I suppose – well, perhaps money has something to do with it. (I worked until I was 71). I was on my own. I've never been married, because I looked after mother and dad ... I paid [National

Insurance] until I was 65, and so got some extra on my pension. But they started to take a lot in tax, and so I thought to myself, well that's that, I'll [retire and] struggle through some way and manage.

(Ford and Sinclair, 1987, pp.76–8)

COMMENT

All of the accounts speak to the experience of being older and working class. Those described by Miss Stewart and Tony (Chapter 1, Extract 3.1) also give insights into the way that their experiences were inflected by gender difference. However, the quotation featuring the London sheltered workshop and Extract 3.6 speak to this experience in different ways, as their production hinges on different methodological entry points. The approaches all involved the deployment of qualitative methods – observation, interviews – and so offer relatively in-depth and rich insights into the experiences outlined. However, while the interview with the voluntary worker in the shelter workshop offers some insight into the kind of working environment that circumscribes the lives of its older workers, the feelings and experiences of the workers themselves are absent. A greater understanding of the workshop and its practices may have been generated if some of these workers had been interviewed in tandem with the voluntary worker. In contrast, in the case of Miss Stewart and Tony, we have access to the voices of people at first hand – albeit mediated through their interviews with researchers.

The analysis that accompanies 'Tony's story' exemplifies the strength of the life history or biographical method used by Numa Murard (2002). This grew out of the oral history method. Informed by a strong emancipatory tradition, it aims to give voice to the personal experiences of marginalized and excluded social groups; voices that might otherwise be overshadowed and subsumed within the accounts offered by more powerful social groups like employers and policy-makers (**Holden, 2004**; Bornat, 2002). The life history or biographical method allows Murard to tease out the significance of the language Tony uses when describing his personal life. In this way, he is able to illuminate the complex feelings and social factors informing Tony's transition out of work and into retirement. Applying a similar approach to the account offered by Miss Stewart helps us to understand features characterizing her transition from work to retirement. It enables us to see how her experiences of work and retirement are inextricably linked to earlier moments in her biography – having to leave school at 13, working in a traditionally female and low-paid industry, combining this with care responsibilities for elderly parents. Further, all of these features can be seen as evidencing the way in which her personal life is constituted through difference and inequalities mapped around intersections of class and gender.

4 From 'OAP' to 'third age' citizen? Fractured transitions and uncertain lives

The 1970s marked a period in which the cessation of the 'normal' period of full-time employment at 60 or 65 years had become the accepted orthodoxy. The personal lives of older people had thus become constituted outside the domain of paid employment and within the arena of public and private welfare. As we illustrated in the preceding section, pensions, organized around fixed ages of retirement based on chronological measurements of age, played a crucial role in this process. Further, as also noted, the implementation of pension policies reflected and reproduced entrenched patterns of inequality organized not only around age but also around social divisions of class, (dis) ability, ethnicity and gender. Reflecting the legacy of the nineteenth-century Poor Law, the low level of the Basic State Pension (BSP) meant many older, working-class people experienced impoverished personal lives. This feature was compounded for women, as the gendered assumptions underpinning the post-war settlement 'species of universalism' continued to constitute their identity in relation to unpaid work.

However, just as this orthodoxy was becoming established, it began to unravel. The mobilization and agency of older people informed this process. Pensioner movements continued to organize for greater rights and social equality for older people. Likewise, the late twentieth century saw older voices being mobilized around the concept of the 'third age' – an age loosely defined as consistent with older age and starting at the conventional age of retirement. This reconceptualization turns on constructing older age as a period of opportunity and choice, and so challenges dominant and negative images which construct older people as a 'burden' or dependent. Potentially freed from the compulsions of paid work, it is suggested that the idea of the 'third age' creates space for older people to become more active and fulfilled citizens, through involvement in education, leisure, family, unpaid work and meaningful and satisfying forms of paid work (Laslett, 1989).

Further, 2003 heralded the election of the first pensioner to the Scottish Parliament, purely on a manifesto of promoting greater social equality for older people. However, the agency of older people was not the only factor that informed the unravelling of this orthodoxy. Important structural changes, policy shifts and a complex set of other interests were also involved. In combination, these factors suggest that the personal lives of older people in the twenty-first century are likely to be characterized by increasing levels of risk and uncertainty. This section offers selective insight into some of these features, and the implications they represent for older people.

Figure 3.6 Older people at work, leisure and protest

4.1 Moving towards greater equality in older age? Old Labour, pension reform and the continuity of age-based labour market discrimination and exit

The mid 1970s heralded a period in which the Labour Government introduced a series of reforms in the pension arena that potentially promised a more secure retirement for older, working-class people. Stripping away some of the patriarchal assumptions that had informed the Beveridgean settlement, the 1975 Social Security Pensions Act promised particular benefits for women and other low-paid workers. For example, the dual aspects of many women's lives – involving both unpaid and paid work – were explicitly acknowledged through the introduction of Home Responsibilities Protection (HRP) in the BSP. This meant that women whose contribution records had been interrupted due to unpaid care responsibilities would still qualify for the BSP as long as they had paid contributions for at least twenty years, as opposed to the previous full working lifetime requirement of 39 years. Married women's entitlement to make reduced National Insurance contributions when in employment was also abolished. As the personal account below indicates, opting out of the BSP had meant that, for some women, 'retirement' marked their continuing involvement in low-paid and exploitative forms of employment, rather than a break from it.

> I was married and had five children. I worked all my life, domestic, hospital cook, mother's help, foster mum etc. but because my [NI] stamps weren't paid in full I get £51 per week with my ex-husband's insurance to help. I cannot live on this as my common-law husband does not keep me ... I have four jobs: cleaning.
>
> (quoted in Ginn et al., 2001, p.96)

This, together with the abolition of the half-test referred to above in section 3.2, promised to equalize women's state pension entitlements. Labour also linked the level of the BSP to inflation or average pay. This provided the basis for the pension to increase to its highest level – equivalent to 20 per cent of average male earnings – since its introduction: a level still less than half that of equivalent pensions in France and Germany (Blackburn, 2002, p.67). At the same time the continuity of the derived benefit principle, which makes pensions and other benefits entitlements contingent on marriage, then and now, perpetuates a series of anomolies and inequalities. For example, in a period when marriage and motherhood are becoming increasingly disconnected, cohabiting women are excluded from the rights that married women have to derived state pensions (Ginn et al., 2001, p.46). Further, because marriage institutionalizes a specific form of sexuality (**Carabine, 2004**), derived pension benefits based around this not only exclude heterosexual cohabitees but also exclude gay, lesbian and transgender couples.

Throughout the 1970s and 1980s, the disengagement of older workers from the labour market escalated (Walker, 1991; Phillipson, 1998). A number of factors informed this trend. The contraction of industries employing older workers represented one factor, as did the growth of unemployment. The latter feature triggered government action that actively promoted the process. For example, in 1977 the Job Release Scheme was introduced in order to combat the unemployment of younger workers by encouraging women aged 59 years and over and men aged 64 years and over to leave their jobs.

Reinforcing the constitution of older people as 'other' and dependent, the exclusion of older people from, and their marginalization within, the domain of paid employment, has spawned a series of studies over the last twenty years. These combined to inform the development of a structured theory of dependency (Walker, 1991). This theory has dominated the way in which the lives of older people have been explained from the late 1970s. Involving a blend of Marxist and social reformist forms of analysis, intersections of social inequalities and older age are explained in terms of the twin effects of minimal levels of state welfare pension support and labour market discrimination and exclusion. Further, changes in the domain of paid employment involving the growth of 'non-standard', part-time and other forms of 'flexible' working (see Chapter 1) constituted a multiplicity of different 'work-endings' and retirement pathways, as Phillipson's (1998, p.62) review of research in the area demonstrates. Drawing on a series of different studies, conducted from the 1980s onwards, he identified the following pathways:

- forced early retirement
- voluntary early retirement
- redundancy
- (dis)ability/long-term sickness
- informal care
- unemployment
- discouraged worker
- state retirement.

4.2 Reconstituting older peoples' personal lives in uncertain times

The multiplicity of different 'work-endings' at the close of the twentieth century, combined with the increasing mobilization of older people through pensioner and 'third age' movements, effectively destabilized the institution of retirement and the associated orthodoxy that older age began at the age of 60 or 65 years.

neo-liberal

However, voices from within the pensioner movement were marginalized in the process of reconstitution that ensued. A **neo-liberal** redrawing of the boundaries between paid work and welfare resulted in welfare becoming increasingly contingent on paid work, with the role of the private sector being privileged over the state in the pensions arena. Further, while the Conservative administrations of the 1980s and early 1990s set the parameters of this redrafting, subsequent Labour administrations (while tinkering at the edges) have continued to work broadly within neo-liberal parameters initially set by the Thatcher administration.

Index-linking of the BSP to earning was one of the first things sacrificed in the Conservative Government's mission to rein in social security costs in the 1980s. By breaking the link to earnings, and pegging increases in the BSP to prices alone, the Thatcher administration provided the basis on which the real value of the pension would fall sharply in the medium and long term. Equivalent to just over 20 per cent of average male earnings in the early 1980s, its value in the late 1990s had reduced to just 14 per cent. These and other pensions reforms are estimated to reduce public spending by £12 billion over the next 50 years (Ginn et al., 2001, p.49). The costs of this, measured in terms of the way older working-class people experience their personal lives are profound. Further, New Labour shows no sign of reversing this policy.

Reneging on promises to reinstate the earnings related link to the BSP during its first term of office, this amounts to a covert phasing out of the BSP; the value of which is scheduled to fall to only 10 per cent of average earnings by 2030 (Blackburn, 2002, p.286). This feature is likely to increase pensioners' reliance on mean-tested benefits and the deterrent effect associated with such benefits because of their nineteenth-century Poor Law associations. For example, around 2 million older people eligible to claim means-tested income supplements did not do so in 2000, and government estimates suggest this trend is likely to continue. This means that a large section of the UK's older, working-class population – and particularly older working-class women who tend to have least access to other sources of income – will continue to inhabit personal lives lived in or on the margins of poverty (Ginn et al., 2001).

Partly prompted by the low level of pension provision furnished by the welfare state, around 50 per cent of workers in the UK are members of occupational pensions. Although traditionally promising a relatively affluent retirement future for their members, the security once offered by occupational pension schemes has recently become subject to increasing risk and uncertainty. For instance, large, high profile companies like ICI, Sainsbury and BT closed or changed the terms of their occupational pension schemes from the late 1990s, to their workers' disadvantage.

Jeopardizing the secure retirement incomes of the traditionally privileged middle classes and skilled sections of the working classes, such moves on the part of employers triggered significant levels of political and industrial protest, as both young and older workers mobilized to safeguard their pension rights (Blackburn, 2002).

Figure 3.7 'Pension rage' 1990s

The increasing uncertainty and risk around occupational pensions is likely to compound the inequalities traditionally informing this form of private pension provision; inequalities which, as we see below, are clearly organized around intersecting differences of class, ethnicity, gender and (dis)ability.

ACTIVITY 3.6

Look at Figures 3.8 and 3.9. What do they tell us about who is likely to benefit most and least from occupational pensions in terms of class, ethnicity and gender?

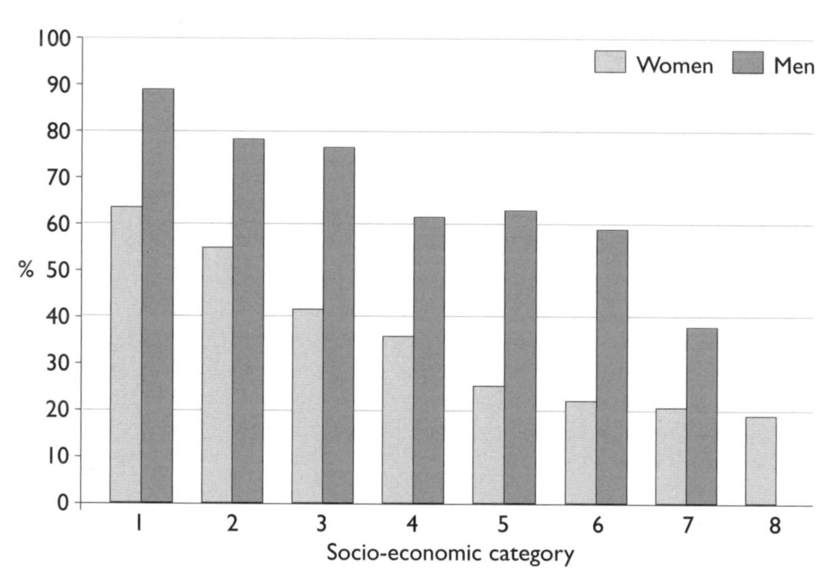

Figure 3.8 Gender and class breakdown of UK population with an occupational pension (Source: based on Ginn et al., 2001, p.55, Figure 4.3)

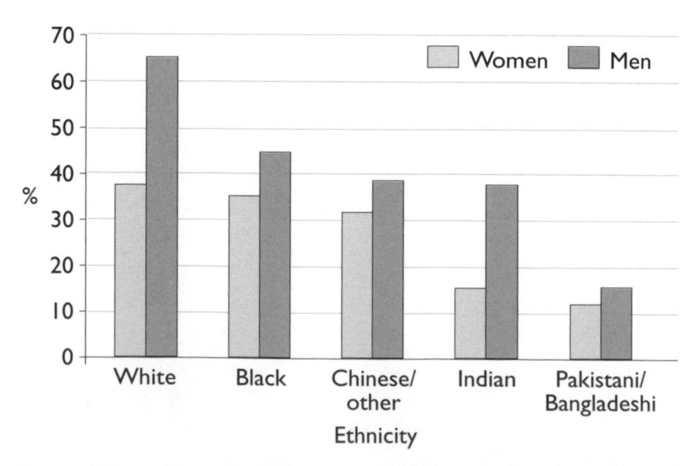

Figure 3.9 Gender and ethnicity of UK population with an occupational pension (Source: based on Ginn et al., 2001, p.56, Figure 4.4)

Figure 3.10 Taking responsibility for your pension: never too young to start?

Occupational pension schemes are predicated on full-time employment over a complete working life. Feminist analyses emphasize how this is most consistent with traditional male working patterns, as women's experiences of paid work are more likely to involve periods of part-time employment, and time taken out of the labour market in order to meet unpaid care responsibilities. Occupational pension provision, therefore, closely reflects labour market divisions (Ginn et al., 2001), the constitution of which reflects and reproduces ingrained patterns of inequality of not only gender but also class, (dis)ability and ethnicity. Women are disproportionately concentrated in low-paid work that is defined as unskilled or semi-skilled. Likewise, racialized minority groups and people defined as having mental and physical disabilities continue to be excluded from, or marginalized within, the labour market. Having significant implications for income levels generated during their working lives, this pattern of inequality is mirrored in the retirement incomes of older people (Bardasi and Jenkins, 2002).

Further, the growth of 'non-standard forms of employment', like part-time working, promises to exacerbate the situation. For example, a total of 223 people responded to a questionnaire survey on 'Women and Pensions' conducted by the Pre-Retirement Association and Help the Aged in 1995 (Peggs and Davies, 2001, pp.92–3). Indicating that all respondents in full-time employment had been offered an occupational scheme, it revealed that employers had not offered part-time workers such a pension scheme. For example, one part-time employee indicated: 'Even if I wanted one [a pension], which I do, I haven't got one – I've got no choice' (Peggs and Davies, 2001, p.92)

Moreover, while employers are now legally required to treat full-time and part-time workers equally in this respect, the insecure nature of some types of part-time work makes it difficult for part-timers to plan for the longer term. This feature means they often have little or no real personal choice in securing an income for their older age – as a second survey respondent indicated:

> I would [join] now...if I had a full-time job...But I think because I regard this job as temporary ... [and] employment has always been conditional ... it's always been very difficult to plan for the future.
>
> (Peggs and Davies, 2001, p.93)

Like the Conservative administrations preceding it, New Labour's downgrading of the state's role as a pension provider has gone hand-in-hand with moves to privilege the role of the private sector. In the case of the Conservatives, this involved offering workers financial incentives to take out personal private pensions. This policy culminated in the widely reported pension mis-selling scandal of the mid 1990s, as it became clear over 20 per cent of the 7 million employees who subscribed to such private pensions had succumbed to high pressure sales tactics and had purchased expensive and inappropriate schemes (Phillipson, 1998). In the case of New Labour, this privileging of the private sector, and the implication that pension provision represented an individual responsibility, involved the launch of Stakeholder Pensions (SHP) in 2001.

While introducing reforms aimed at avoiding a repeat of the mis-selling scandal that plagued the Conservative government's private pension policy, New Labour's SHP policy, and the assumptions on which it is based, nonetheless raises a number of important questions – as we see below.

ACTIVITY 3.7

Read through the following quotation, taken from government publicity material, aimed at promoting take-up of SHP. As you do so, think about the kind of personal life it constructs and assumes.

> Parveen is a self-employed fitness trainer in her late twenties, earning around £14,000 a year. She has recently bought a flat with a friend, and now that the initial expenses are out of the way she thinks she can afford to start a pension. She has considered the information on stakeholder pensions, including the 'decisions trees' and this helped her to decide that a stakeholder pension would be suitable for her.
>
> (quoted in Blackburn, 2002, pp.314)

Now read Extract 3.7 by Polly Toynbee, which offers a commentary on the quotation above, and see how your responses compare.

Extract 3.7 'Prudent Parveen is the chancellor's fictitious saver'

Parveen is the star of the government's guide to stakeholder pensions. ... So who is this model citizen ...? ... She seems surprisingly certain about her future life. ... [S]he is quite sure she will not have children and will not need rainy-day money, her savings untouched until she is 65. Parveen is a paragon of prudence. With a mortgage on £14,000 pay (she plainly lives far from the South East), 'Guardian' [newspaper] writers, using average mortgage figures, reckon that after tax, national insurance, council tax, mortgage and energy bills, she has about £6,480 a year or £135 a week to live on. So what made her decide that a pension was right for her? Shouldn't she have put any savings into an ISA where she could get the money back if she ever gets sick, loses her job or just needs it? Did she have a financial adviser? If so, she was mis-sold this pension. I called the Department of Social Security in whose stakeholder guide Parveen features. Would it be possible to interview her? ... 'Um, well, actually she's an example.' Oh? 'She's not real.' Just as well since a real-life Parveen

> might be going hungry to pay for her old age. No, Parveen is just a decoy duck, displayed to entice real life Parveens. There are, the government says, five million sitting ducks at whom stakeholders are primarily targeted. They earn between £10,400 and £20,000, and currently have no pensions. However research suggests that most people on below average earnings can't afford pensions. (A third of those who take out personal pensions default within a few years, losing most of their money.)
>
> (Toynbee quoted in Blackburn, 2002, pp.314-5)

Take up of SHP has been much lower than anticipated, with research indicating that half of the target audience have not heard of the scheme, and that two-thirds have no plans to take out a SHP. This suggests that large sections of the UK's population will continue to rely on the ever-diminishing returns of the BSP and the impoverished personal life this frequently involves.

5 Conclusion

As we have seen, pensions are both inherently personal and political. Pensions and other social policies are heavily implicated in shaping the way older people experience their personal lives, and the way in which these personal lives have become constructed as 'other'. Providing a means by which older lives could be 'divided up' and divided out of the domain of paid employment, and reconstituted through the arena of public and private welfare, this process is also informed by differences and inequalities of class, (dis)ability, ethnicity, gender and sexuality. Pension reforms implemented by the Conservatives and New Labour in the latter part of the twentieth century and early part of the twenty-first, place the onus of responsibility on individuals to build a financially secure older age. They are therefore consistent with other welfare reforms that emphasized notions of **responsibilization** implemented over the same period. Bearing the continuing legacy of the nineteenth-century Poor Law, the extent to which such policy prescriptions can be reconciled with the uncertainties and inequalities that shape the lived reality of employment and retirement is however questionable.

responsibilization

The apparent 'freeing ' of individuals from the putative fetters of the welfare state has further been articulated through wider, sociological readings of the position of older people in society. These have some resonance with the demands older people make for themselves through pensioner movements and arguments mobilized through the concept of the 'third age'. So, for example, Giddens has asserted:

> Pensioner – the very term sounds incapacitating and in fact designates a dependent person. Welfare systems here define old age, not as a status worthy of respect, but as a disqualification from full membership of society. Ageing is treated as 'external', as something that happens to one, not as a phenomenon actively constructed and negotiated ... The majority of people over 65 want to do

> some form of paid work ... There simply isn't enough money to go around to continue to finance universal pension schemes ... Older people can and should ... be regarded as part of the wealth creating sectors of society.
>
> (Giddens, 1994, pp.170–84)

There are some clear similarities between the reading of older age developed by Giddens and that offered by older people within 'third age' and pensioner movements. Both foreground notions of agency to suggest that older age is not an imposed event. Nor is it, they suggest, something that simply happens. Instead both readings conceptualize older age as an experience and identity older people actively shape for themselves. In making this case, deterministic and reductionist explanations of older age – whether based around the dynamics of capitalism or biology – are effectively challenged. Nonetheless, there are a number of important tensions between the two, and these coalesce around the issue of work. Giddens' prescription for a secure personal life and full citizenship in older age turns on privileging a continuity of paid employment and a residual welfare state, as a way out of older age dependency and poverty. In contrast, voices within the pensioner movement emphasize expanding the choices available to older people: choices which, they argue, should include the option to make the transition into retirement and out of the compulsions of paid employment without fear of living their lives in poverty. Further, as the uncertainty and politicization of pension provision escalates, younger people are adding to these calls, as they anticipate their own older age. In making this case, they are challenging the legacy of the nineteenth-century Poor Law, the work–welfare relation it enshrines, and the shadow of poverty it continues to cast over the personal lives of many older people.

Further resources

Gilleard and Higgs (2000) more fully develop some of the ideas explored by Giddens (1994) in their useful and comprehensive introduction to post-structural readings of older age. Elder's (1977) life history account offers compelling insights into the intersections of class and gender through a socialist lens, and represents an early and interesting example of the life history and biographical method. Chamberlayne et al. (2000) provide comprehensive and thoughtful insights into biographical methods and their uses. The Joseph Rowntree Foundation's *Transitions After 50* research series involves a number of investigations into different aspects of older people's lives. Information about this series is available from the Foundation's website. In terms of journals, *Ageing and Society* is an excellent source of up-to-date research on various aspects of older people's lives, and related academic debates. Work, Employment and Society and *Critical Social Policy* both occasionally report on research around older age.

A wide range of relevant Internet sites are also available, including (all websites were last accessed on 13 January 2004):

- Joseph Rowntree Foundation – http://www.jrf.org.uk

- Age Concern England – http://www.ace.org.uk
- Centre for Policy in Ageing – http://www.cpa.org.uk
- The ESRC Growing Older Programme – http://www.esrc.ac.uk
- Ageing and Ethnicity Web – http://www.aeweb.org

References

Arber, S. and Ginn, J. (1995) *Connecting Gender and Ageing*, Buckingham, Open University Press.

Bardasi, E. and Jenkins, S. (2002) *Income in Later Life: Work History Matters*, Bristol, Policy Press and Joseph Rowntree Foundation.

Blackburn, R. (2002) *Banking on Death or, Investing in Life: The History and Future of Pensions*, London, Verso.

Bornat, J. (2002) 'Doing life history research' in Jamieson, A. and Victor, C.E. (eds) *Researching Ageing and Later Life*, Buckingham, Open University Press.

Braverman, H. (1974) *Labour and Monopoly Capital: The Degradation of Work in the Twentieth Century*, New York, Monthly Review Press.

Carabine, J. (ed.) (2004) *Sexualities: Personal Lives and Social Policy*, Bristol, The Policy Press in association with The Open University.

Chamberlayne, P., Bornat, J. and Wengraf, T. (eds) (2000) *The Turn to Biographical Methods in Social Science: Comparative Issues and Examples*, London, Routledge.

Coates, K. and Silburn, K. (1970) *Poverty: The Forgotten Englishmen*, London, Penguin.

Elder OAP, G. (1977) *The Alienated: Growing Old Today*, London, Writers and Readers Publishing Cooperative.

Fergusson, R. (2004) 'Remaking the relations of work and welfare' in Mooney, G. (ed.) *Work: Personal Lives and Social Policy*, Bristol, The Policy Press in association with The Open University.

Fink, J (2004) 'Questions of care' in Fink (ed.) (2004).

Fink, J. (ed.) (2004) *Care: Personal Lives and Social Policy*, Bristol, The Policy Press in association with The Open University.

Ford, J. and Sinclair, R. (1987) *Sixty Years On: Women Talk About Old Age*, London, The Women's Press.

Foucault, M. (1973) *The Birth of the Clinic: An Archaeology of Medical Perception* (trans. A.M. Sheridan-Smith), London, Tavistock. (First published in 1970.)

Foucault, M. (1977) *Discipline and Punish: The Birth of the Prison* (trans. A.M. Sheridan-Smith), London, Penguin.

Foucault,M. (1979) *The History of Sexuality, Volume 1: An Introduction* (trans. R. Hurley), London, Allen Lane. (First published in 1976.)

Graebner, W. (1980) *A History of Retirement: The Meaning and Function of an American Institution 1885–1978*, New Haven, CT, Yale University Press.

Giddens, A. (1994) *Beyond Left and Right: The Future of Radical Politics*, Oxford, Polity Press.

Gilleard, C. and Higgs, P. (2000) *Cultures of Ageing*, London, Prentice Hall.

Ginn, J., Street, D. and Arber, S. (eds) (2001) *Women, Work and Pensions : International Issues and Prospects.* Buckingham, Open University Press.

Goldson, B. (2004) 'Victims or threats? Children, care and control' in Fink (ed.) (2004).

Goffman, E. (1961) *Asylums: Essays in the Social Situation of Mental Patients and Other Inmates,* New York, Doubleday.

Hancock, P., Hughes, W., Paterson, K., Russell, R., Tulle, E. and Tyler, M.J. (eds) (2000) *The Body, Culture and Society: An Introduction*, Buckingham, Open University Press.

Harper, S. and Thane, P. (1989) 'The consolidation of old age and a phase in life' in Jefferys, M. (ed.) *Growing Old in the Twentieth Century*, London, Routledge.

Holden, K. (2004) 'Personal costs and personal pleasures: care and the unmarried woman in inter-war Britain' in Fink (ed.) (2004).

Hughes, G. (1998) 'A suitable case for treatment' in Saraga, E. (ed.) *Embodying the Social: Constructions of Difference,* London, Routledge in association with The Open University.

Hussey, S. (2001) 'An inheritance of fear' in Botello, L. and Thane, P. (eds) *Women and Ageing in British Society Since 1500,* Essex, Pearson Education Limited.

Jamieson, A., Harper, S. and Victor, C. (eds) (1997) *Critical Approaches to Ageing and Later Life*, Buckingham, Open University Press.

Johnson, J. and Bytheway, B. (1997) 'Illustrating care: images of care relationships with older people' in Jamieson et al. (1997).

Laslett, P. (1989) *A Fresh Map of Life: The Emergence of the Third Age*, London, Weidenfeld and Nicholson.

Laws, G. (1997) 'Spatiality and age relations' in Jamieson et al. (1997).

Lewis, G. and Fink, J. (2004) '"All that heaven allows": the worker citizen in the post-war welfare state' in Lewis, G. (ed.) *Citizenship: Personal Lives and Social Policy*, Bristol, The Policy Press in association with The Open University.

Macnicol, J. (1998) *The Politics of Retirement in Britain 1878–1948*, Cambridge, Cambridge University Press.

Midwinter, E. (1997) *Pensioned Off*, Buckingham, Open University Press.

Mooney, G. (2004) 'Exploring the dynamics of work, personal lives and social policy' in Mooney (ed.) (2004).

Mooney, G. (ed.) (2004) *Work: Personal Lives and Social Policy*, Bristol, The Policy Press in association with The Open University.

Newman, J. and Mooney, G. (2004) 'Managing personal lives: doing "welfare work"' in Mooney (ed.) (2004).

Murard, N. (2002) 'The shortest way out of work' in Chamberlayne, P., Rustin, M. and Wengraf, T. (eds) *Biography and Social Exclusion in Europe: Experiences and Life Journeys*, Bristol, Policy Press.

Peggs, K. and Davies, M. (2001) 'Women and pensions: perspectives, motivations and choices' in Ginn et al. (eds) (2001).

Phillipson, C. (1998) *Reconstructing Old Age*, London, Sage.

Richardson, R (1989) *Death, Dissection and the Destitute*, London, Pelican.

Skeggs, B. (1997) *Formations of Class and Gender*, London, Sage.

Shaw, J. (1971) *On Our Conscience: The Plight of the Elderly*, London, Penguin.

Shildrick, M. (2004) 'Silencing sexuality: the regulation of the disabled body' in Carabine (ed.) (2004).

Thane, P. (2000) *Old Age in English History: Past Experiences, Present Issues*, Oxford, Oxford University Press.

Thomson, R. (2004) 'Sexuality and young people: policies, practices and identities' in Carabine (ed.) (2004).

Townsend, P. and Wedderburn, D. (1965) *The Aged and the Welfare State*, London, Bell.

Vincent, D. (1991) *Poor Citizens: The State and the Poor in Twentieth Century Britain*, London, Longman.

Walby, S. (1986) *Patriarchy at Work: Patriarchal and Capitalist Relations in Employment*, Cambridge, Polity Press.

Walker, A. (1991) 'The social construction of dependency in old age' in Loney, M., Robert, B., Clarke, J., Cochrane, A. and Graham, P. (eds) *The State or the Market: Politics and Welfare in Contemporary Britain*, London, Sage.

CHAPTER 4

Remaking the Relations of Work and Welfare

by Ross Fergusson

Contents

1 Introduction

On 29 February 2000, a 6-year-old boy in his first year at Buell School, Beecher, in the town of Flint, Michigan, in the USA, took a .32 calibre handgun to school and shot 6-year-old Michaela Roland dead with a single bullet. The boy had been staying with his uncle because his mother, Tamarla Owens, had been evicted from her home for lapsing on her rent payments, despite working up to 70 hours a week in two jobs to maintain her two children. Tamarla Owens was not there that morning to see her son find the gun and take it to school because she had already set out on her three hour round-trip bus journey to Oakland County, where she worked as a waitress and as a bartender in Dick Clarke's American Grandstand Grill. She was required to make the journey as a condition of the State of Michigan's welfare-to-work programme.

Beecher is the one-time home of General Motors and a huge car production plant, long since derelict and surrounded by a community in which 87 per cent of children live below the official poverty line. With no work available nearby, Tamarla Owens joined the daily bus-full of workers who went to service the affluent residents of Oakland County in return for US$5.50 (about £3.70) an hour. Dick Clarke's restaurant chain sought special tax breaks for its service to the community in placing people on the programme.

In the County Sheriff's Office immediately after the shooting, Tamarla Owens's son was given crayons and paper. He drew a picture of a child, alone, beside a tiny house (see Figure 4.1).

Figure 4.1 Tamarla Owens's son's drawing

Tamarla Owens is a black lone mother. Her story was made famous in Michael Moore's Oscar-winning documentary film, *Bowling for Columbine* (2002), about the mass school shooting in Littleton, Colorado in April 1999. In the film, the driver of Tamarla Owens's bus says that she went to work every day.

Her manager at the Grandstand Grill commends her as a good worker. And the Sheriff argues forcefully that the welfare-to-work programme should be closed down, because it prevents parents with sole responsibility from caring for their children.

Figure 4.2 Tamarla Owens

The US 'workfare' programmes (as they are often known) of the 1990s have been celebrated as successes and taken-up as profitable private enterprises by firms as prestigious as Lockheed Martin, the giant armaments manufacturer, which runs many of them. The Temporary Aid for Needy Families Programme was established by the Personal Responsibility and Work Opportunity Reconciliation Act (PRWORA) of 1996. These programmes have been venerated as having solved 'the welfare problem' (Rogers, 1999; Clark and Hein, 2000; Peck, 2001). And they have epitomized the ways in which welfare policies are developed around particular constructions of personal lives, and go on to shape those lives in profound ways. Few will be as profound as the ways in which Michigan's programme shaped Tamarla Owens's life. But, despite the exceptional nature of the Buell School tragedy, Tamarla Owens's story carries within it many of the key narratives of the transformation of welfare policy through welfare to work. It is emblematic of them, in that Tamarla Owens is black, poor and a lone mother. But, it is also typical since it highlights a range of issues concerning how personal lives and social policies intersect. It raises questions about the sources of her poverty in a town whose main economic base has collapsed. It challenges social priorities when financial self-sufficiency and parental responsibility are in conflict. And it opens debate about whether the purpose of workfare is to save the state money, to reduce labour costs, to train an unskilled workforce or to discipline a population. Cutting across all these questions, Tamarla Owens's story raises issues about how 'race', gender, sexuality and class shape the ways in which 'the personal' is interpreted in the development of social policies, and how these policies might work to 'remake' those facets of the personal lives of welfare subjects. Addressing these questions, the issues they raise, and the theoretical frameworks they invoke, are the central aims of this chapter.

Where the articulation of welfare with work is closest, in workfare regimes like those of the USA, the impact of policy on almost every aspect of 'the personal' is potentially profound. For Tamarla Owens, it is not just daily routines that are directly determined by policy, but it is also how her life is ordered, the way she experiences the community she lives in, how it regards her, and who she becomes, that are affected. These also affect the personal lives of those around her – tragically so if the Sheriff's interpretation of events holds. But, in less extreme forms, in more moderate regimes that connect welfare to work, ways of conceptualizing rights and entitlements are shifting, 'common-sense' ideas about welfare are changing, and how welfare subjects are constituted is being reworked in ways which are built on, and have consequences for, how we understand personal lives. Understanding how welfare and work are connected in contemporary social policy does not just give us an insight into an important aspect of the workings of the welfare system. It also provides a significant way of understanding how individuals and groups become constituted as welfare subjects. The processes through which this takes place are the first and central theme of this chapter.

Though we know little of Tamarla Owens's personal history, it is likely that some aspects of her personal life resemble the stereotypical constructions and representations that underpin discourses which lead to workfare reforms. She will have been regarded as welfare dependent, since she lacked work, perhaps because she had limited skills or qualifications, and, especially, as she was a lone parent. The so-called 'trap' of needing to work to maintain children, but being unavailable to work while caring for them, has been the most intractable welfare conundrum with which governments grappled during the 1990s in pursuit of their commitment to reducing welfare spending (see **Thomson, 2004**). Pathologizing constructions of blackness, lone parenthood and welfare dependency became key discourses in the steady shift of welfare policies towards workfare. How welfare, in the form of income maintenance, touches the lives of different groups unequally is the second theme of this chapter.

The events in Flint, Michigan, raise critical questions about the social, political and economic purposes of workfare. Is it primarily helping to keep pay and taxes low and match people to jobs? Is it providing work experience that will help unemployed people into jobs? Or is it serving as a deterrent to Tamarla Owens and others having more children? The first of these questions imagines the purposes of workfare to be economic; the second views it as developmental; the third as disciplining personal conduct. Determining which of the three purposes of workfare is supportable and whether they are compatible or contradictory is the third theme of the chapter.

Assessing these explanations calls for evidence about the circumstances that give rise to workfare programmes. Most social scientists would also want to hear Tamarla Owens's own account of the programme and its impact on her personal life. But, her account alone would not allow us to reach an informed view about the programme. If we are to understand the programme's impact on personal lives in the wider context of welfare provision, taxation and labour markets, for example, we would need some broader evidence about its costs and effects on employment. We would want other accounts that represented a diverse range of people and experiences. We might also want to consider categories of people and evidence of inequalities in the ways they are affected. So, there is a wide range of evidence that would inform a debate about how workfare constructs the intersection of policies and 'the personal'. Finding appropriate evidence and judging its value for assessing workfare is the fourth theme of the chapter.

Assessing and interpreting evidence cannot be undertaken without a theoretical framework within which disconnected facts can be formed into a reasoned argument. No amount of evidence about the circumstances of those who are assigned to workfare will produce an assessment of it unless it is woven into a coherent theorized narrative. Four very different theories provide the framework for the chapter. Neo-Marxism focuses on the contradictory place of welfare in market-based societies committed to the maximization of profits. Post-structuralism looks at the networks of power that lie behind the relations of work and welfare, and aims to understand how the actions and conduct of unique, autonomous individuals are governed in them. And feminism looks at the distinctive position of women and at the production of differences and inequalities of gender, through the power relations of welfare structures and personal interactions of individuals. In addition, this chapter highlights key aspects of a neo-liberal approach, in particular neo-liberalism's concern with optimizing economic rationality and minimizing welfare to secure the unhampered working of markets.

Aims To summarize, then, this chapter aims to:

- Provide insights into the ways in which the relations between work and welfare are made and remade in different places and at different times.
- Consider how these changing relations contribute to constituting welfare subjects.
- Show how welfare provision that is connected to work affects the lives of different welfare subjects in different and unequal ways.
- Assess the relative influences and effects of the economic, developmental and social purposes of welfare programmes based on work.
- Identify appropriate evidence for assessing such programmes, and make a critical evaluation of it.
- Consider the different ways in which a range of theoretical frameworks make sense of work-based welfare, and interpret and assess evidence about it.
- Begin to develop a critical evaluation of these theoretical frameworks and their respective capacities to explain, justify or criticize work-based welfare.

Workfare is a particular way of remaking the relations between work and welfare, and it epitomizes some of the ways in which policies and 'the personal' intersect. The forms taken by these relations often shift at critical transition points in personal lives: at retirement, as Chapter 3 has shown; and when people begin work or become parents, as this chapter will show. To pursue the themes we have set out, we need, first, to trace some of the ways in which the relations between welfare and work have been repeatedly remade historically. Embodied in every different version of these relations are distinctive constructions of how 'the personal' has shaped policies and how policies have shaped personal lives.

2 The contingent relations of welfare and work: from workhouse to workfare?

As we saw in Chapter 1, everyday talk, public discourse and political debates sometimes treat the concepts of 'welfare' and 'work' as separate spheres of activity, or even binary opposites: welfare or work. This can occur in different ways, for example:

- an explicit connection is drawn between welfare and work, as though they were directly dependent upon one another: welfare and work, work for welfare, welfare to work;
- the connection is implicit: welfare and work as interweaving patterns over a lifetime;
- the connection is treated as an objective, perhaps in the phrase **welfare to work**;
- the dependency is more explicit, as in 'working for welfare'; and
- in some versions, it is clear that welfare is not offered without work, as is suggested by collapsing the two words: 'workfare'.

welfare to work

All these mixes of the concepts of 'welfare' and 'work' are captured in the word '**contingent**': it refers to a set of relations in which welfare and work necessarily connect, but in a very wide variety of ways, from potential link to complete interdependency.

contingent

It would be possible to take distinctive welfare systems and 'map' them according to the different ways in which the relations between welfare and work have been made at different times, for different social groups and in different places. But, even the briefest mapping leads rapidly towards an important, and perhaps rather startling, realization: the decades that followed the post-war welfare settlement in the UK were historically unique in a number of ways, because they established a degree of separation between the *entitlement* to welfare and the *obligation* to work.

Two points of contrast highlight this. In the UK, the involvement of the centralized state in the relief of the poor after the 1834 Poor Law Amendment Act made the contingent nature of welfare–work relations more highly visible than they had ever been. As Chapter 3 showed, the 'welfare' system drew unemployed men, their families and unmarried mothers into workhouses as their sole access to welfare, and so established the principle that state welfare was conditional on commodified work. On the same principle, a century later in the USA nationally provided state welfare began with Roosevelt's New Deal, and the Works Administration Programme, that allowed states to require the involvement of those seeking benefits in public works.

Between these two starting points, the welfare polices that took Tamarla Owens on the bus to Oakland County, and the recent development of welfare-to-work programmes in the UK, have two long and disparate histories. In the UK, the Poor Law shaped provision for the unskilled, for some women and for most racialized minority groups for the best part of a century. The conditional connection between welfare and work was incrementally relaxed for other groups between 1911 and the post-war settlement. From then until the late 1970s, as we have noted, welfare entitlement and work obligation remained much more loosely connected for *most* of the population.

In the USA, unconditional entitlement was largely restricted to lone parent families with dependent children. The pressures on them to participate in 'public works' or 'community-based' programmes grew during the 1960s, shifted towards a stronger emphasis on support and training in the 1970s, then began a transition from facilitative welfare to work incentives, to mandatory work-for-welfare conditions, with sanctions for those who refused or withdrew, during the 1980s and 1990s (Burghes, 1987; Peck, 2001). In 1996, the Personal Responsibility and Work Opportunity Reconciliation Act (PRWORA) made all benefit entitlement entirely conditional upon work, except for lone parents whose first child was below school age. This is the form of relations referred to as **workfare**.

workfare

A parallel trend affected the UK from the 1980s onwards, once the disruption of the post-war welfare settlement had begun (Lewis, 1998). At first, the focus was largely on facilitative incentives, and there was a gradual move towards job-search requirements, participation in workshops and careers advice and vigorous encouragement of lone parents to take work. In 1986, 16 to 18-year-olds lost all benefit entitlement and were required to join youth training programmes, many of which entailed work placement. In 1997, New Labour's New Deal marked the highly significant switch to mandatory forms of participation in work placement or training.

The contingent relation between work and welfare has moved – unevenly over time and place – between extremes of conditionality and separation, with long periods of more complex relations that varied for different social groups and between localities. Early in the twenty-first century, in the UK and the USA, there is a powerful trend towards a return to the conditional nature of welfare with which state involvement began. What underlies this pattern of the rise and fall of unconditional entitlement to welfare for some provides a key to understanding how welfare policies and personal lives constitute one another.

Three rationales have been used by those who advocate conditional relations between welfare and work. **Economic–regulatory** rationales are based on the workhouse principle of 'less eligibility' (see Chapter 3), which sought to encourage participation in the labour market by depriving workhouse inmates

economic–regulatory

of material comforts. If the conditions of welfare provision are equal to or better than the conditions of those earning the lowest rates of pay, they leave employers short of workers and exert inflationary pressure on wages. So, if the least skilled workers are to choose low paid jobs, not welfare, benefit levels must always be less desirable, or 'less eligible'. Here, Tamarla Owens's low wages provide some income and reduce the wage bill of employers like Dick Clarke.

personal–developmental

Personal–developmental rationales stress the importance of developing the skills base of the workforce in a competitive international economy. For those on the margins of work and welfare, enhancing employability is the key to reducing welfare costs and strengthening the economy. This may be best achieved by subsidized work experience, by job creation through public works programmes, or through education and training. Here, it is the skills gained from the experience of working that will benefit Tamarla Owens, while also serving the interests of restaurant-goers.

social–disciplinary
worklessness

Social–disciplinary rationales focus on the supposedly debilitating effects of welfare as a response to **worklessness**, stressing instead habits of industriousness to an impoverished and supposedly 'demoralized' class which becomes feckless and idle when lacking employment. On this reading, the workhouse was inspired by inculcating good behaviour and policing 'degenerate' behaviour. It is the moral effects of welfare dependency that are damaging. **Remoralizing** the poor by making welfare dependent on participation in work is therefore the main purpose of work programmes. It is the act of being on the early morning bus every day and being a good worker that benefits Tamarla Owens.

remoralizing

These rationales overlap, yet each embodies distinctive assumptions about the personal lives of those in need of welfare. In some cases, this is no more than a broad theory about human conduct. Neo-liberals who have drawn on the economic–regulatory rationale, for example, build their argument around the belief that people are rational economic actors who make calculated self-interested choices to optimize their own well-being. Reformists who use the personal–developmental rationale trace the need for welfare in shortcomings in individuals' abilities to compete for jobs. Alongside deprived backgrounds and poor provision, they portray personal lives marred by lack of self-respect and confidence. In contrast, neo-conservatives use the social–disciplinary rationale to depict an underclass of demoralized welfare dependants who lack hope. Neo-conservative remoralization discourses and their constructions of personal lives have exerted a particularly strong influence over the shifting contingency of welfare and work, notably in the USA, but also in the UK.

ACTIVITY 4.1

Read the following quotations from two influential US authors. Make a note of how each quotation construes the place of 'the personal' in welfare and identify any significant differences in their approaches.

> ... surprisingly little has been made of the distinction between the behaviors that make sense when one is poor and the behaviors that make sense when one is not poor.
>
> (Murray, 1994, p.156)

> Self-sufficiency [is] no longer taken to be an intrinsic obligation of healthy adults.
>
> (Murray, 1994, p.180)

> A greater number [of poor adults] are simply defeatist about work or unable to organize their personal lives to hold jobs consistently.
>
> (Mead, 1997, p.12)

> ... bureaucracy – unpopular though it is – increasingly must manage the lives of those who are seriously poor.
>
> (Mead, 1997, p.14)

COMMENT

Personal lives are regarded as the source of welfare dependency, but the first two quotations see claimants as rational, the second two as demoralized. Charles Murray's (1994) work, from which the first two quotations come, was highly influential on welfare policy-making in the USA in the 1990s. It focused on the formation of a welfare underclass, particularly amongst black American lone mothers and unemployed fathers. He identified what he viewed as their **rational self-interest** in responding to the '**perverse incentives**' of the US welfare system in the 1960s and 1970s to qualify for welfare by having 'illegitimate' children as a means to gaining income and security in the face of poor job opportunities. While his work is infused with assumptions and implications about the personal lives of black Americans, his focus remains on their pursuit of their own best short-term interests by 'using' an ill-conceived welfare system to their advantage (see also Morris, 1998).

rational self-interest

perverse incentives

Lawrence Mead (1997) is the author of the second two quotations. He shared many of Murray's views of welfare, but had a significantly different analysis. To Mead it was the personal conduct of impoverished welfare claimants that was the key to their dependency. Their need for welfare is a reflection of their worklessness, which in turn is the product of individual de-motivation, despair and self-defeat that result from a '**culture of poverty**'. As the third and fourth quotations suggest, Mead was not persuaded by the standard explanations for dependency. To him, the main cause of poverty 'is no longer social injustice but the disorders of (dependants') private lives' (Mead, 1997, p.15). This view is echoed by some conservatives in the UK. Green (1999), for example, depicts the stereotypic self-destructive behaviour of an unqualified, unskilled school-leaver and father of illegitimate children, for whom only a change of attitude from within will bring an escape

culture of poverty

from dependency. It is this 'new politics of conduct' (Deacon, 1997, p.xv) and its social–disciplinary rationale that underpin their arguments for constructing a binding connection between work and welfare.

It is vividly clear that these commentators locate poverty and the need for welfare in personal lives and 'pathological' behaviours. It is unskilled men, lone mothers and the black population whose personal lives are implied to underlie the need for welfare. The influence of these commentaries on government policies has been extensive, as much because of their work of legitimizing and authorizing perceptions and representations as by originating them (Deacon, 1997; Clarke, 2001). And it is through these processes of discursive construction, in which particular readings of individual circumstances become sedimented into dominant truths about the causes of poverty and 'dependency', that representations of personal lives come to shape social policies.

3 Personal agency, participation and refusal: gathering evidence

While it is difficult to exaggerate the impact of this construction of 'welfare dependency', particularly in the USA, this construction does not go unchallenged. A very wide range of groups of people who are poor or who are subject to discrimination succeed in shaping welfare arrangements by evading, refusing or resisting policies. Historically, there are numerous examples of collective agency in resisting and reshaping welfare policies. In the USA, Fox Piven and Cloward (1977) trace the history of poor people's movements that began around the time of Roosevelt's New Deal, and continued with the considerable successes of the industrial workers' movement and the civil rights movement. Some comparable movements are well-known in the UK, most notably the hunger marches and the Jarrow March of the 1930s depression, but there are also numerous other effective protests against poverty by welfare rights groups, claimants' unions and feminist campaigns against cohabitation rules in the 1970s and 1980s.

More recently, resistance to workfare policies has taken a number of forms. Least common, but with a stronger history in Canada and the USA, are active forms of explicit political protest. Swanson (1997) describes an extended campaign that delayed the introduction of workfare in British Columbia in the mid 1990s. Protesting groups took their cause to the United Nations on the grounds that workfare breaches the UN Covenant on Social Economic and Cultural Rights, which requires signatory nations to allow their citizens to earn a living by 'freely chosen' work. In Quebec, resistance was registered by community groups who, as prospective employers, were eligible to take on workfare clients. They boycotted the programmes as inequitable and as causing 'job substitution' (Shragge and Deniger, 1997). Swanson describes trades unions' protests in New Brunswick over job substitution, which attracted much popular local support, and successful prosecution of a legal grievance. Abramovitz (1996) catalogues an extensive range of protests by

Figure 4.3 Protest against reductions in Works Progress Administration payments, Washington DC, 1937

women activists in the USA against workfare reforms. These may have made some contribution to the continuing protected position of lone mothers while their first child remains below school age under the PRWORA.

Such resistance undoubtedly represents only a small part of the picture. But, although workfare polices have a major impact on the lives of those who come within their ambit, the processes of policy implementation are not smooth and mechanical. Both in express protest, and in their efforts to accommodate their lives to policy demands, groups and individuals act to obstruct or amend policies. Horton and Shaw's (2002) study of the Los Angeles workfare programme found disappointment among claimants with humiliating and rigid bureaucratic procedures, which produced complaint and resistance. Bringing together claimants produced solidarity, raised collective awareness of the faults of the programme, and expressed criticism of the policy-makers' ignorance of their difficulties. Kingfisher's (1996) analysis of women's narratives about US welfare found them appropriating dominant views for subversive, resistant purposes. They appeared to accept and adopt the categories used by policy-makers, while deploying them to define themselves outside these categories as responsible mothers, committed workers and as reluctant to be dependent. Through such 'reverse discourses', Kingfisher argues, women confront the contradictions of the system.

There are also important questions about the extent to which withdrawal and non-participation constitute resistance. In his extensive study of youth training in the 1980s and 1990s in the UK, Mizen (1994) argues that participation in schemes was infused with scepticism, reluctance and a deeply instrumental attitude on the part of trainees who saw through bogus claims of quality training and subverted attempts to manage them. Rates of refusal and early leaving were consistently high, thus subverting many of the programmes' personal development claims. Hollands's (1990) study pointed to the ways in which schemes fostered 'workless cultures', involving deliberate, and sometimes politicized and collectivized, avoidance.

How far these responses go beyond cultures of avoidance and non-cooperation to constitute resistance is less clear, not least because it is exceptionally difficult to find evidence of the significance of refusals and withdrawals in the evaluation data on workfare programmes. One way of getting a glimpse of how far people participate, avoid or resist welfare to work is to look at the evidence from the first mandatory programme in the UK – the New Deal for Young People (NDYP). Since 1998, 18 to 24-year-olds who have been claiming job seekers allowance (JSA) for six months have been required to join the programme. Following a 'Gateway' period of intensive counselling, advice and job search guidance with a Personal Adviser, clients choose between a job with a training component (subsidized placement with an employer, the Environmental Task Force or a community project), and full-time education or training. Clients who gain subsidized employment are paid at the market rate set by their employer. Others receive a weekly allowance fractionally above the minimum JSA rate. Clients are sanctioned by withdrawal of the allowance for repeatedly refusing placements, absenteeism or drop-out. In practice, some clients remain in place for the whole programme, some leave during the Gateway period during their placement on a job or course, or before they complete a job search afterwards.

It is difficult to gather clear information about the point at which they leave, what happens to some leavers immediately afterwards and the longer-term outcomes. Government data used to monitor the NDYP comes in the form of monthly statistics, which provide some basic information.

ACTIVITY 4.2

Examine Table 4.1 carefully. Make notes on what you can gather about participation, drop-out and completion, and about differences between the groups identified. As you do so, think about the kinds of explanations you would expect to find for the differences between social groups in patterns of participation and outcomes from NDYP.

COMMENT

There are clearly some major differences, as well as many areas of similarity, between all the social groups identified regarding which options they follow and what they move on to. Many different explanations might be offered. We will return to the more significant differences and explanations later. What is beyond any doubt, at this stage, is that it is impossible to judge, on the basis of this kind of evidence alone, who refuses to participate and how these patterns reflect differences in personal lives. One possible source of explanation of differences in this data is that employment opportunities for young people differ greatly between different parts of the country. Such variations might help us to

Table 4.1 Position at end of December 2002 of those who had their first 18 to 24-year-old NDYP interview in October 2001, by client characteristics, Great Britain

	All	%	Male	%	Female	%	People with disabilities	%	Whites	%	Ethnic minorities	%	No qualifications or below NVQ Level 2	%	Qualifications NVQ Level 2 or above	%
9,942 who have had a first New Deal interview in October 2001 of which:	**9942**		**6964**		**2956**		**1226**		**7745**		**1747**		**3569**		**1099**	
As a percentage of all	**100**		**70**		**30**		**12**		**78**		**18**		**36**		**11**	
On an option:	**323**	**100**	**244**	**100**	**77**	**100**	**57**	**100**	**246**	**100**	**57**	**100**	**156**	**100**	**41**	**100**
Employment	34	11	26	11	8	10	9	16	29	12	5	9	18	12	8	20
Education and training	158	49	115	47	41	53	29	51	108	44	37	65	78	50	19	46
Voluntary sector	60	19	38	16	22	29	9	16	46	19	11	19	23	15	11	27
Environment task force	71	22	65	27	6	8	10	18	63	26	4	7	37	24	3	7
Had left New Deal (1):	**8779**	**100**	**6096**	**100**	**2667**	**100**	**1043**	**100**	**6855**	**100**	**1530**	**100**	**3048**	**100**	**955**	**100**
For an unsubsidized job	3191	36	2268	37	916	34	356	34	2595	38	468	31	1060	35	421	44
For other benefits	1259	14	705	12	554	21	183	18	1066	16	153	10	463	15	92	10
For other known destination (2)	754	9	507	8	246	9	80	8	541	8	165	11	221	7	71	7
Unknown destination	3575	41	2616	43	951	36	424	41	2653	39	744	49	1265	42	358	38

Notes:

(1) The breakdown of this category is the immediate destination on leaving; the individual's position at the end of the month may have changed.

(2) This includes young people, who, on leaving New Deal, continue to claim JSA.

Percentages may not add up to 100 due to incomplete data or rounding.

Source: based on DWP, 2002, Table 10

understand much better the causes and effects of participation in (and refusal of) welfare-to-work programmes. Sunley et al. (2001) analysed the spatial distribution of unemployment and the success rates of NDYP leavers in securing jobs (see Figures 4.4 and 4.5).

ACTIVITY 4.3

Compare Figures 4.4 and 4.5, beginning with a locality that you know well, then look at north–south differences and national differences, and finally compare the largest conurbations with other localities. Make notes on the relationship between high and low levels of youth unemployment, and high and low levels of entry into jobs.

- Is there a spatial match between the proportions of unemployed and of those gaining jobs after NDYP?
- If so, is it uniform or variable?
- If it is variable, is there a difference by region or by size of area?
- What interpretations come to mind about patterns and variations?

COMMENT

There are clearly major differences between localities, and some close correspondences between levels of local youth unemployment and the job successes of leavers. Again, we will return to these points. For now, it is important to note that although this additional evidence offers some important pointers to the significance of patterns of participation and withdrawal, it is by no means sufficient to make sense of them. Other kinds of evidence are needed.

---

4 An auditor reports

Some analysis of the data shown in Figures 4.4 and 4.5 is needed to set it in a wider context. We need to know how many openings were created after the NDYP was launched, who participates in the programme, and with what outcomes. Not only would this answer questions about the significance of participations and withdrawals, it would allow insights into the rationale for NDYP. A report by the National Audit Office (NAO), *The New Deal for Young People* (2002), is an authoritative statement to Parliament on the programme's value and cost-effectiveness. The focus of the report is quite specific: is NDYP a good use of public funds and does it contribute to the economy?

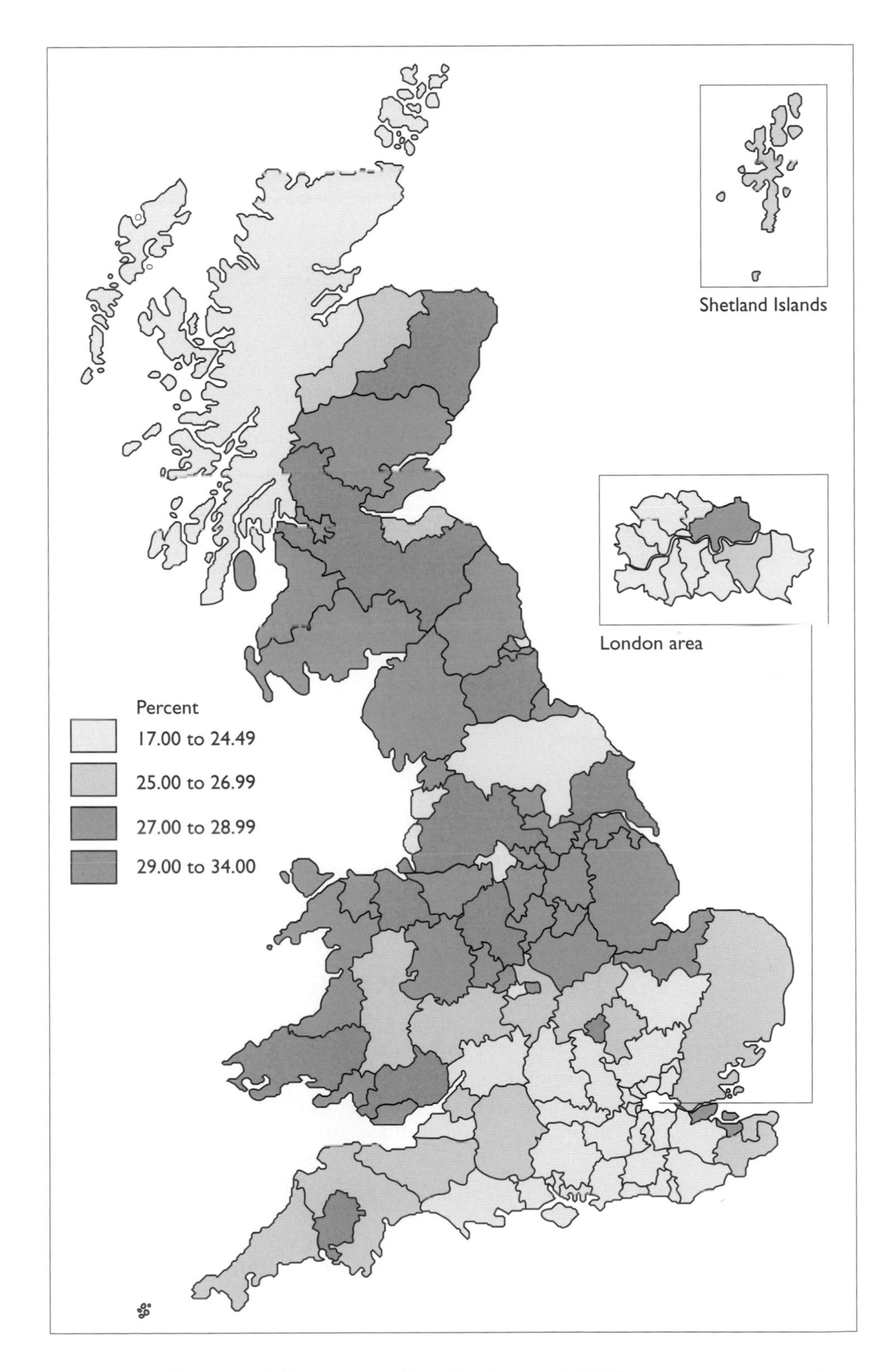

Figure 4.4 Youth unemployment by New Deal areas, 1997 (Source: based on Sunley et al., 2001, p.489, Figure 2)

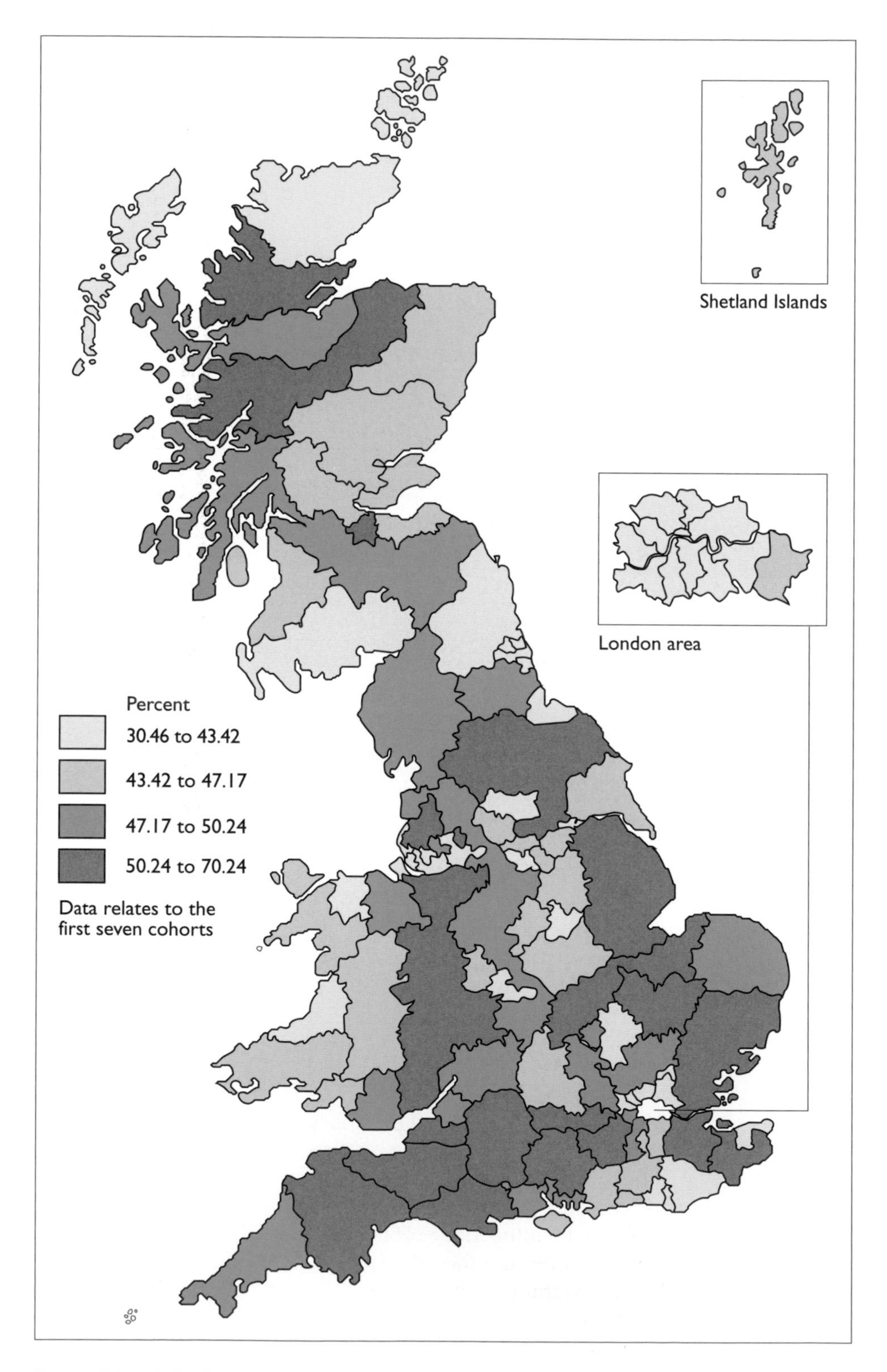

Figure 4.5 NDYP participants moving into unsubsidized jobs by New Deal areas, as at April 2000 (Source: based on Sunley et al., 2001, p.490, Figure 3)

ACTIVITY 4.4

Read Extract 4.1, and make brief notes on the NAO's assessment of the value and effectiveness of NDYP, on the criteria it employs to come to its conclusion, and on the data that was used.

Extract 4.1: 'NAO report on the New Deal for Young People'

How far the New Deal for Young People has met its objectives

5 The government met its target of getting 250,000 under 25-year-olds off benefit and into work before the end of the 1997 to 2002 Parliament in September 2000. By the end of October 2001, some 339,000 participants in the New Deal for Young People had ceased claiming job seekers allowance and had experienced at least one spell in employment, including subsidized employment. Of these, some 244,000 young people had left for sustained unsubsidized jobs. A further 30 per cent of leavers left to unknown destinations. Research indicates that 56 per cent of participants who left the programme and for whom no known destination was recorded (some additional 107,000 young people) had left to go into a job. However, some young people placed into sustained jobs (lasting more than 13 weeks) will have returned to unemployment within that period without reclaming job seekers allowance.

6 A large majority of the young people placed into sustained jobs remained out of unemployment for a substantial period. However, as might be expected in a dynamic labour market, some young people placed into jobs subsequently returned to a period of unemployment. This is a positive outcome as long as they remain employable, actively seek work and do not return to long-term unemployment ...

...

Impact of the programme on the national economy

8 The New Deal for Young People achieved its stated target of helping 250,000 young people into work in September 2000. But the economic impact of the programme cannot be measured simply in terms of the number of young people placed into jobs. For example, many of them would have found a job anyway because of natural labour market turnover and the general expansion of the economy. The overall impact of the programme therefore needs to be viewed in the context of wider labour market dynamics, as many young people will become unemployed and leave employment without any labour market intervention. Also, the headline figure of the number of young people placed into work does not measure the additional benefit for those who have participated in the programme in terms of their improved longer-term labour market position.

9 Research commissioned by the Employment Service into the first two years of the programme's operation estimated that the New Deal for Young People had reduced youth unemployment by 35,000 and increased youth employment by 15,000.

10 Our analysis suggests that these estimates of the direct effects of the programme were reasonable. Because of inherent difficulties in evaluating the programme, they needed to be placed within a fairly wide range of plausibility, but it is clear that there is a positive effect.

11 The research also estimated that the programme indirectly had increased employment in groups other than 18 to 24-year-olds by 10,000. Based on this research into the direct and indirect effects of the New Deal for Young People, we estimate that national income has grown by a minimum of £200 million a year.

12 The government had spent £668 million on the programme by March 2000. After taking into account the programme's impact on other parts of the government budget, its estimated net cost was around £140 million a year. Applying this to our estimates of the programme's impact on levels of employment, the average annual cost per additional person of any age in employment lies within the range of £5,000 to £8,000 ...

Our estimates of the effect of the New Deal for Young People on youth unemployment and youth employment

Effect	Plausible range of estimates
Reduced youth unemployment	25,000–45,000
Increased youth employment	8,000–20,000

(NAO, 2002, pp.2–4)

COMMENT

The NAO's assessment is equivocal. The increase in youth employment is proportionately very small. The report is careful to differentiate new jobs from existing jobs that employers transfer to NDYP in order to gain the subsidy. It expresses concern about the 30 per cent of leavers to unknown destinations, and about the subsequent unemployment of those who get work when they leave. It draws attention to poor provision for those who are 'harder to help', and the declining trend in the numbers of leavers beginning jobs that results from the practice of placing the 'easiest' recruits first. Finally, while the net cost of £140 million is exceeded by the estimated net growth of £200 million in the national income, the annual cost per trainee of up to £8,000 is several times the cost of the trainees' 'allowance', partly because of the subsidy to employers.

The criteria upon which the report bases its assessments are exclusively quantitative. Aspects of the programme that 'were not measurable' are ignored. Questions about how it was experienced by young people and employers are not addressed. There is therefore no measure of 'value added' to participants' skills. Nevertheless, the report confirms a number of important points. Few jobs are created and the impact on youth unemployment is relatively modest. There is no saving on welfare costs, but a very small gain in overall economic output. And while there is still a lack of clarity about drop-out, refusal, withdrawal and ineffective outcomes, it seems likely that the 30 per cent who left for unknown destinations were withdrawals before completion. The duration of jobs gained beyond 13 weeks is uncertain. This strongly suggests refusal or resistance alongside a substantial proportion of successful placements.

To interpret these findings, and to consider how New Deal policies constitute a response to and a shaping of personal lives, clear frameworks for interpretation are needed. We begin with two that offer opposing analyses.

4.1 Neo-liberal interpretations of welfare to work

Neo-liberalism begins from an emphasis on the free market, individual freedom and responsibility. Neo-liberal approaches use the 'less eligibility' principle. Welfare is thought to distort 'free' markets, because it either removes incentives to work, or drives up entry-level pay to rates that are not economical for employers. Neo-liberals tend to advocate what Peck (2001) terms the 'hard' **Labour Force Attachment** model of working for welfare, which places claimants directly into labour markets as a condition of welfare. This is thought to break cycles of dependency by reducing welfare costs and containing wage inflation, following the economic–regulatory rationale. In practice, this model is often conflated with the conservative-inspired social–disciplinary rationale, in which mandatory attachment brings good habits of work. Both facets are visible in Tamarla Owens's experiences in Michigan. 'Softer' versions locate the problem in inadequate skills and work experience. This is the **Human Capital Development** model, based on personal–developmental rationales.

Labour Force Attachment

Human Capital Development

Advocates of the Labour Force Attachment model would argue that NDYP is not a workfare programme. It does not reduce welfare costs, enforce immediate labour market entry, stimulate competition for the lowest paid jobs or even demonstrably help to control wage rates. It is closer to the Human Capital Development model. On its criteria, the NAO's (2002) findings reveal that the programme has succeeded in the core aims of removing large numbers of young people from the unemployed register and obliging them to make themselves employable.

4.2 Neo-Marxist interpretations of welfare to work

Neo-Marxists interpret welfare-to-work programmes as doubly alienating. First, the programmes deny workers control over the conditions of their 'employment' by forcibly constructing their relations with employers. Second, they deepen social inequalities because they are concerned with people who are weakest in the competitive labour market. Neo-Marxists view economic regulation as the principle purpose of welfare to work. Its task is to manage the **contradictions of the capitalist welfare state** (Offe, 1984) by reconciling the tensions between welfare provision and capital accumulation

contradictions of the capitalist welfare state

during the transformations in work that Chapter 1 describes. Welfare states are said to be moving away from stable full employment and management of the market economy within a national policy framework (the **Keynesian Welfare National State**), and towards a regime in which welfare depends on work, competitiveness requires continuous change in the pursuit of efficiency, and policy decisions are taken in the context of cost-cutting globalized production (the **Schumpeterian Workfare Postnational Regime**) (Jessop, 2000). The implications of the latter for welfare are that costs too must be minimized, following the 'less eligibility' principle. So must the costs of the cheapest labour, if affluent Western welfare regimes are to compete in global markets.

Keynesian Welfare National State

Schumpeterian Workfare Postnational Regime

Neo-Marxism, therefore, draws attention to a number of NDYP's shortcomings. The capacity of the programme to create employment is very limited. Costs per 'trainee' remain high, so it is not reducing welfare expenditure. There is no audit of enhanced skills. And with large numbers of leavers to unknown destinations, its social–disciplinary value is also in doubt. These criticisms are reinforced by Sunley et al. (2001) in their spatial analysis, which concludes that NDYP may be least effective in the very localities in which it is most needed as the analysis in Figures 4.4 and 4.5 suggest. And the data in Table 4.1 for job placements show that it magnifies existing labour market inequalities. Analyses therefore conclude that economic regulation is the main purpose of such programmes. Grover and Stewart (1999; 2000), for example, argue that the objective of the programmes is to contain wage inflation by drawing into employment inactive people who will accept entry-level wages. Peck and Theodore (2000, p.120) argue that they 'intensify competitive pressures at the bottom of the labour market and enforce low paid work'. NDYP adheres to the 'less eligibility' principle by shaping the critical '**reservation wage**': the minimum amount of pay for which employees individually decide they are prepared to work.

reservation wage

Young women are in a 30:70 minority on NDYP (see Table 4.1). As Chapter 1 showed, there is now a concentration of women in part-time, lower paid, and generally less skilled work sought by poorly qualified young people. Marxist feminists would explain this in terms of young women's adaptability in labour markets, and their historically lower reservation wage as 'second earners' and a 'reserve army of labour', which can be called upon in boom times, or when the wage demands of the primary labour force threaten employers' profits.

4.3 Finding 'the personal' in policy: responses, refusals and resistances

The reservation wage is one of many meeting points between personal lives and social policies. Personal lives fundamentally condition the rate of pay at which everyone individually decides they can or must work. Policies like New Deal necessarily regulate that level.

ACTIVITY 4.5

Read Extract 4.2 from interviews with three lone mothers who were considering the option of registering for the New Deal for Lone Parents (NDLP), and make a note of how their personal lives shape their responses.

Extract 4.2

I'm on a career break from my job at – at the moment and working part-time in the local library. I am waiting until my little boy is at full-time school before I return to work. I had a lone parent interview because at the library where I work I was offered 12 hours a week. So I phoned them up to ask about my benefits, how it would affect them. (The Personal Adviser) put all the figures in the box, and it came out that I was going to be worse off. If it had been 16 hours, it would have made a big difference.

...

I had a visit from the lady from the social, and she said to me, 'I know you are determined to work, but you know is it really worth it, especially when you start talking about childcare and all the different bits and pieces?' I said to her 'It might not be worth it, but I prefer to be out keeping my brain active as opposed to just sitting at home'. Because when I'm at home it's just housework, ironing, cooking and I hate it you know.

...

I'm not a material person, but I think most people would agree that it's not worth putting yourself through all that and being only £20 better off. I suppose that a majority of single parents would agree with that. What's the point? It's more hassle than it's worth, getting the kids organized, getting them out, getting yourself ready, getting yourself out, getting back. I mean, on top of your work you're coming home, looking after these children, making the tea, bathing them, putting them to bed. You really have to have an incentive, you really have to make it worth your while. I know it's a bad attitude to take, but I really would need to get more than £20 a week extra.

(Dawson et al., 2000, pp.100, 114–15)

COMMENT

The balance of how policy pressures and financial interests meet for these three women is finely poised. For the first, a difference of four hours pay is critical; for the second, the marginal disincentive to work is negligible; for the third the marginal gain is inadequate. The critical allowance thresholds for NDLP are determined politically to strike the balance between incentivizing work and avoiding wage inflation. But, whether they function as intended is determined by the individual circumstances, beliefs and attitudes of lone parents. There are elements of neo-liberal rational self-interest in all three

responses, but how these are expressed is also inflected by personal–developmental concerns for the first two women, and by the neo-conservative social–disciplinary rationale embraced by the second and resisted by the third.

Participation in NDLP is voluntary, in NDYP it is a condition of welfare. The threat of benefits sanctions gives NDYP some power to shape behaviour. But, the examples of Sid's and Jolene's experiences below illustrate how differing individual circumstances radically affect this power:

> Sid left his Subsidized Employment Option as a catering assistant in a nursing home because 'it wasn't really a catering job, it was a skivvy's job'. He thought he would learn how to cook and get some proper catering experience. However, most of the work involved microwaving pre-prepared [*sic*] food. Sid left the Option knowing he would be sanctioned. However, he knew he could rely on his parents to financially support him during the period of sanction.
>
> ...
>
> Jolene undertook a Voluntary Sector Option at a local community centre. After three weeks, she became ill with flu and was out of work for over a week. She had rung her employer on the first day of illness but did not realize she should have done this for every day of the illness. Even though she had a doctor's certificate, she was sanctioned for two weeks. Jolene was upset that she was sanctioned. For the two weeks she found it difficult to survive. She lives on her own and had to borrow money from friends to pay for electricity and food. She also received £2 a day from a crisis fund.
>
> (O'Connor et al., 2001, p.75)

Evaluation studies report participants leaving under threat of sanctions (O'Connor et al., 2001). This undoubtedly involves adjustments to their personal reservation wage thresholds. It is here that the scope for agency in resisting and evading programmes is greatest, and that refusal of placements shown in Table 4.1 may reflect determination to dilute the force of policies that shape personal lives. Faced with a Personal Adviser (PA) who is determined to place them regardless of suitable options, some young people leave for stop-gap work. Ritchie (2000) reports that nearly two-thirds of those who leave, do so when unwanted placements loom large. Underlying the statistics of early leaving, non-participation and unknown destinations, are innumerable stories of planned non-entry, last minute evasions, and multiple re-registrations. They may be dismissed as chaotic manifestations of disorderly lives or they may constitute resistance. Only research about intent and motivation would be able to illuminate this issue further.

Such actions carry particular meaning amongst minority ethnic groups. The evaluation study of NDLP by Dawson et al. (2000) marks a sharp differentiation between the social integration of black non-participants in the programme, all of whom were already involved in work or training, and Bangladeshi women, who were unlikely to participate because of family support networks and commitments to care for their children. A study by Kalra et al. (2001) amongst Bangladeshis and Pakistanis found that many who left after an initial interview with their PA, did so to avoid NDYP. Local personal networks accounted for its poor reputation amongst those who described bad placement experiences and negative attitudes towards Asian clients on past programmes.

These studies show how personal lives, constituted through particular racialized identities, respond to the lived experience of programmes, and may include culturally-based forms of collective refusal. Behind these responses and resistances lie narratives of persuasion and attrition, adjustment and submission. PAs will have striven to engage the attention and win the trust of their clients, drawing out their interests, perhaps trying to fashion them to approximate available options. But, the outcomes of such encounters are inextricably bound in a complex web of individual histories, circumstances, networks and dispositions that make up the personal lives of clients. Some options may be unappealing, resonate with negative past experiences, or fit badly with firmly held views or cultural mores which clients are not prepared to compromise.

5 Personal Advisers, personal lives

What is clear from a wide range of New Deal evaluations (Dawson et al., 2000; O'Connor et al., 2001; Lewis et al., 2000) is that PAs provide a critical interface between the programme and its clients. The prominence of 'personal' in their title carries several meanings. Clients are allocated to PAs on a one-to-one basis, with the implication of a relationship, and of continuity. It also implies personal advice, which crosses the boundary of the informational into the distinctive needs of a particular individual. The way in which this relationship is realized is a key to understanding how policy and 'the personal' meet. Historically, the contact between welfare officials and 'clients' has taken different forms; this is revealing about how the relationship is constituted. We explore this next.

ACTIVITY 4.6

Look at Figures 4.6 and 4.7. Pick out any signs that suggest how the relationship between official and client is constituted, inferring what you can from the finer detail.

COMMENT

It is clear that these images portray two very different conceptions of how welfare officials and their clients should interact. Figure 4.6 is archetypal, symbolizing millions of similar gendered encounters between a bureaucrat–official of the old welfare state, and a waiting line of massed, anonymous claimants. All the participants are male and white. The geography of the room speaks of separation of official from claimant. A counter keeps them safely apart, and the steel framework above it suggests that there are shutters which can be erected when needed. The attire of the various actors too tells of separation: the smart white-collared, besuited official with his plastered hair and studious spectacles facing the mass of flat-caps and uncustomary neck-ties, some hidden under mufflers – all markers of class distinction. Their engagement is impersonal. The gaze of the official and of

Figure 4.6 Men seeking work at the Labour Exchange, Wigan, 11 November 1939

Figure 4.7 New Deal interview, Hackney Job Centre, London, 2003

the applicants alike is downwards. They are concerned with paper records, the symbolic bureaucratic administration of statutory entitlements according to predetermined criteria. The official searches for cards that represent applicants and the applicants testify in writing to their eligibility. No words are spoken at the moment captured in the photograph, and we might imagine verbal exchanges to be brief, structured and predictable. The encounter shown in Figure 4.6 is an act of regulation.

In Figure 4.7, there is still little difficulty in distinguishing between the official and the client, but the highly formalized style, attire and geography of their distinct roles is absent. Both participants (and those behind them) are on the same side of the desk, with nothing separating them. The clues about their respective positions are less obvious. The female adviser seems smartly, but informally, dressed. The male client is dressed more casually. Their gendering is typical of their roles: most PAs are women, most NDYP clients are male. Their 'race' too reflects the overrepresentation of young black men on the programme. Their encounter has the hallmarks of something genuinely interpersonal – they are holding one another's attention with direct eye contact, and they are there to converse, not read and fill in forms. He speaks, she listens. The PA seems engaged with her client as a unique individual. This is closer to autonomous, personal contact between subjects rather than to the ritualized enactment of roles. It suggests an encounter that might be developmental, rather than regulating or disciplining. Yet one actor (the PA) holds most of the power, symbolized by her computer, with fast access to records, personal details and information about jobs.

The two encounters shown in Figures 4.6 and 4.7 symbolize very different ways of understanding – and theorizing – how policies and personal lives meet. The first is premised on a coherent, organized state machine in which agents act as part of a chain of command, following a rule-based script in fixed, consistent ways. Such encounters are de-personalized and bureaucratized versions of the social–disciplinary rationale that underpinned the workhouse regime. This reading accords with some 'orthodox' Marxist analyses of how the state exercises power through institutions. Few now claim that officials slavishly serve 'the state', and there is ample evidence that 'street-level bureaucrats' (Lipsky, 1980) variously adjust, adapt, dilute, ignore or even subvert procedures and directives when their discretion dictates. Wright (2003) found clear evidence that job centre staff are strongly influenced by their own beliefs and values, which lead them to categorize clients and deal with them using sharply differentiating moral assessments. This reading fits the personalized interaction in Figure 4.7, in which the relative autonomy of both actors is acknowledged. Each speaks not according to a script, but by using their discretion to negotiate an outcome within broad rules, which are open to interpretation, can be 'worked round' and cannot prescribe action. If the purpose remains social–disciplinary, the techniques fit the personal–developmental rationale. This interpretation is closer to post-structuralist theories of **governmentality**. These argue that it is through such encounters that relations of persuasion and power are enacted. Following Foucault's theories about the processes through which people's conduct of themselves is governed, Rose (1999) argues that:

governmentality

> To dominate is to ignore or to attempt to crush the capacity for action of the dominated. But to govern is to recognize the capacity for action and to adjust oneself to it. *To govern is to act upon action.* This entails trying to understand what mobilizes the domains or entities to be governed: to govern one must act

> upon these forces, instrumentalize them in order to shape actions, processes and outcomes in desired directions. Hence, when it comes to governing human beings, to govern is to presuppose the freedom of the governed. To govern humans is not to crush their capacity to act but to acknowledge it and to utilise it for one's own objectives.
>
> (Rose, 1999, p.4, emphasis added)

The task of PAs, then, is to find what motivates (or mobilizes) their clients, to shape it in ways which can be realized through the programmes on offer (to instrumentalize it), and to induce them into those programmes. Part of this will involve careful listening to individual priorities and preferences. It may also involve persuasion that one activity leads to another more desirable possibility. And part may involve inducing a realistic approach to what is available.

personal responsibility

The more difficult these processes of negotiation, compromise and adjustment, the greater will be the need for pressure through establishing norms by means of discourses that assert that welfare is always the product of someone's work, and that it is a matter of **personal responsibility** to be the provider of one's own welfare by working. As welfare subjects become imbued with this thinking, through their relationship with their PA, they begin to rely less on being governed by the PA's interventions, and begin instead to govern themselves.

governance

reconstituting

Rose (1999) argues that welfare-to-work programmes epitomize the **governance** of disapproved social behaviour, through moral pressures upon individual conduct. What might once have been treated as social–disciplinary issues are recast as behaviours in need of remoralization, through which the dominant discourses of PAs get inside the thinking of unemployed people and harness their energies towards making *themselves* ready for employment. Their clients become party to the belief that they are responsible for their own employment, and that expecting welfare support without work is socially irresponsible. In this way, PAs are charged with **reconstituting** their clients as responsible, self-governing subjects, and as worker–citizens of enterprising economies. Social–disciplinary purposes are largely masked by personal–developmental practices. And it is in this way that social policies shape personal lives. What is less clear is how far this theory allows that such strategies may fail, in the face of resistance.

Feminist post-structuralists would inflect this interpretation by focusing on the predominance of women in PA roles, who are presumed to use the skills of responsiveness that women develop as daughters, sisters, wives and mothers to negotiate potentially conflicting interests by appreciating the needs of others and accommodating them. It is a key tenet of feminist epistemology and methodology that 'the personal', and lived experience, are at the centre of theoretical and empirical work. Feminism often works outward from 'the personal' through dilemmas and contradictions towards the policies that frame them, rather than vice versa. This has profound implications for the kinds of evidence that make it possible to understand how welfare and work are contingent upon one another and the way that personal lives intersect with welfare policies. Such evidence is located in millions of encounters in which welfare subjects are constituted, *or resist being constituted*, as responsible self-governing worker–citizens. Hence, it is only qualitative studies that can successfully unpack the biographies of personal lives in order to track the power relations of work and welfare. In this case, tables, maps and audits offer little insight into how 'the personal 'and social policies are mutually constitutive, and how constitution is resisted. This chapter began with Tamarla Owens's biography, and it is to another that we now turn to advance this argument.

6 A short biography of Mandy: comparing theories about work and welfare

Figure 4.8 Exclusion from welfare: the price of resistance?

Mandy's biography has some striking parallels with Tamarla Owens's, but also some clear differences from it. It comes from an evaluation report on NDYP. Despite its brevity, it illustrates the potential of beginning from 'the personal' to show how social policies constitute welfare subjects.

ACTIVITY 4.7

Read Extract 4.3. Write a sentence about how you think neo-liberals, neo-Marxists, governmentality theorists and feminists would make sense of the way in which NDYP policies and Mandy's personal life 'frame' one another. Keep in mind the part played by Mandy's PA in the processes involved, and any aspects of Mandy's conduct that represent resistance to the processes of her own constitution as a responsible, self-governing welfare subject. Note too any comparisons and contrasts with Tamarla Owens's story.

Extract 4.3 'Mandy'

Mandy, now aged 21, left home when she was 16 due to a conflict with her family. After a period of sleeping rough, she was temporarily housed in a hostel for young women where she lived for a few years. About a year before starting NDYP, Mandy moved from the hostel into a flat. However, she found it difficult to make the transition to independent living, especially with managing her money and paying for bills.

On joining NYPD, Mandy enrolled in full-time education to gain secretarial skills. However, she found it hard to adjust to being in education again. She also felt that there was no support for her to make this transition. She became disenchanted with the [Education] Option and eventually left after two and a half months. Mandy moved on to Follow-through [the stage of NDYP once clients have been on an Option] where she was sanctioned for not completing her Option. The loss of benefit was very problematic for her, adding to her already mounting debt and her difficulty with managing money. This financial crisis led to her being evicted from her flat. After a short time of sleeping on various friend's [*sic*] floors, she moved in with her mother temporarily. At the time of interview, she was still there, but acknowledged that the situation was far from ideal. She was worried that if the relationship deteriorated again, she did not have anywhere else to go.

(O'Connor et al., 2001, p.76)

COMMENT

NDYP threatened to take Mandy's personal life to the edge of crisis. She was clearly already extremely vulnerable, and young women who 'sleep rough' easily fall prey to sexual exploitation. Mandy's admission to a hostel suggests this was recognized. However, once she was subject to NDYP this recognition apparently lapsed. She joined a course for which she was ill-prepared, perhaps under pressure from her PA. The withdrawal of her allowance as a sanction for leaving the Education Option (normally at a PA's discretion) presumably caused her to spend her housing benefit on immediate essentials, leading to rent arrears and eviction. This clearly upset a delicate balance that had begun to move her from vulnerability towards independence. In an attempt to hurry her progress, NDYP returned Mandy to the circumstances that put her on the streets.

From a neo-liberal interpretation, paradoxically, Mandy's history epitomizes the benefits of welfare to work. It is because there are sanctions with painful consequences that NDYP promises success. Aged 16, Mandy was a welfare dependent who had her own flat – a 'perverse incentive' her working peers might envy and emulate. NDYP removed the artificial protection of unconditional welfare and exposed Mandy to work and the costs of independence. Her return to her mother's home would help her realize that it was rash to leave the course and lose the flat. The shock of the sanction is the PA's 'tough love' that should break Mandy's dependency. It is likely to have pushed her into low-paid work (meeting the economic–regulatory purpose) or study (meeting the personal–developmental purpose), and promised to discipline a supposedly disorderly life.

A neo-Marxist analysis takes a very different starting-point. Once she left home, Mandy had no means of subsistence. By making welfare conditional upon work, NDYP again put Mandy at risk of the depredations of street life. She was an exploited victim of an inequitable system whose economic relations either drive people like Mandy directly into low-paid work or require them to gain skills that later bind them to it. Her brief engagement with NDYP would probably have lowered her reservation wage. She was also apparently pushed towards a course for which she was not ready. A job placement would have helped more with her debt problems. But as we saw, paradoxically, NDYP is least able to provide jobs where they are most needed. By initiating the sanction, Mandy's PA acted as a rule-following state agent, who seemingly had little regard for the counterproductive consequences of her actions. By triggering Mandy's eviction from her flat, the sanction escalated an understandable act of resistance into a personal crisis, returning her to live with her 'estranged' mother. This is characteristic of the contradictions of state welfare. In an effort to make welfare conditional on work for reasons of social discipline or economic regulation, vulnerable people are precipitated into the very crises that make the most costly demands on welfare.

Post-structuralist analyses offer differing readings of Mandy's experience. In a Foucauldian reading, the discourses of welfare to work employed by her PA have, in this case, been unable to move Mandy to inhabit the subject position of a working welfare-recipient, en route to becoming a self-governing, responsible worker–citizen. Her 'personal' has prompted her to refuse to be constituted in this way, because the discourses have not been able to override her dislike of the college course, or her problematic relationship with her mother. Though it may have been neither deliberate nor conscious, Mandy resisted the dominant discourses.

A reading based on post-structuralist theories of governmentality interprets Mandy's experiences differently. It sees the crisis that follows the withdrawal of her benefits as one episode in a continuing history of welfare interventions. In different ways, each intervention is part of a process of *acting* on Mandy's own autonomy as an actor – that is, of enabling Mandy to govern herself more effectively. The allocation of her own flat presupposed her freedom to shape her own life. Her PA will have worked to establish her interests, acknowledged her capacity to be responsible and aimed for the best match with placement options. This time, the intervention failed. As an autonomous agent, Mandy chose to quit the course. She may have done so in the knowledge that she would be sanctioned, but it is far from certain that she knew that this in turn would result in eviction. The programme governs its subjects through persuasion, but also through more coercive measures by withdrawing benefits. Mandy is being induced to govern herself both through steering by her PA, and by being put under financial pressure. Though this episode did not induce Mandy to govern herself in the way envisaged, it may be that she has learned the price of refusing 'guidance', and (as neo-liberals would also suggest) would act differently on a future occasion, out of self-interest.

Feminist analysis would emphasize Mandy's vulnerabilities as a very young woman, especially to male sexual exploitation and unwanted pregnancy. It would take up the hints that Mandy's mother is a lone parent, for whom bringing up a teenager may have been stressful. It would point out that the effects of treating families as the back-stop when welfare is withheld impact almost entirely on women. Marxist-feminists would see the actions of Mandy's PA as reproducing a gender-differentiated dual labour market, by steering her towards secretarial work and a subordinated labour market position. Post-structuralist feminists would draw attention to the absence from the account of Mandy's voice, and her mother's, and of details of their relationship. They would also remind us that we know nothing of her PA's working life in which she juggled the tensions between discipline and development, and between her own responses to Mandy and formal NDYP requirements (see Chapter 2). Without this information, interpretation is speculative.

7 Workfare lives: evaluating theories

Figure 4.9 Tamarla Owens

These theoretical readings of how NDYP 'met' Mandy's life offer important insights, but none provides a definitive interpretation – and all require evaluation that looks critically at their epistemological bases, internal coherence, resilience to contrary evidence and robustness against other theoretical positions. Here, we can embark only on the briefest of evaluations, by taking the starting-points of each theory in turn and offering a critical voice from other theories.

To begin with neo-liberalism, it is a key premise that the market is the primary means of coordinating economic activity, including the allocation of people to jobs. This assumes that rational actors make judgements about their earnings prospects to decide their best options – training to improve employability, as in Mandy's case, or accepting subsistence-level earnings, as Tamarla Owens did. To neo-liberals, both Mandy and Tamarla Owens would have used information they gleaned in their everyday lives to make such decisions. But other theories take issue with the neo-liberal model of the market as a self-regulating set of relations. Post-structuralists point to the innumerable human interventions needed to match workers to places in workfare programmes. When workers are as inexperienced as Tamarla Owens and Mandy, they learn to govern themselves

Figure 4.10 Hungry and homeless: 'Mandy's' past, present and future?

responsibly only through the help of welfare para-professionals. Mandy had to be induced into recognizing her need for a qualification; Tamarla Owens had to be led to see for herself the 'need' to make a long, inconvenient daily journey. Neither rational self-interest nor direct force alone could mobilize them. The two had to be brought together and explained, and then reworked through Mandy's and Tamarla Owens's own processes of reasoning, of their own volition. And in Mandy's case the intervention was not successful, albeit for different reasons from the failure of intervention in Tamarla Owens's case. Evidence of the critical processes through which personal lives individually embrace, accommodate or refuse the requirements of workfare programmes is visible only in the moments in which para-professionals 'act upon action', and 'instrumentalize' the self-interest of the governed, in pursuit of the objectives of those who govern.

Alternatively, we can take neo-Marxism as a starting-point. Here, the stress is on the economic–regulatory purposes of programmes that would see Mandy and Tamarla Owens as unskilled workers who are being prepared for their place in the labour market. It is typical that Mandy as a white woman is steered towards the skilled role of secretary, and Tamarla Owens as a black woman towards the low-skill role of waitress. Mandy refuses this role and makes herself vulnerable. Tamarla Owens conforms and excels but remains financially insecure, while her employer's profits rise on the surplus generated from her poverty pay. Both women end up homeless. For neo-Marxists, this is the work of a relatively autonomous state and its agents. Despite its contradictory position on welfare, the state generally works to the advantage of capital, in this case by depressing the pay of the poorest, so keeping welfare 'less eligible'. In doing so, workfare programmes assure a continuing supply of appropriately prepared labour that can rise and fall roughly in harmony with the economic cycles of growth and retrenchment. But to neo-liberals, such action by the state is inconceivable: it is the market that coordinates the allocation to jobs and sets wage levels. Mandy is poor because she left home without a job or the skills to gain one. Tamarla Owens is poor because she had children without a partner or a job. They have been exposed to the harsher effects of competitive markets. If markets are to be the engine of enterprise and reward for individual effort, it is inevitable that they produce dramatically unequal outcomes. In time, these two women's skills will accumulate more marketable value if they choose to develop them. Questions may remain only about why poverty is reproduced so consistently in the same families and social groupings. To most neo-liberals (and all neo-conservatives) the answers reside in essentialized differences in the aptitudes and energies of individuals and groups. To post-structuralists, they reside in how such essentialisms are constructed discursively and 'realized' in specific local conditions of personal poverty or personal advancement.

Reversing the argument, we can begin from post-structuralist theories of governmentality. We might put the case that it is those who 'act on the actions of others' at ground level who shape personal lives and govern the social world. It is only through interactions between unique individual client–subjects and PA's wide discretion that this can occur under workfare arrangements. To neo-Marxists and Marxist feminists, though, PAs are at best semi-autonomous agents of the state, whose power to govern is merely 'lent', within prescribed parameters. Discretion may be exercised, and agents may sometimes break rules undetected, but workfare drives most clients into work primarily because those who refuse lose their income. It was the implicit threat of sanctions that made Mandy sign up for the course, and their application by a dutiful PA that made her homeless. The same threat drove Tamarla Owens onto the bus every day despite the needs of her son. The threats may have been unspoken by the PA, but they were nonetheless embodied in state power, which was enacted by Mandy's PA when she stopped her allowance.

On this reading, a post-structuralist theory of governmentality is misleading in its claim that the freedom of the governed is taken for granted and that coercion is not used. So long as coercion exists as a last resort, all interactions take place in its shadow. Rose's (1990, 1999) acknowledgement of the freedom of human beings to act and his reading of the ways in which it is harnessed by para-professionals only makes sense if coercive powers linger as threats. His theory then falls prey to the same criticisms as are levelled at some Marxist theories: the state is wrongly attributed with overwhelming, deterministic powers, whereas there is clear evidence that these are evaded and resisted by the street-level bureaucrats mentioned earlier, among others.

In the face of these arguments, Foucauldian post-structuralist theories seem more persuasive. Individuals are led towards inhabiting particular subject positions through the powers of discourses, but are also able to resist becoming constituted as subjects. But, in turn, this version of post-structuralism is criticized for being impermeable to empirical verification. The processes whereby subjects become constituted are buried in protracted interactions and recurrent episodes of incremental persuasion and attrition. Every case is unique and so cannot provide a basis for generalization. And the interactions that underlie them require insights into the psychodynamics, cognitions and changed beliefs and morals of newly constituted subjects. The key issue, as always, is one of interpretation.

From another theoretical position, feminists have pointed to the gendered nature of the way in which workfare has 'made' personal lives, either through women's distinctive position in the labour market, or through particular subjectivities available to women without work. The allocation of Mandy and Tamarla Owens to stereotypically gendered activities (as secretarial student and waitress) underlines the tendency of workfare schemes to reinforce old inequalities. Both women are single; both their lives are framed by lone parenthood – Mandy as daughter, Tamarla Owens as mother. And both suffer poverty that has made them homeless in troubling circumstances. In this sense they represent the condition of many whose financial position as single women is precarious. The challenge to feminism is to analyse how gender is cross-cut by other sources of inequality in the ways policies shape personal lives. To Marxist feminists, it is the combination of their class and gender that unite Mandy's and Tamarla Owens's experiences. Tamarla Owens's experience as a black person deepens her disadvantage, but does not qualitatively alter it.

In contrast, for post-structuralist feminists, living blackness as a working-class woman's identity in the face of welfare policies is an entirely different experience from living whiteness. Tamarla Owens, by virtue of her blackness and by her location in the USA, is constituted in different ways from Mandy, who as a British white woman is constituted as part of a dominant social group. The relation between their differences (as gendered, as racialized) and their inequality is itself different for each of them, because of where they live as well as who they are. This is most obvious when seen through the formal procedures by which each of them became drawn into workfare. Mandy's age alone was the condition of her entry, as a young unemployed person aged 18 she would have been exempt in the USA. Tamarla Owens's gender, 'race', and her lone parenthood conjointly made her the essentialized target of workfare. But this is only so in the US context: in the UK she would have been eligible for benefit without work, and would not perhaps have had to undertake a long journey to a distant job that involved leaving her 6-year-old son in someone else's care with tragic consequences.

Despite their very considerable differences, and the very different kinds of evidence they draw upon, it is clear from these brief exchanges between theoretical frameworks that 'the personal' and social policies meet and remake one another in multiple and complex ways. Making welfare directly conditional upon work represents an unusually focused response to particular perceptions of personal lives, and the material circumstances and social conducts associated with them. And as policies become moulded to the contours of these perceptions, their capacities, in turn, to shape those lives become greater. The groups and their lives that are at the centre of these complex relations between work and welfare are highly variable by place, over time and in different political contexts. How the policies they produce are encountered, conformed to and resisted by the active agents who are their subjects is equally closely inflected by time, place and political priority. But, it is through the shifting contingent relations between work and welfare that some of the most powerful connections between personal lives and social policies are made.

Further resources

There is a wide range of material available on welfare to work. Peck (2001) is undoubtedly the definitive study in terms of policy development in the UK and the USA. Major sources of data on all UK New Deal programmes are on the Department for Work and Pensions (DWP) website, http://www.dwp.gov.uk/asd/ndyp.asp, and the more analytical Working Brief series which is updated very regularly by the Centre for Economic and Social Inclusion on its website, http://www.cesi.org.uk/. Large numbers of evaluation studies have also been published and these too are listed on the DWP website at http://www.dwp.gov.uk/publications/2003/index.asp. (All these websites were last accessed on 2 December 2003.)

Critical academic research studies are much scarcer. For an overview of NDYP and studies of it see Fergusson (2002; forthcoming). Primary studies include

Kalra et al. (2001) and Ritchie (2000). There is a richer critical research literature on workfare in the USA and Canada, including important contributions by Kingfisher (1996), Shragge (1997) and Fox Piven et al. (2002), which are much more concerned with qualitative (and personal) effects of programmes.

On governmentality theory, the key source is the influential but much contested work of Nikolas Rose (1990; 1999), who takes forward Foucault's very brief writings on this approach.

References

Abramovitz, M. (1996) *Regulating the Lives of Women: Social Welfare Policy from Colonial Times to the Present* (revised edition), Boston, MA, South End Press.

Burghes, L. (1987) *Made in the USA: A Review of Workfare – a Compulsory Work-for-Benefits Regime*, London, Unemployment Unit.

Clarke, J. (2001) 'US welfare: variations on the liberal regime' in Cochrane, A., Clarke, J. and Gewirtz, S. (eds) *Comparing Welfare States* (2nd ed), Buckingham, Open University Press.

Clark, J and Hein, J. (2000) 'The political economy of welfare reform in the United States' in Smith, D. (ed.) *Welfare, Work and Poverty: Lessons from Recent Reforms in the USA and the UK*, London, Institute for the Study of Civil Society.

Dawson, T., Dickens, S. and Finer, S. (2000) *Evaluation of the New Deal for Lone Parents: Report on Qualitative Studies with Individuals*, Employment Service, Department of Work and Pensions.

Deacon, A. (1997) *From Welfare to Work: Lessons from America*, London, Institute of Economic Affairs.

DWP (Department for Work and Pensions) (2002) *New Deal for Young People and Long-Term Unemployed People Aged 25+, Statistics to December 2002,* http://www.dwp.gov.uk/asd/asd1/new_deal/new_deal_young_feb2003.asp (accessed 3 February 2004).

Fergusson, R. (2002) 'Rethinking youth transitions: policy transfer and new exclusions in New Labour's New Deal', *Policy Studies*, vol.23, nos.3 and 4, pp.173–90.

Fergusson, R. (2004) (forthcoming) 'The poverty of policy evaluation: the New Deal, social inequality and the eclipse of research', Faculty of Social Sciences, The Open University.

Fox Piven, F., Acker, J., Hallock, M. and Morgan, S. (eds) (2002), *Work, Welfare and Politics: Confronting Poverty in the Wake of Welfare Reform*, Eugene, OR, University of Oregon Press.

Fox Piven, F. and Cloward, R.A. (1977) *Poor People's Movements: Why They Succeed, How They Fail*, New York, Pantheon Books.

Green, D. (1999) *An End to Welfare Rights: the Rediscovery of Independence*, London, Institute of Economic Affairs.

Grover, C. and Stewart, J. (1999) '"Market Workfare": social security, social regulation and competitiveness in the 1990s', *Journal of Social Policy*, vol.24, no.1, pp.73–93.

Grover, C. and Stewart, J. (2000) 'Modernizing social security? Labour and its welfare-to-work strategy', *Social Policy and Administration*, vol.34, no.3, pp.235–52.

Horton, J. and Shaw, L. (2002) 'Opportunity and control: living welfare reform in Los Angeles county' in Fox Piven, Acker, Hallock and Morgan (eds) (2002).

Hollands, R.G. (1990) *The Long Transition : Class, Culture and Youth Training*, London, Macmillan.

Jessop, B. (2000) 'From the KWNS to the SPWR' in Lewis, G., Gewirtz, S. and Clarke, J. (eds) *Rethinking Social Policy*, London, Sage.

Kalra, V.S., Fieldhouse, E.A. and Alam, S. (2001) 'Avoiding the New Deal: a case study of non-participation by minority ethnic young people', *Youth and Policy*, vol.72, pp.63–79.

Kingfisher, C. (1996) *Women in the American Welfare* Trap, Philadelphia, PA, University of Pennsylvania Press.

Lewis, G. (1998) 'Coming apart at the seams: the crises of the welfare state' in Hughes, G. and Lewis, G. (eds) *Unsettling Welfare: the Reconstruction of Social Policy*, London, Routledge.

Lewis, J., Mitchell, L., Sanderson, T., O'Connor, W. and Clayden, M. (2000) *Lone Parents and Personal Advisers: Roles and Relationships*, DSS (Department of Social Security) Research Report, No. 122.

Lipsky, M. (1980) *Street-Level Bureaucracy: Dilemmas of the Individual in Public Services,* New York, Russell Sage Foundation.

Mead, L. (1997) 'From welfare to work: lessons from America' in Deacon, A. (ed.) (1997).

Mizen, P. (1994) *The State, Young People and Youth Training:In and Against the Training State,* London, Mansell.

Morris, L. (1998) 'Legitimate membership of the welfare community' in Langan, M.(ed.) *Welfare: Needs, Rights and Risks*, London, Routledge.

Murray, C. (1994) *Losing Ground: American Social Policy, 1950–1980* (tenth anniversary edition), New York, Basic Books.

NAO (National Audit Office) (2002) *The New Deal for Young People*, HC639, London, HMSO.

O'Connor, W., Ritchie, J. and Woodfield, K. (2001*) Experiences of New Deal: Qualitative Profiles of Young Participants,* Employment Service, March, No. P5988.

Offe, C. (1984) *Contradictions of the Welfare State*, London, Hutchinson.

Peck, J. (2001) *Workfare States*, New York, The Guilford Press.

Peck, J. and Theodore, N. (2000) '"Work first": workfare and the regulation of contingent labour markets', *Cambridge Journal of Economics*, vol.24, no.1, pp.119–38.

Ritchie, J. (2000) 'New Deal for Young People: participants' perspectives', *Policy Studies*, vol.21, no.4, pp.301–12.

Rogers, J. (1999) 'Getting Wisconsin to work', *Economic Affairs*, vol.19, no.3, pp.28–34.

Rose, N. (1990) *Governing the Soul: The Shaping of the Private Self*, London, Routledge.

Rose, N. (1999) *Powers of Freedom: Reframing Political Thought*, Cambridge, Cambridge University Press.

Shragge, E. (ed.) (1997) *Workfare: Ideology for a New Underclass*, Toronto, Garamond Press.

Shragge, E. and Deniger, M.A. (1997) 'Workfare in Quebec' in Shragge, E. (ed.) (1997).

Sunley, P., Martin, R. and Nativel, C. (2001) 'Mapping the New Deal: local disparities in the performance of welfare-to-work', *Transactions of the Institute of British Geographers*, vol.26, no.4, pp.484–512.

Swanson, J. (1997) 'Resisting workfare' in Shragge, E. (ed.) (1997).

Thomson, R. (2004) 'Sexuality and young people: policies, practices and identities' in Carrabine, J. (ed.) *Sexualities: Personal Lives and Social Policy*, Bristol, The Policy Press in association with The Open University.

Wright, S. (2003) 'The street-level implementation of unemployment policy in Millar, J. (ed.) *Understanding Social Security: Issues for Policy and Practice*, Bristol, Policy Press.

CHAPTER 5

The Shifting Relations of Work, Welfare and Personal Lives

by Gerry Mooney

Contents

1 Introduction

This book is concerned with the complex and shifting relations between work, personal lives and social policy. Drawing on the analyses offered by Marxism, feminism and post-structuralism, each chapter has explored the mutual constitution of personal lives and social policy. The central theme running throughout is that work represents a site of policy intervention through which our personal lives come to be delineated and regulated. In the process, a distinction is mobilized between self-reliant 'independent' workers and those who are considered welfare 'dependent'. As we have seen, social policy in the UK has in different ways over the past two centuries mobilized discourses of 'normal', 'deviant' and 'pathological' in this context. The dominant constructions of work as paid employment operate through the discourses, practices and policies of welfare to identify and pathologize particular groups as, for example, 'work-shy', 'feckless', 'workless' and an 'underclass'.

Aims

The aims of this book have been to explore the following themes:

- Work represents a channel through which personal lives and social policy are mutually constituted.
- Work has occupied a central place in the history of social policy in the UK; it is a key site through which different social policies and practices come to shape and regulate personal lives.
- There is a complex interplay between work and personal lives which means that these two domains also help comprise and form the other.

That there has been a close interrelationship between work and welfare has been a constant of UK social policy though, as we have seen in the different chapters, these are often constructed as separate fields of interest. That the diverse links between them carry normative assumptions about how our personal lives should be ordered is also an ever constant (if at times implicit) thread underpinning this relationship. However, this is not to deny the changes that have taken place: changes in the organization of work, especially the intensification of work and 'anti-social' patterns of shift working that have impacted on life outside paid work and shaped the rhythms and structures of domestic work and 'home life'. In other ways, particular aspects of our personal lives are exploited through the increasing use of, for example, emotional labour, not only in welfare work but also in call centres and in the 'customer-service' sectors (see Chapter 2). In other words, while there are clear continuities in the relations between work and social policy, there are also what we have identified here as shifts. These have repercussions for how the personal lives of those concerned should be ordered and, if necessary, shaped and regulated through the practices of welfare policy.

A number of significant shifts have been identified in:

- the meanings attached to work;
- the organization of paid employment;
- the development of 'non-traditional' forms of paid work and the spread of 'flexible' working of different kinds;

- pension polices and in the constructions of 'retirement' and 'the retired';
- the welfare policies pursued by UK governments in the 1980s, 1990s and early 2000s, to a more 'workfarist' regime.

There are, then, related issues that come together to form the central storyline of this book, and the aim of this final chapter is to revisit these by considering some important developments in work-related social policies in the UK in the early 2000s to consolidate your understanding of these.

2 The centrality of work in social policy

Let us begin with two brief quotations from the politicians, Frank Field and Harriet Harman, who in the mid 1990s were central in developing New Labour's visions of a 'modernized' welfare regime.

> Being without work permeates everything. It changes how women regard men, for example. It not only leads to crime but also affects how the probation service then deals with the criminal. What kind of hope can you build into a person's life if there is no chance of work and of therefore beginning to plan what type of life they may lead with their partner.
>
> (Field, 1995, p.9)

> Lone mothers say that work is about more than money, although that is important. Work for them means that they do not have to depend on benefits. They can show their children that income is about work rather than benefits ... They want to work so that they can set an example to their children, and can bring them up to understand that life is about work and not just claiming benefits.
>
> (Harman, 1997, p.7)

Figure 5.1

Important as it is here, for us, the significance of these ideas is not in what they tell us about New Labour's then vision of a reformed welfare state, but in the ways in which they mobilize particular understandings of the relationship between work and personal lives. As we saw in Chapter 4, in the early twenty-first century 'work' as paid employment has come to be increasingly central to the organization of welfare policy in the UK. This has encompassed much more than specifically work-related benefits and/or income maintenance policies such as unemployment benefit and tax credits. The moral compulsion to work and the idea that work structures wider social relations and behaviour in ways that are considered to be 'normal' are evident from the comments by Field and Harman. In its 2001 General Election manifesto for instance, the Labour Party (2001, p.24) referred to paid work as the 'best anti-poverty, anti-crime and pro-family policy yet'. Work has been central to New Labour's vision of a 'modern' welfare state, as it was with the Conservatives in the 1980s and 1990s. New Labour's welfare 'reforms' would be, as Chancellor Gordon Brown expressed it (1999, p.1), 'putting work at the centre of the welfare state'. The discourse of work under New Labour has thus permeated a broad range of social policy areas.

There are a number of important and wide-ranging implications of this workfarist shift (see Grover, 2003; Peck, 1999; Peck and Theodore, 2000). For this chapter, paid work is shown to have great significance in shaping the content and trajectory of our everyday lives. Workfarism is not just about labour discipline, but is also about discipline and behaviour in other areas of day-to-day life. It is about bringing up children to recognize the moral value of paid work, which is crucial given that they are increasingly constructed as the 'citizen–workers' of the future (Lister, 2003). And it is about undertaking behaviour that either improves the possibility of securing paid work in the first place, and undertaking personal development and/or life long learning thereafter. It is the responsibility of individuals to equip themselves with the capabilities to manage the insecurities and opportunities open to them. Work, then, has become more central to the organization of our personal lives with penalties and sanctions for those whose behaviour does not correspond to the moral imperative sanctioned by the government. Workfarism is about much more than welfare to work however. Importantly, it is also, as we saw in Chapter 1, about defining work in particular ways.

ACTIVITY 5.1

In Chapter 4, Ross Fergusson explored the 1996 Personal Responsibility and Work Opportunity Reconciliation Act in the USA in terms of a shift to a more workfare based welfare regime. Study carefully the following list of activities (Boyer, 2003, p.79) defined by policy-makers as fulfilling the work requirement of this Act.

- unsubsidized employment
- subsidized private-sector employment
- subsidized public-sector employment
- work experience
- on-the-job training
- job search and job readiness assistance
- community service programmes
- vocational educational training (not to exceed 12 months)
- training in job skills directly related to employment

- education directly related to employment
- secondary school attendance
- provision of child care to an individual who is participating in a community service programme.

In what ways is work being defined here, and what forms of work are being marginalized? Reflecting on the themes of Chapters 2 and 3, how might workfare impact on voluntary workers and on older workers outside the formal labour market?

COMMENT

As Fergusson has noted, this Act resulted from far-reaching changes in the US welfare system in the mid to late 1990s where, as with the UK, there was a shift to a workfarist regime. Under the Act, what counted as work varied from state to state, as long as it was defined in relation to the twelve activities listed above. Boyer (2003, p.76) argues that through the new policy agenda work is largely defined in terms that are place-based: as an activity that takes place outside the home. As we saw in Chapter 1, the consequences of this for care work are significant, as it has become even more marginalized (in policy discourse and practice) and it remains associated primarily with women and the home (see **Fink, 2004**). Yet, at the same time, care work has been central to welfare 'reforms' in both the USA and the UK, not least because so-called welfare dependent women with children have been encouraged to place their children in child care (formal or informal) in order to enter the labour market. While the development of workfare in the USA has been more pronounced than in the UK, we can also detect in UK social policy the ways in which welfare to work and other related policies have devalued forms of non paid work and/or informal work. So, for example, voluntary unpaid work is afforded little value because it is not seen as providing a route to an independent existence.

The distinction that was made between welfare and work in the UK and in the USA in the early 2000s was, in part, the product of enduring legacies of nineteenth- and twentieth-century notions of 'dependency'. Work has long been portrayed as the 'best' form of welfare, even in the context of the universal rights-based welfare system developed by William Beveridge. As Jones and Novak remind us:

> Social Security has never been just a system for maintaining those without sufficient income; throughout its history this aim has been over-ridden by the perceived need to fashion benefits according to the requirements of the labour market ... The principle of less eligibility entombed in the 1834 Poor Law Amendment Act – that relief of poverty should always be made less attractive than the condition of the low paid – lives on, driven relentlessly downwards by the deteriorating conditions of the labour market itself
>
> (Jones and Novak, 1999, pp.56–7)

However, the shift from the welfare system envisaged by Beveridge to the more workfarist regimes of the early twenty-first century – both carrying particular constructions of the separation between work and social security/

Figure 5.2

welfare – has also involved a shift towards more in-work related benefits. In this respect, it is possible to argue that welfare to work did not represent a distinct shift from welfare dependency to paid labour, since under New Labour in-work benefits such as tax credits and work-based subsidies for lone mothers gradually came to replace more 'universal' out-of-work benefits. Welfare to work for many people resulted not in permanent paid employment in any case, but episodic rounds of work and unemployment. The important shift to recognize though is that in-work benefits came to gradually, but steadily, replace out-of-work benefits.

The relationship between work and welfare, then, is an ever-changing one, but it is also complex and contested. The shift to in-work welfare payments carried with it far-reaching consequences for how lives should be lived and organized. As we saw in Chapters 3 and 4, the personal lives of marginalized groups such as young unemployed people and older retired people have been increasingly structured by the vagaries of the labour market and the dictates of the welfare system. Through all of this the moral politics of individual responsibility, duty and obligations were ever present.

Think back to Chapter 4. What insights did post-structuralist analyses bring to our understanding of how welfare subjects and their conduct are governed through welfare-to-work programmes?

3 'Family friendly' employment and the pursuit of work–life 'balance'

The emphasis on workfarist policies such as welfare to work sits somewhat uneasily with other policies that are slowly, but steadily, emerging and that seek to regulate work and personal lives in other ways. Here, the notion of work–life balance (WLB) has been particularly influential and so it is to this issue that we now turn in order to examine further how personal lives become ordered through their intersections with work and social policy.

The growth of 'new' working patterns, the spread of new forms of 'flexible' working and changes in work organization have, for many, disrupted the rhythms of what were in the recent past regarded as 'traditional' in working life (see Chapter 1). What has emerged is the '24/7' society in which, for example, all-day supermarkets, call centres, petrol stations and leisure centres grow to meet the needs of those working longer and more varied hours. Indeed, some supermarkets promote and publicize themselves as fitting around the complex demands of home and work. The rise of the so-called '24/7' society both reflects and contributes to significant changes in the organization of paid work.

Many workers have experienced an increase in the hours they are expected to work – and in the times when they are expected to work or to be ready to work if called upon. The rise of a long hours culture has been well documented (see Perrons, 2003; Taylor, 2002) and, as we saw in Chapter 2, long hours and round-the-clock shift working was, and remains, the norm for many welfare workers. UK workers work the longest hours and receive less paid holiday time than their counterparts in the European Union (EU). This affects different groups of workers in different ways. For example, there has been an increase in the number of fathers who complain that they have less and less time to spend with their family and children (National Family and Parenting Institute, 2000), while growing numbers of workers protest that they cannot take their holiday entitlements or find time for leisure and other pursuits. Parents, spouses and partners comment that they often 'pass like ships in the night', with little time spent together. The fear of job loss drives many people to engage in longer and longer hours at work or in work-related activities. It is through these cultures and practices of paid employment that we can begin to understand how workers are encouraged and coerced into demonstrating their commitment to work. Moreover, as we saw in Chapter 3 with the increasing emphasis placed on individuals taking more responsibility for their own financial security in retirement, such a commitment also reflects an assumption that paid employment is the means by which poverty in older age can be avoided.

For sociologist Richard Sennett (1998), the consequence of these developments is a growing 'imbalance' between the values that are required to maintain family life and those necessary for working life, which leads, in his words, to a 'corrosion of character' (Sennett, 1998). Here Sennett is referring to a largely vanished world of work in which personal character mattered and which contrasts with the 'new' world of risk and flexibility in which people have to constantly reinvent themselves to maintain employability. In this new world, workers are wholly disposable and lack any long-term relationships with the organizations for which they work. Sennett's concern with this 'imbalance' between work and personal life is reflected in the emergence of so-called 'family friendly' employment policies and in policies that are being developed to enhance WLB. 'Family friendly' and WLB have become increasingly important discourses in employment policy although we can see, following the previous chapters, how work and personal lives continue to be constituted as separate domains. In the UK, in the early 2000s, several government departments, for example, the Department of Trade and Industry (DTI, 2001) and Department for Employment and Education (DfEE, 2000), promoted WLB policies and ideas. In April 2003, following (in the minimum way allowed) EU directives, new government legislation was passed allowing parents (both female and male) with children under 6 years and with disabled children up to 18 years to request 'flexible' forms of work from their employer, including part-time work. Companies are not compelled to agree to these requests however. Here, 'flexible' forms of work means something very different to that discussed in Chapters 1 and 2. The drive is from workers to secure work patterns that allow them to meet the demands of different areas of their lives (and to enjoy some of the pleasures) in contrast to employer-led flexibility motivated by a desire to maximize profitability. Struggles over conditions of employment have long been part of work place relations between employers and workers, and WLB is no exception. In July 2003, 2,500 British Airways (BA) check-in staff based at London Heathrow and Gatwick airports took unofficial strike action against management plans to impose a new clocking-in system, amidst fears that this would lead to an increase in the number of hours they were expected to work. With around seventy five per cent of BA's customer service staff women, and with a number of single parents among them, there was considerable concern that this would impact on child care. Media coverage of the strike provided the following comment from one union leader about those taking part in the strike:

> Our members are not traditionally militant workers. Many of them have family responsibilities and just want to retain some balance between work and home lives.
>
> (Fraser, 2003, p.18)

And this analysis of their demands:

> It was a twenty-first century dispute where low-paid, mainly women, workers stood up and demanded dignity, respect and consultation from their employer. I believe that this dispute proves that time is the new money, and work–life balance and the quality of people's lives will become a major part of the collective bargaining agenda.
>
> (Maguire, 2003, p.3)

Reconciling family life and working lives is not only a dilemma for groups of workers like those at BA. It also poses problems for the UK government in the early 2000s. On the one hand welfare to work, as we have seen, is premised on a 'work-first' agenda, while WLB is concerned with combining paid work and family life. In other respects New Labour has also sought to promote family life (Dean, 2002; Home Office, 1998). However, the tensions underlying this are evidenced in the UK government's unwillingness to adopt the full range of 'family friendly' and WLB policies that are evident elsewhere in the EU. As Duncan (2002) has noted, New Labour's drive to make the UK a competitive economy based on flexible labour markets sat somewhat uneasily with the more rights based agenda of the EU. WLB policies in the UK thus far have amounted to little more than encouraging employers to adopt more 'family friendly' working practices.

The idea that all parents can successfully combine the demands and responsibilities of paid work and family life has been central to New Labour's vision of a modern welfare system, a system in which work participation is maximized and welfare minimized. Along with the workfarist strategies explored by Fergusson in the preceding chapter, 'family friendly' and WLB policies have become little more than strategies to maximize labour market participation. As Perrons (2003, p.69) argues: '... within this perspective, flexible working seems to be more concerned with accommodating life to rather demanding and unquestioned working hours rather than one of reorganizing work to allow time for domestic and caring responsibilities'.

The notion of 'flexibility' has been central to discussions of WLB. But, as we saw in Chapters 1 and 2, 'flexibility' is a somewhat fluid and ambiguous term. 'Flexibility' for the employer is not the same as 'flexibility' for the worker. WLB policies have been promoted by the UK government as a means of increasing productivity and enhancing employee commitment. Thus, WLB has been narrowly defined in terms of economic imperatives and a business agenda. It is not the individual or the family that is being promoted 'first' here, but instead once more the need to work.

WLB also carries with it some sense that people can increasingly negotiate and shape their own working lives; that through work, people can become active agents creating their own futures. The emphasis on individual responsibility does not end with the securing of paid employment or with bringing up children to recognize the duties and obligations of working. As we saw in Chapter 1 (section 4.2) the emergence of the idea of an 'end of career' has resulted in more emphasis on individuals being able to engineer their own career, their own marketability through 'personal development' such as training and 'life-long learning'. But beyond this, what has also been constructed is an emphasis on individuals taking responsibility for decisions about their work histories, their finances and their pensions. Clearly, some groups of very well paid workers can exercise a high degree of control over their working lives. It is likely that high-income dual earner households are in a much better position to finance WLB (though many do not achieve this) than so-called workless or 'work-poor' households. However, the cost of paid child care alone is prohibitive for many households and parents often struggle to combine the demands of paid employment, domestic work and the care of children. Home workers also toil to create any sense of a WLB. We need here, then, to distinguish between the position and opportunities open to highly paid professional households and those workers who, for whatever reason, are in low-paid, insecure or part-time employment and struggle as a result to attain even the basic working rights, let alone any sense of a WLB.

The pursuit of WLB and 'family friendly' employment policies is at odds both with the realities of the modern work place and the experiences of the growing armies of poorly paid domestic workers that are, in the late 1990s and early 2000s, increasingly servicing middle-class homes in the UK, Ireland, the USA and elsewhere around the globe (see Ehrenreich and Hochschild, 2003). In allowing others to achieve a WLB, including growing numbers of professional women, these mainly female migrant workers suffer from a culture of long hours and ill-health:

ACTIVITY 5.2

Read the following excerpt from a feature by Barbara Ehrenreich (based on Ehrenreich and Hochschild, 2003) that was published in *The Guardian* in 2003. How might Marxist and feminist approaches interpret the experiences being articulated here and the question of domestic service in the twenty-first century?

> Even ritual work takes its toll on those assigned to perform it. Turnover is dizzyingly high: cleaning is a physically punishing occupation, something to tide you over for a few months, not year after year. The hands-and-knees posture damages knees; vacuuming strains the back; constant wiping and scrubbing invite repetitive stress injuries. In my three weeks as a maid, I suffered nothing more than a persistent muscle spasm in the right forearm ... but the damage would have been far worse if I'd had to go home to my own housework and children, as most of my co-workers did, instead of returning to my motel and indulging in a daily after work regimen of ice packs and stretches. Chores that seem effortless at home, even almost recreational when undertaken at will for 20 minutes or so at a time, quickly turn nasty when performed hour after hour under relentless time pressure.
>
> (Ehrenreich, 2003, p.20)

COMMENT

Marxist and feminist theoretical approaches draw attention to the class and gender relations that underpin and surround paid work. In the context of this piece, Marxists would highlight the alienating conditions that characterize such forms of domestic labour, the dehumanization that is central to repetitive, monotonous and physically and emotionally draining work. For feminists, ethnographic research of the kind conducted by Ehrenreich illuminates the gendered nature of paid domestic work and disrupts gendered assumptions that hard physical labour is carried out by men in the 'public' world of work rather than by women in the 'private' sphere of the home. Marxist-feminist accounts would highlight the ways in which class and gender relations intersect in particular ways to produce patterns of inequality that are reflected here in the use of migrant female labour by middle-class professional women.

The alienation of paid employment for these and millions of other workers, and the lack of any meaningful control over their working life means that WLB is a fiction for many. It is here that inequalities of power are founded.

Opportunities in the work place (wherever that is located) and opportunities for a WLB are structured by social divisions. In the different chapters in this book we have seen that social divisions and inequalities of class, gender, ethnicity and age are central to the relationship between work, personal lives and social policies. WLB is no exception. For workers on poor and irregular wages, such as the migrant maids who were the subject of the study by Ehrenreich and Hochschild referred to in Activity 5.2, WLB has little real meaning. Here, the class, gender and ethnic position of these vulnerable workers structures their life chances in very different and unequal ways from the highly paid professionals whom they service. We saw other patterns of power and inequality in Chapter 2 where we considered the ways in which different forms of voluntary work had become, in recent decades, more central to the delivery of welfare. While we argued then that not all voluntary work is freely chosen, where it is, this contributes to a very different sense of WLB than for those voluntary workers who seek, through voluntary work, a route to more formalized paid employment.

We can see that the tensions between welfare to work and WLB policies reflect the ways in which New Labour sought to construct welfare, work and personal lives as separate spheres or arenas. The idea that we can 'balance' work and life implies some sense of a division between them. But, as we have argued throughout this book, work and personal life are not easily separated, but overlap and shape each other in many different ways. Many people gain meaning to their life through their work, while others see paid employment as an opportunity to make choices about lifestyle or as a necessary condition of their everyday life. The notion of a WLB implies a somewhat arbitrary separation between work and 'other' aspects of personal life such as family, friendships and social networks. It also carries with it an increasing emphasis on the individual, and their duties and obligations. Discourses of independence, dependency and personal responsibility are mobilized and the dominant subject of social policy remains the free individual, organizing their personal life around the rhythms of work and of the market.

4 Explaining the shifts: the neo-liberal agenda

In the previous section we used some key areas of New Labour social policy in the early 2000s to illustrate how ideas and discourses of welfare to work and WLB carry with them particular understandings of the ways in which work and personal lives *should be* ordered and organized. But, the underlying shifts on which these policies have been premised were more far reaching and significant than were the strategies to which they gave rise. New Labour has represented an uneasy amalgam of neo-liberal, conservative and social-democratic political thinking. European ideas of 'social inclusion' shaped some important areas of the Labour Government's anti-poverty programmes. We should recognize though that there are no equal partnerships here. It is all too evident that the dominant influence on New Labour has been neo-liberalism. This is reflected in, for instance, the emphasis on individual as opposed to collective responsibilities in relation to work, WLB and pension provision, as discussed in Chapter 3. Personal lives have come to be embedded in a policy context that prioritizes the individual over the collective. The emergence of this neo-liberal socio-economic agenda has been central to many of the different shifts we have explored in this book.

Since the 1980s, social policy has become increasingly tied to macro level economic policies that revolve around the restructuring of employment and supporting the operation of the market. In other words, social policy has become increasingly located in wider concerns relating to the socio-economic order. We are referring here to a range of social policies, from area-regeneration strategies through to education policies (see Stedward, 2003), not just in relation to welfare to work and other in-work related policies. This is not to argue that prior to this period there were no links between economic and social policy. It is more to claim that social policy under the Conservative Government during the 1980s and 1990s, and under Labour in the late 1990s and early 2000s, became much more integrated with the pursuit of 'flexible' labour markets; a strategy that successive governments have come to identify as the key to enhancing the UK's economic competitiveness in global markets. This stands in marked contrast to the protection of 'universal' rights that was so central to the Beveridgean–Keynesian welfare system of the post-1945 era. However, there are also important continuities with the past in that with Beveridge, benefits and rights were also closely related to labour market participation and also demanded particular kinds of behaviours, responsibilities and moralities (**Lewis and Fink, 2004**).

Neo-liberalism carries with it a harsh anti-welfarism along with a strong antipathy to collective relationships – especially when structured by the state. In this respect the role of governments is to create the conditions for free markets to operate in an unregulated way, as well as enhancing entrepreneurialism and enterprise. Welfare to work and other workfare type social policies reflect these assumptions in a number of different ways, based as they are on a commitment to 'work first, welfare second' and on the idea that work-based 'independence' must always be preferable to welfare-based 'dependency'. In other ways, the neo-liberal agenda and the shifts associated with it operate to increase productivity and profitability by intensifying work, and by reinforcing greater employer and managerial control over the labour process in different work settings. The alienation, as well as the growing stress that workers experience in their daily employment, are exacerbated by these neo-liberal market-driven agendas which promote the speeding-up of work, and casualization strategies of different kinds, as well as promoting employer-flexible strategies (see Chapters 1 and 2). In this respect WLB and 'family friendly' employment policies are attractive to those advocating a neo-liberal agenda, as they did not affect the central dynamics and relations of the workplace.

Neo-liberalism is the product of human agency and of politics. It is also resisted by human agency in different ways and by different groups and individuals, such as the fire fighters of Chapter 2, the pensioners' movement of Chapter 3 and some of those who excluded themselves from the New Deal in Chapter 4. Individual workers struggle daily to gain some meaning from their work, while coming together with their fellow workers to secure better conditions and some security from employment. While neo-liberalism is dominant, it does not 'rule' unopposed. And even when and where it is dominant, it often co-exists in an uneven and uneasy relationship with other ideologies and discourses. New Labour's social policies were, as we have seen, characterized by tensions and contradictions – for example between the more social-democratic impulses (coming both from the EU and from Labour's political past) that gave rise to a diverse array of social inclusion programmes and to the promotion of social justice – as well as the work ethos based on neo-liberal understandings; and the more conservative influenced emphasis on family and community.

Bringing neo-liberalism to the analytic lens illustrates still further the dynamic and changing relationship between personal lives, work and social policy. We can see that the politics of neo-liberalism has been a key factor in the ways in which this relationship is constructed and ordered. It has driven labour market 'flexibility' (or growing risk and uncertainty) and growing employment-based inequalities, through to the increasing use of the market (and associated managerial strategies) in the provision of welfare and public services, commonly referred to as 'privatization'. Elsewhere, there is more emphasis on individuals taking responsibility for the organization of their lives, their pensions (as we saw in Chapter 3) or in ensuring their continuing employability through a commitment to personal development.

By focusing on the neo-liberal agenda we can begin to add to our understandings of the shifts explored in the different chapters in this book. In Chapter 1, the insecurity of employment that characterizes the lives of many workers is part of the neo-liberal emphasis on labour market flexibility and competitiveness. The changing world of welfare work that was the subject of much of Chapter 2 is also indicative of the neo-liberal shift. The 'contracting out' of care services from local authorities to private firms, along with the increasing penetration of the market into the 'heartland' of the NHS and public services, is among the clearest indications of this along with the steady managerialization of the public sector. In Chapter 3, individual-centred notions of responsibilization have increasingly come to dominate discussions of pension provision. While in Chapter 4, welfare to work has in other ways prioritized the role of the individual in securing paid employment. In each the emphasis on the individual, the key agent of liberal theory, is all too evident.

In the different chapters in this book, Marxism, feminism and post-structuralism have been utilized to inform our understanding of the shifts that have taken place in the 'work–personal lives–social policy' interface in recent decades. They each contribute in different ways to an appreciation of the far reaching consequences of the neo-liberal agenda, including the growing emphasis on labour market flexibility and the stress on people constructing and managing their own careers, work opportunities and lives in retirement. The politics of neo-liberalism plays a different role here to the theoretical frameworks used in this book in that it has become the hegemonic, if not unchallenged, common sense in the world in the early twenty-first century: a common sense that has had a pervasive impact on the personal lives of different groups of workers, those in retirement and those excluded from paid employment in different ways.

5 Conclusion

While the promise of an 'end of work' has long been proclaimed, work as paid employment has come to take on new meaning and significance in the late twentieth and early twenty-first centuries. While there are enduring legacies of the past, work has become constructed and sedimented as the key marker through which we signify our responsibility and commitment to the duties and obligations of citizenship (see **Lewis, 2004**). Developments in social policies have been concerned to engineer particular behaviours, norms and values, based around a commitment to paid work. It is through paid work that we become 'socially included' and are alleviated from the worst effects of poverty. It is through paid work that we become independent citizens faced with a world of opportunities and choices. It is through paid work that a host of 'social problems' from crime and 'disorder' through to 'inadequate' parenting and delinquency can be addressed.

In this world of work, however, the personal lives of different people are affected in diverse, uneven and unequal ways. Work in all its forms – formal paid employment, unpaid domestic labour, voluntary work, community activism among others – is an arena around which wider social divisions are played out in particular ways and where personal lives are constituted and shaped by the daily battle to survive through negotiation and resistance. But, we should not forget that our personal lives have also shaped social policies through individual and collective struggles for improved welfare services, for a healthy working environment and for a 'decent' living wage. The relationships between work, personal lives and social policy, then, are formed in the complex intersections of power, inequality and struggle.

References

Boyer, K. (2003) 'At work, at home? New geographies of work and care-giving under welfare reform in the US', *Space and Polity*, vol.7, no.1, pp.75–86.

Brown, G. (1999) Speech by the Chancellor of the Exchequer to the CBI Annual Dinner, Treasury News Release 80/99, 18 May 1999, http://www.hm-treasury.gov.uk/newsroom_and_speeches/press/1999/press_80_99.cfm (accessed 20 January 2004).

Dean, H. (2002) 'Business versus families: whose side is new labour on?', *Social Policy and Society*, vol.1, no.1, pp.3–10.

DfEE (Department for Education and Employment) (2000) *Creating a Work–Life Balance: A Good Practice for Employers*, London, HMSO.

DTI (Department of Trade and Industry) (2001) *The Essential Guide to Work–Life Balance*, London, HMSO.

Duncan, S. (2002) 'Policy discourses on "reconciling work and life" in the EU', *Social Policy and Society*, vol.1, no.4, pp.305–14.

Ehrenreich, B. (2003) 'A grubby business', *The Guardian Weekend*, 12 July, pp.16–21.

Ehrenreich, B. and Hochschild, A.R. (2003) *Global Woman: Nannies, Maids and Sex Workers in the New Economy*, London, Granta.

Ferguson, I., Lavalette, M. and Mooney, G. (2002) *Rethinking Welfare*, London, Sage.

Field, F. (1995) *Making Welfare Work: Reconstituting Welfare for the Millennium*, London, Institute of Community Studies.

Fink, J. (ed.) (2004) *Care: Personal Lives and Social Policy,* Bristol, The Policy Press in association with The Open University.

Fraser, D. (2003) 'Perfect timing', *Sunday Herald*, 27 July, p.18.

Grover, C. (2003) 'New Labour, welfare reform and the reserve army of labour', *Capital and Class*, 1979, Spring, pp.17–23.

Harman, H. (1997) Speech at London School of Economics on the launch of the Centre for the Analysis of Social Exclusion, Department of Social Security 97/244, 13 November 1997, http://www.newsrelease-archive.net/coi/depts/GSS/coi4548d.ok (accessed 20 January 2004).

Home Office (1998) *Supporting Families*, Cm 3991, London, HMSO.

Jones, C. and Novak, T. (1999) *Poverty, Welfare and the Disciplinary State*, London, Routledge.

Labour Party (2001) *Ambitions for Britain: 2001 General Election Manifesto*, London, The Labour Party.

Lewis, G. (ed.) (2004) *Citizenship: Personal Lives and Social Policy,* Bristol, The Policy Press in association with The Open University.

Lewis, G. and Fink, J. (2004) '"All that heaven allows": the worker citizen in the post-war welfare state' in Lewis, G. (ed.) (2004).

Lister, R. (2003) 'Investing in the citizen–workers of the future: transformations in citizenship and the state under New Labour', *Social Policy and Administration*, vol.37, no.5, pp.427–43.

Maguire, K. (2003) 'Compromise deal ends £50m strike at BA', *The Guardian*, 31 July, p.3.

National Family and Parenting Institute (2000) *Is Britain Family-Friendly? The Parents' View*, http://www.nfpi.org.uk/data/publications/ (accessed 20 January 2004).

Peck, J. (1999) 'New labourers? Making a new deal for the "Workless Class"', *Environment and Planning*, vol.17, no.3, pp.345–72.

Peck, J. and Theodore, N. (2000) '"Work first": workfare and the regulation of contingent labour markets', *Cambridge Journal of Economics*, vol.24, no.1, pp.119–38.

Perrons, D. (2003) 'The new economy and the work–life balance: conceptual explorations and a case study of new media', *Gender, Work and Organization,* vol.10, no.1, pp.65–93.

Sennett, R. (1998) *The Corrosion of Character: Personal Consequences of Work in the New Capitalism*, London, W W Norton.

Stedward, G. (2003) 'Education as industrial policy: New Labour's marriage of the social and the economic', *Policy and Politics*, vol.31, no.2, pp.139–52.

Taylor, R. (2002) *The Future of Work–Life Balance*, Swindon, ESRC.

Acknowledgements

Grateful acknowledgement is made to the following sources for permission to reproduce material within this book:

Text

Chapter 1: *Extract 1.3:* Murard, N. (2002) 'The shortest way out of work' in Chamberlayne, P., Rustin, M. and Wengraf, T. (eds) *Biography and Social Exclusion in Europe: Experiences and Life Journeys*, Bristol, The Policy Press; ***Chapter 2:*** *Figure 2.5:* Butler, P. (2003) 'Staying Power', *The Guardian Society,* 19 February 2003 © The Guardian; Batty, D. and Whitely, J. (2003) 'Crippled by ambition', *The Guardian Society,* 19 February 2003 © The Guardian; Batty, D. (2003) 'Draining the South', *The Guardian,* 11 March 2003 © The Guardian; ***Chapter 3:*** *Figure 3.3:* 'Tortoise goes into retirement', *Oxford Journal,* 16 August 2002. Reprinted by permission of Oxford Courier Ltd.; ***Chapter 4:*** *Extract 4.1: The New Deal for Young People*, Report by the Controller and Auditor General, HC 639 Session 2001–2002, 28 February 2002. Crown copyright material is reproduced under Class Licence Number C01W0000065 with the permission of the controller of HMSO and the Queen's Printer for Scotland.

Figures/Illustrations

Figure 1.1: © Peter Seabrook; *Figure 1.2:* © Hulton Archive; *Figure 1.3 (left):* © Jess Hurd/Report Digital; *Figure 1.3 (right):* © Gerry McAnn/Report Digital; *Figure 1.4 (top):* © John Harris/Report Digital; *Figure 1.4 (bottom left):* © Paul Herrmann/Report Digital; *Figure 1.4 (bottom right):* © John Harris/Report Digital; *Figure 2.1 (left):* © The Advertising Archive; *Figure 2.2 (right):* © The Advertising Archive; *Figure 2.3 (top):* © John Harris/Report Digital; *Figure 2.3 (centre left):* © John Harris/Report Digital; *Figure 2.3 (bottom left):* © Joanne O'Brien/Report Digital; *Figure 2.3 (right):* © Paul Herrmann/Report Digital; *Figure 2.5:* © Frank Baron/The Guardian; *Figure 2.6:* © Jess Hurd/Report Digital; Herrmann/; *Figure 3.2:* © Mike Abrahams/ Network; *Figure 3.3:* © Marc West/Courier Newspapers, Oxford; *Figure 3.4:* © Courtesy of McCarthy & Stone plc; *Figure 3.5:* © Florence White. Courtesy of West Yorkshire Archive Service; *Figure 3.6 (top):* © James F Hunkin; *Figure 3.6 (bottom left):* © Paul Carter/Report Digital; *Figure 3.6 (bottom right):* © National Pensioners Convention; *Figure 3.7:* © Sean Dempsey/P A Photos; *Figure 3.10:* Neil Bennett, *Private Eye*, 12 July 2002. Copyright Pressdram Ltd 2003. Reproduced by permission. *Figure 4.1:* © The Flint Journal. All rights reserved. Reprinted with permission. Photo by Steve Jessmore; *Figures 4.2:* © The Flint Journal. All rights reserved. Reprinted with permission. Photo by Steve Jessmore; *Figure 4.3:* © Underwood & Underwood/Corbis; *Figure 4.4:* Sunley, P. et al. (2001) 'Mapping the New Deal: local disparities in the performance of welfare-to-work', *Transactions of the Institute of British Geographers,* vol.26, no.4, Blackwell Publishing Ltd.; *Figure 4.5:* Sunley, P. et al. (2001) 'Mapping the New Deal: local disparities in the performance of welfare-to-work', *Transactions of the Institute of British Geographers,* vol.26, no.4, Blackwell Publishing Ltd.; *Figure 4.6:* © Hulton Archive; *Figure 4.7:* © Network Photographers; *Figure 4.8:* © John Birdsall Social Issues Photo Library; *Figure 4.9:* © The Flint Journal. All rights reserved. Reprinted with permission. Photo by Steve Jessmore; *Figure 4.10:* © John Birdsall Social Issues Photo Library; *Figure 5.1:* © Dave Simonds; *Figure 5.2:* © Dave Simonds.

Every effort has been made to contact copyright holders. If any have been inadvertently overlooked, the publishers will be pleased to make the necessary arrangements at the first opportunity.

Index